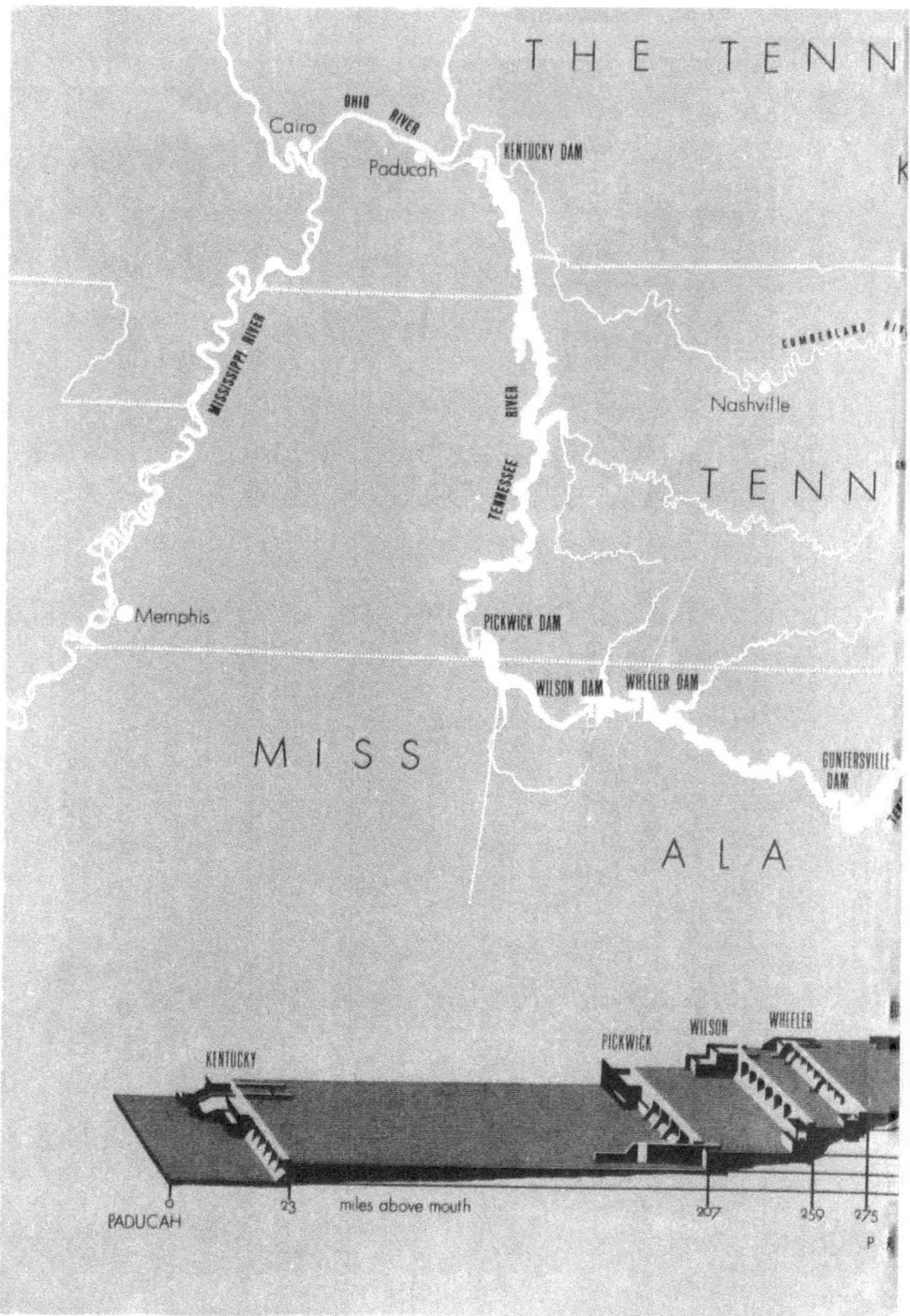

THE TENN

Cairo
OHIO RIVER

Paducah
KENTUCKY DAM

MISSISSIPPI RIVER

CUMBERLAND RIV

Nashville

TENN

TENNESSEE RIVER

Memphis

PICKWICK DAM

WILSON DAM   WHEELER DAM

MISS

GUNTERSVILLE
DAM

ALA

KENTUCKY

PICKWICK   WILSON   WHEELER

PADUCAH   0   23   miles above mouth   207   259   275

ESSEE VALLEY

Y   V A

POWELL RIVER
CLINCH RIVER
HOLSTON RIVER   Bristol

SOUTH HOLSTON DAM
WATAUGA DAM

NORRIS DAM   CHEROKEE DAM

Knoxville

FORT LOUDOUN DAM

T FALLS DAM   DOUGLAS DAM   FRENCH BROAD RIVER   N C

WATTS BAR DAM   LITTLE TENN   FONTANA DAM   Asheville

WATTS BAR STEAM PLANT   CALDERWOOD DAM
                             CHEOAH DAM
                             SANTEETLAH DAM
                HIWASSEE RIVER   HIWASSEE DAM
CHICKAMAUGA DAM   NANTAHALA DAM   GLENVILLE DAM
                        No. 1   APALACHIA DAM
LES BAR DAM   OCOEE DAMS No. 2
                             No. 3   CHATUGE DAM
Chattanooga   BLUE RIDGE DAM   NOTTELY DAM

                                    Storage Dams On Tributary Streams

RIVER   G A

                    HIWASSEE   NORRIS   FONTANA   CHEROKEE

                                 WATTS BAR   FORT LOUDOUN

RSVILLE   HALES BAR   CHICKAMAUGA   806
                                                                 740
                                                                 675
                                                                 655
                                                                 593
                                                                 550
                                                                 593
                                                                 408
                                                                 354
                                                                 300

349   431   471   530   604   650

                                                   KNOXVILLE

feet above sea level

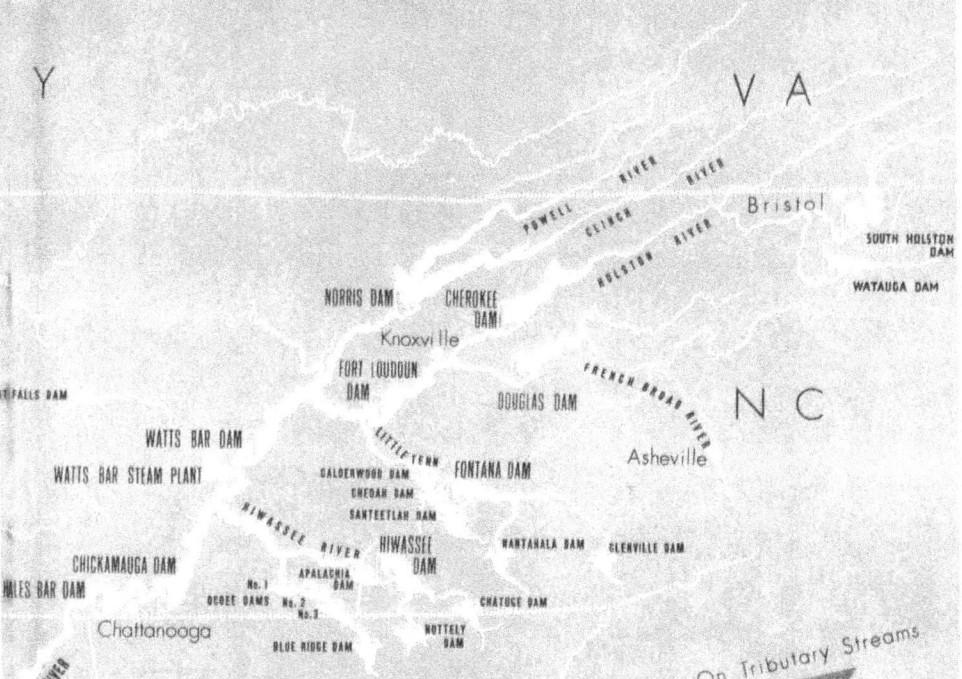

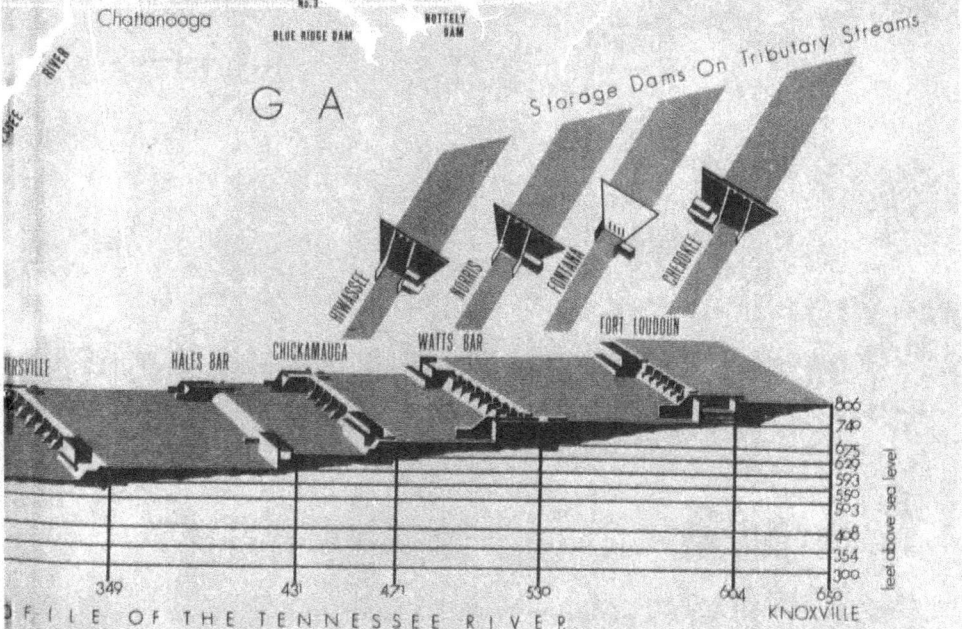

FILE OF THE TENNESSEE RIVER

THE TENNESSEE VALLEY AUTHORITY

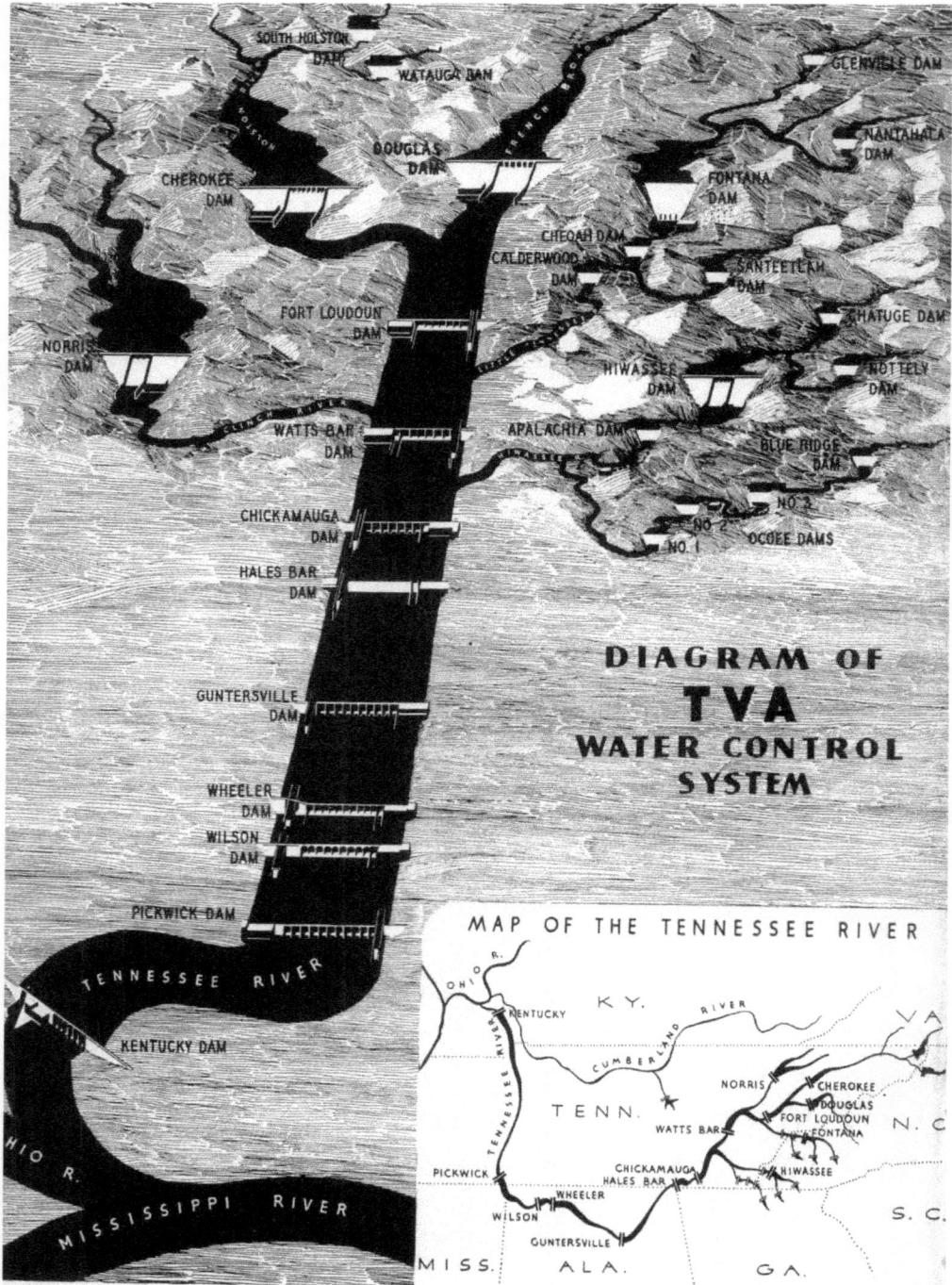

DIAGRAM OF
TVA
WATER CONTROL
SYSTEM

MAP OF THE TENNESSEE RIVER

THE TENNESSEE VALLEY AUTHORITY

Study in Public Administration

C. HERMAN PRITCHETT

Assistant Professor of Political Science
The University of Chicago

CHAPEL HILL · 1943

NIVERSITY OF NORTH CAROLINA PRESS

TYPOGRAPHY, PRINTING, AND BINDING IN THE U. S. A
KINGSPORT PRESS, INC., KINGSPORT, TENNES

TO MY MOTHER AND FATHER

Preface

ANY PERSON who undertakes to write about the Tennessee Valley Authority is in the position of the fabled blind man before an elephant. Although it is a single government institution, and only in its tenth year, the activities of the T.V.A. have been so diverse, its implications so far-reaching, its methods so novel, and its goals so challenging, that the task of appraisal and description is one of large proportions. The present study attempts only such part of that task as is within the author's grasp. His approach to the T.V.A. is primarily that of a student of public administration who finds concentrated in this public agency more of valuable administrative history and experience than has accumulated during the longer lives of dozens of more prosaic government departments and bureaus. The purpose of this book is, so far as may be possible within a reasonable compass, to tell that history and analyze that experience.

This concentration upon the administrative aspects of the T.V.A. does not mean that the author has no concern for the purposes of the Authority's program or the social and economic effects of its activities. Indeed, the limits of the study have been purposely, and of necessity, drawn to include some consideration of these matters, for to an unusual degree the T.V.A. has sought to develop methods of administration suited to its larger purposes. To understand T.V.A. administration it is necessary to understand the T.V.A. program, and a section of this book is devoted to each of those subjects. It has not, however, been possible to attempt any real appraisal of the effect of the Authority's program upon the economic and social life of the Tennessee Valley, a subject which would require another book for adequate consideration. The best description of what the T.V.A. has meant in terms of effect upon people and ways of life is found in the excellent volume by Willson Whitman entitled *God's Valley*, published in 1939. The present author recommends that book as a supplement, or perhaps as an antidote, to this work.

Limitation of this study largely to the administrative features of the T.V.A. experience calls for no apology. In the midst of a world struggle whose outcome will be determined in large part by relative efficiency of the various governments in organization and utilization of their resources, the vital importance of effective public administration becomes too obvious to need underlining. Thirty years ago Brooks Adams said: "It is in dealing with administration, as I apprehend, that civilizations have usually, though not always, broken down, for it has been on administrative difficulties that revolutions have for the most part supervened." Naturally a study of T.V.A. administration is not going to reveal how to win the war or stop civilizations from crumbling. But the contribution of the T.V.A. to the developing art of public administration is by no means an inconsiderable one, and it deserves the closest attention of thoughtful citizens who realize that an honest, enlightened, and imaginative public service is under modern conditions essential to national existence.

It would be disingenuous for the author to pretend that he has no biases in connection with the T.V.A. The example set by Vernon Parrington in frankly confessing that his great *Main Currents in American Thought* was written from the standpoint of a Jeffersonian liberal is a good one. The present author readily admits to a bias in favor of the T.V.A. and what it has done. He does not consider that one need be a disciple of Karl Marx or even of Norman Thomas to hold that the natural resources of our great rivers should be developed by and in the interests of the people. He does not feel that government ownership and operation of public utilities is a death blow to the profit system. He feels that the world-wide trend toward statism, which has been greatly accelerated by the necessities of the present world catastrophe, must be resisted and kept within definite limits in the United States if we are to remain a free and democratic nation. But in his judgment public operation of power monopolies falls well within those limits, and he is quite willing to compare the democracy of the T.V.A. with that of the Commonwealth & Southern Corporation.

In the preparation of this study the author has had the invaluable advice and encouragement of his chief, Leonard D. White, chairman of the administrative committee of the Political Science Department at the University of Chicago, for which he wishes to express the deepest appreciation. An earlier study of the T.V.A. was prepared by the author as a doctoral dissertation under the supervision of Marshall E. Dimock, formerly associate professor of political science at the University of Chicago, later Second Assistant Secretary of Labor, and now with the War Shipping Administration. The author's obligations to Marshall Dimock are many. He is also indebted to Charles E. Merriam for years of encouragement and guidance, and it was in a Merriam seminar that the author's interest in government corporations first took form.

The author wishes especially to acknowledge the assistance he has received from Gordon R. Clapp, general manager of the T.V.A., and from many other officials and employees of the Authority, past and present, of which the following is only a partial list: Frank J. Carr, Paul Ager, Edwin Lamke, Paul David, Glenn Smith, George Gant, Arthur S. Jandrey, Richard Niehoff, Carl Richey, Milton V. Smith, Thomas Hall, E. B. Shultz, C. H. Garity, C. W. Farrier, William J. Hayes, E. G. Wiesehuegel, Lee S. Greene, Clifford J. Hynning, Kenneth V. James, Lawrence L. Durisch, T. L. Howard, and Misses Alice Dewar, Laverne Burchfield, and Mary Agnes Gordon. The excellent bibliographies prepared by Harry Bauer and Miss Alice M. Norwood of the T.V.A. Technical Library have been of great assistance. The Technical Library staff, particularly Ernest I. Miller and Bernard Foy, were very helpful. W. L. Sturdevant, T.V.A. director of information, very kindly supplied data requested. Diagrams in the book are used by courtesy of the T.V.A.

The final chapter of this book has appeared in substantially the same form as an article in *The Virginia Quarterly Review*. Material in several other chapters has been taken from articles by the author published in *Social Forces, Public Administration Review,* the *Tennessee Law Review,* and the *Southwestern Social Science Quarterly*.

The author was an employee of the T.V.A. Social and Economic Division from 1934 to 1937, but it goes without saying that the T.V.A. has absolutely no responsibility for the present study. The author also had the privilege of serving as research associate to Dr. Herman Finer, of the London School of Economics, who made a study of the T.V.A. for the Committee on Public Administration of the Social Science Research Council in 1937–1938. The present book, however, is purely the product of the author's own research, and has no connection whatever with Dr. Finer's study. Financial assistance for typing of the manuscript was received from the Public Administration Research Fund of the University of Chicago. The author's deepest obligation is to his wife, who has had to live with this project.

The data of the study are drawn from many sources, and are believed to be reliable. For the gloss which covers them, the author alone is responsible.

C. Herman Pritchett

Chicago
August, 1942

Contents

List of Tables

List of Maps and Charts

Introduction

1: The Muscle Shoals Problem

> "The continued idleness of a great national investment in the Tennessee Valley leads me to ask the Congress for legislation necessary to enlist this project in the service of the people."
> —*Franklin D. Roosevelt (1933)*

ON MAY 18, 1933, Congress created what was in many ways the most unique government agency ever set up in the United States. Its program and its organization differed in important respects from traditional governmental patterns. It was a strange hybrid among the regular departments, bureaus, and commissions in Washington—a semi-independent, quasi-autonomous government corporation. While it was a federal agency, yet it had a local habitation and name, its direct sphere of operations being the 40,000 square mile watershed of the Tennessee River and its tributaries.

Its task was in broadest terms one of regional development. It was directed to promote, by its own efforts and by its example, the control, conservation, and wise utilization of the natural resources of the Tennessee Valley. It was authorized to build dams, and to operate them for the promotion of navigation, the control of floods, and the generation of power. It was directed to concern itself with conservation of the Valley's soil, to experiment with the manufacture of fertilizer and to use the product in a program of education toward improved soil-preserving agricultural practices. It was envisaged as an agency which, unhampered by state lines or departmental jurisdictions, would examine into the peculiar economic and social problems of its area, considering all the factors that go to produce human well-being, and would then build out of the abundant resources available an integrated program of regional rehabilitation. Its name came from President Franklin D. Roosevelt, who recommended the creation of this agency in a message to Congress on April 10, 1933. It was called the Tennessee Valley Authority.

In the years since 1933 the reputation of the T.V.A. has gone around the world. It has built great and beautiful dams, which have made of the Tennessee River a chain of inland lakes. It operates the most comprehensive system of water control ever developed in a major watershed. It runs one of the biggest power businesses in the nation. But it is not only what the T.V.A. has done that has made it famous; it is also *how* it has been done. Indeed, the major emphasis of this book is upon the administrative achievements of the T.V.A., which are in their way as spectacular as the dams and powerhouses. These achievements include the demonstrations which the Authority has given in use of the business corporation for public purposes, in non-political management of a major public service, in wholesome federal decentralization, in a dynamic personnel program, in cooperation rather than competition with state and local government agencies—in short, in the meaning and potentialities of able and effective public management.

But before discussing either the what or the how of the T.V.A., some attention must be given to the why. Why was an organization set up with this unusual form and wide range of responsibilities? Why was the Tennessee Valley selected as the area of its operations? The answer to these questions requires the telling of a complicated story. For the T.V.A. Act of 1933 was the end product of a chain of circumstances set in motion by the National Defense Act of 1916. The span between those two dates was in a real sense the formative period of the T.V.A., when under the name of the "Muscle Shoals problem" congressional debate and public discussion shaped the solution which was ultimately adopted. It is impossible to understand the T.V.A. without knowing what went on during that period.

THE MUSCLE SHOALS PROJECT

The basic factor in the situation was one of geography and topography—the fact that the Tennessee River drops 134 feet in a stretch of 37 miles near Florence, Alabama. The rapids, pools, and exposed rocks of this section of the river were known from the time of white settlement as the Muscle Shoals. Because it constituted an obstruction to navigation on the Tennessee River, Muscle Shoals received national attention as early as 1824 from Secretary of War John C. Calhoun. The water power potentialities of the site were recognized before the turn of the century.

For a long time circumstances prevented an effective attack on either of these problems. It is true that between 1828 and 1890 various canal projects aiming to circumvent the shoals were undertaken under both federal and state auspices, but none of them was completely successful. In 1899 Congress gave its consent to construction of a dam at the shoals for a private power development, but this authorization was allowed to lapse unused. In 1906 the Muscle Shoals Hydroelectric Power Company (later taken over by the Alabama Power Company) began an attempt to secure congressional approval for a joint navigation and power project there, in which the government was to bear a substantial portion of the cost. The company, however, ran into the conservationist temper of the times, newly aroused under President Theodore Roosevelt, and despite a ten-year campaign failed to get control of this important water power site.[1]

So it was not until the first World War, when the United States experienced a sudden need for a domestic supply of nitrates, that the type of development to be undertaken at Muscle Shoals was finally determined. Nitrates are essential to the manufacture of explosives, and have a constant peacetime use in fertilizers. The war in Europe aroused anxiety over American dependence upon Chile

1. See Joseph S. Ransmeier, *The Tennessee Valley Authority: A Case Study in the Economics of Multiple Purpose Stream Planning* (Nashville, 1942), Chap. 2; Jerome G. Kerwin, *Federal Water-Power Legislation* (New York, 1926).

for this essential material. Fixation of atmospheric nitrogen, although comparatively new, had proved feasible, but large amounts of power were required in the only two processes then known (the arc and the cyanamid). Consequently, when the National Defense Act of 1916 was drafted, the problem of securing nitrates for munitions and fertilizers was linked with the provision of adequate hydroelectric power. Section 124 of that Act authorized the President, by investigation, to determine the best means for the production of nitrates by the use of water power or other cheap power, to designate sites on navigable or non-navigable rivers for the exclusive use of the United States, and to construct dams, locks, powerhouses, or other types of plants for the generation of power to be used in the production of nitrates. These plants were required to be operated solely by the government, and not in conjunction with any private enterprise.

Under this authority President Woodrow Wilson late in 1917 designated Muscle Shoals as the site for nitrate plant development, and authorized the construction of a gigantic dam there to supply power for the plants. Two nitrate plants were constructed at Muscle Shoals pursuant to this program. The first was an experimental plant for the production of ammonium nitrate by the Haber process. Only one of the three units in the plant was entirely completed, and continuous operation was never achieved. The second plant was designed for the production of ammonium nitrate by the cyanamid process, but it did not get into production until after the war was over. Consequently there was no occasion for full operation of the plant, and after a test run early in 1919 it was maintained in standby condition. The cost of this plant and appurtenant properties, including two steam generating plants to supply power until the dam was completed, was $69,000,000. At Nitrate Plant No. 1 the cost was almost $13,000,000.[2]

The combined navigation and power project at Muscle Shoals, the original plans for which were drawn up by the Corps of Engi-

2. The history of Muscle Shoals development up to 1925 is summarized in *Majority and Minority Reports of the Muscle Shoals Inquiry*, House Doc. 119, 69th Cong., 1st sess. (1925), pp. 11–37.

neers in 1916, called for the construction of three dams, of which the one designated as Dam No. 2 (later named Wilson Dam) was the most important.[3] The first allotment of funds for acquiring the necessary lands and undertaking construction of this dam was made in November, 1917, but little progress had been made by the time of the armistice. However, the work was pushed on vigorously until April, 1921, when funds ran out with the project about 35 per cent completed. Additional money was appropriated in 1922, and the dam was then finished, the first power being generated in September, 1925. Eight hydroelectric units with a capacity of 184,000 kilowatts were installed in the powerhouse, and space was provided for the installation of ten more units. The cost of the Wilson Dam project was placed at around $47,000,000.

Out of the nucleus of physical properties which thus came into existence there developed a 15 year struggle over the peacetime disposition to be made of the nitrate plants and dam. A complete history of the Muscle Shoals controversy would fill several volumes. Here it will be possible only to trace out the lines of development which make intelligible the product of that controversy.

MUSCLE SHOALS AS A FERTILIZER PLANT

The National Defense Act had definitely provided for the peacetime use of the nitrate plants in the manufacture of fertilizer, and this was the approach taken by the War Department after the armistice. Mr. Arthur Glasgow, fixed nitrogen director under Secretary of War Newton D. Baker, spent months in attempting to get the fertilizer industry interested in taking over and operating the plants. He found that no private interests would consider the proposition even on what he considered the most generous terms, their attitude undoubtedly being due to the fact that the first plant was an admitted failure and the second would require extensive alteration to fit it for commercial production of fertilizer.

3. Dam No. 1 was a small navigation dam, intended to provide a slack-water approach to the lower lock of Wilson Dam, and was completed in 1926. Dam No. 3 was to be located 15 miles upstream from Wilson Dam, completing the navigation project and adding to the power at Wilson Dam. This dam was not constructed until after the T.V.A. had taken over the project, and is the present Wheeler Dam.

Of necessity, Mr. Glasgow then turned to government operation, and recommended that all the fixed nitrogen assets of the War Department be taken over for operation by a government owned corporation. A bill was drawn up giving effect to this plan, and was introduced in both houses of Congress in November, 1919, at the request of Secretary Baker.[4] It provided for organization of the United States Fixed-Nitrogen Corporation, to be controlled by a board of directors appointed by the Secretary of War. Under the direction of this board the corporation was to conduct a commercial fertilizer business and, after the completion of Wilson Dam, to operate the hydroelectric plant and use and sell the power developed there.

The Glasgow bill made little progress in the Sixty-sixth Congress. The Senate finally passed it, after much revision, in January, 1921, but it never reached the floor of the House. Only a few of the factors affecting the fate of the bill can be mentioned. Many Senators objected to setting up the government in competition with the private fertilizer industry. There was general doubt whether operation under the plan proposed would materially benefit the farmers. It was pointed out that the plants were of little value without cheap Wilson Dam power, and that there was no certainty the dam would be finished, a further appropriation having just been refused. A highly critical report by a House committee, charging politics in the selection of the Muscle Shoals site and gross waste under Army Ordnance officials in constructing the plants,[5] led many to believe that the entire development was tainted.

With this failure of the first attempt to utilize the Muscle Shoals properties, the problem became one for the Harding administration, which almost immediately adopted a policy of liquidation. In March, 1921, Secretary of War John W. Weeks invited proposals from private concerns for acquisition of the plants. No offers were received. At the Secretary's request, the Chief of Engineers then advertised for bids on the properties. On July 8, 1921, Henry Ford

4. S. 3390 and H. R. 10329, 66th Cong.; text of bill, 60 *Cong. Rec.* 812–13 (1920).
5. House Report 998, 66th Cong., 2d sess. (1920).

responded with his famous offer. He proposed to buy the two nitrate plants and accompanying steam power plants for $5,000,000,[6] and promised to use them for the production of nitrogen and other fertilizer compounds to be sold at a profit not exceeding 8 per cent. His offer also included the completion of Wilson Dam and the construction of the proposed Dam No. 3 for the government at cost, the dams and power plants then to be leased to him for a period of 100 years.

Following the Ford proposal, and stimulated by it, a variety of other offers came to the War Department, which turned them all over to Congress for consideration. The primary interest of southern congressmen, who were most vocal on this matter, was to utilize Muscle Shoals so as to reduce the cost of fertilizer, of which the South is the country's largest consumer. Ford's representatives intimated that, operating at Muscle Shoals, he could cut the cost of commercial fertilizer in half. The magic of the Ford name was sufficient to convince many congressmen that he would achieve this purpose, although careful consideration of the proposal ought to have indicated to them that Ford was chiefly interested in the power available at Muscle Shoals, which he was proposing to obtain at a ridiculously low figure. The associated power companies of that area, who had submitted a proposal simply for utilization of the power at Muscle Shoals, saw they had no chance of competing with Ford unless they too were willing to promise fertilizers, and so they revised their offer to that effect.[7] However, none of the offers except Ford's was able to generate any considerable congressional or popular enthusiasm, and although the Sixty-seventh Congress failed to take any action on the various Muscle Shoals proposals, the Ford proposition got a House majority in the next Congress on March 10, 1924. That it was not accepted in the Senate was due primarily to Senator George W. Norris.

6. The government subsequently realized $3,472,487 by sale of one of the steam power plants alone. The Ford offers are contained in House Doc. 167, 67th Cong., 2d sess. (1922), and House Report 143, 68th Cong., 1st sess. (1924).

7. House Doc. 192, 67th Cong., 2d sess. (1922); House Docs. 158, 173, 68th Cong., 1st sess. (1924).

Senator Norris first gave evidence of his interest in Muscle Shoals in 1921, when he introduced a bill providing for government operation of the properties there. As chairman of the Senate Committee on Agriculture and Forestry, which was handling Muscle Shoals measures, he was in a strategic position to resist the turning over of Muscle Shoals to private interests, a step which he felt to be indefensible. Only a reading of the voluminous hearings before his committee can indicate the amazing degree to which he educated himself on this question. He got the opinion of experts as to what could and what could not be expected of the nitrate plants. He studied the problems of power production on the Tennessee River. He went over with a critical eye the various proposals which were laid before Congress by private interests, and the report which he wrote for his committee on the Ford offer was so devastating as to make further support of that plan almost impossible.[8]

One of the principal results of Senator Norris' activity during this early period was to debunk the extravagant conceptions widely entertained as to the fertilizer potentialities of the Muscle Shoals plants, and to contribute toward the adoption of a more realistic view. His first bill, introduced in 1921, which he admitted was only tentative, followed the Glasgow bill in providing for a government corporation to take over the properties and utilize them for fertilizer and power production.[9] The corporation was authorized to manufacture a completed fertilizer in order to prevent a monopoly of the fertilizer business, to establish selling agencies, and if necessary to sell directly to farmers. The more Senator Norris investigated the problem, however, the more he came to doubt that the nitrate plants could be thrown into commercial production of fertilizer, or that operation at Muscle Shoals could effect a substantial reduction in nitrogenous fertilizer prices. It seemed evident to him that continued fertilizer experimentation, not commercial production, was the most promising method of aiding the farmers and utilizing the plants.

8. Senate Report 831, 67th Cong., 2d sess. (1922).
9. S. 3420, 67th Cong.

Consequently, for the Sixty-eighth Congress he drew up a new bill which entirely separated the functions of power production and fertilizer manufacture.[10] He proposed to turn over the nitrate plants to the Secretary of Agriculture, by whose staff they were to be operated for experimental purposes. The Wilson Dam power plant was to be run by a separate corporation, federally owned; it would supply power to the nitrate plants, but have no other connection with them. This bill was substituted by the Senate committee for the House-approved Ford bill, and when the Senate failed to choose between them during the 1924 session, Ford withdrew his offer. Because of this effect of Senator Norris' intervention, he was bitterly denounced by professional friends of the farmer in the Senate as having betrayed the cause of agriculture.

The belief in the fertilizer potentialities of Muscle Shoals was kept alive by the report, in December, 1925, of the Muscle Shoals Inquiry, a commission appointed by President Calvin Coolidge.[11] The majority of this commission concluded that the Shoals properties should be dedicated to their original purpose of providing fixed nitrogen compounds, with utilization of power generated at Wilson Dam purely incidental. They recommended that all the properties be leased as a unit to a private operator for not more than 50 years, under certain safeguarding conditions. With this report before it, the Sixty-ninth Congress continued a rather half-hearted attempt to secure a satisfactory fertilizer lessee. A Joint Committee on Muscle Shoals, composed of three members from each house, was set up and directed to conduct negotiations toward leasing the plants, but the bids received were too unfavorable to the government to be considered seriously.[12]

The experience was sufficiently disillusioning to impress even

10. Senate Report 678, 68th Cong., 1st sess. (1924); bill originally numbered S. 3214.

11. House Doc. 119, 69th Cong., 1st sess.

12. During this period the power companies retired in favor of some associated chemical companies, headed by the Cyanamid Co. Officials of the American Farm Bureau Federation were enlisted in support of the Cyanamid bid, apparently by dubious methods. See Stephen Raushenbush, *The Power Fight* (New York, 1932), pp. 184–95.

the House Committee on Military Affairs, which announced that if
the situation remained unchanged by the convening of the Seven-
tieth Congress, "this committee should give the matter of operation
at Muscle Shoals by a Government corporation full and careful consideration." [13] Accordingly, when that time arrived an entirely new
bill was worked out by this committee, providing for the creation of
a government corporation to engage in fertilizer experimentation,
production of fixed nitrogen, and the sale of surplus power. The
authorization to manufacture only fixed nitrogen, rather than a completed fertilizer, was inserted in the bill because of congressional
opposition to government competition with the private fertilizer
industry. The House passed this bill on May 16, 1928, and after the
conference committee had worked into it several of Senator Norris'
power provisions, it was accepted by both houses on May 25, 1928.

President Coolidge gave the bill a pocket veto. So the fight had
to be commenced all over again, and in the meantime the House
had repented of its consent to a measure embodying such a degree
of government ownership. The Military Affairs Committee went
back to the theory that Muscle Shoals must be utilized for fertilizer
production and experimentation under private operation, stated its
belief that "all possible means for negotiating a satisfactory lease
for the disposal of Muscle Shoals had not been availed of," [14] and
drafted a bill authorizing the President to establish a board to appraise the properties and undertake to secure leases. This bill was
passed by the House on May 28, 1930, but it was not satisfactory to
the Senate, and it was nine months later before the two houses compromised on a measure which limited the leasing principle to the
nitrate plants and provided for outright government ownership and
operation of the power plant.

Once again congressional agreement was frustrated when President Herbert Hoover vetoed this bill on March 3, 1931. [15] His veto
was principally concerned with government operation of the power
properties, which is a subject for later consideration. He did, how-

13. House Report 2303, 69th Cong., 2d sess. (1927), p. 2.
14. House Report 1430, 71st Cong., 2d sess. (1930), p. 9.
15. Senate Doc. 321, 71st Cong., 3d sess.

ever, indicate his belief that the nitrate plants could not be leased under the terms of the bill. He made the rather remarkable suggestion that the Muscle Shoals problem, with which six Congresses had labored, really concerned only the states of Alabama and Tennessee, and that a commission representing those states, as well as national farm organizations and the Army Engineers, should be set up with authority to lease the plants. Following this suggestion, a Muscle Shoals Commission was appointed, which concluded that it was feasible to use the properties for production of commercial fertilizer, experimentation for the betterment of agriculture, and the manufacture of chemicals.[16] The commission recommended that Congress empower the President to conclude a 50-year lease for all the properties, preferably with a farmer-controlled corporation. A leasing bill subsequently passed the House in 1932, but no further action was taken.

The recommendation of this Hoover commission seems a striking bit of perversity, for if the experience of some 14 years had indicated anything, it had shown the unattractiveness of the Muscle Shoals nitrate plants to private fertilizer operators. The potential lessees who had appeared were all, it is safe to say, interested in the power available at Muscle Shoals, not in the nitrate plants. One of these was unusable, the other had grown progressively out of date and uneconomical as the years passed and new technological developments occurred. The electric furnaces were still standing in Nitrate Plant No. 2, and could still turn out their quota of ammonium nitrate. For the government they furnished a useful safeguard if ever nitrates were needed in a hurry and without particular regard to cost. But this was all that could be said for the Muscle Shoals nitrate plants by 1933.

MUSCLE SHOALS AS A POWER PLANT

Wilson Dam was not completed and ready to generate power until September, 1925. Even then it was not a satisfactory power plant, because of the extremely variable supply of water in the Ten-

16. Senate Doc. 21, 72d Cong., 1st sess.

nessee River. In the dry summer months the flow of the river frequently became a mere fraction of that available in other seasons, a condition which greatly reduced the amount of firm year-round power which a plant must be prepared to guarantee to customers. It was to increase the average flow at Wilson Dam that Dam No. 3, 15 miles upstream, was planned as part of the Muscle Shoals development. By retaining flood waters at this dam and then releasing them in dry seasons, the flow of the river at Wilson Dam would be leveled out and firm power production greatly increased.

It was undoubtedly the power potentialities at Muscle Shoals which led Henry Ford to interest himself in the proposition. His proposal that the two dams be leased to him for 100 years at an absurdly low rental figure roused to action the power companies of the southern area, which allegedly had been hanging back in the hope that Muscle Shoals would become a white elephant and could then be acquired at its junk value. The proposals made by the power companies were unquestionably better than Ford's from a financial point of view, and they involved only a 50 year lease, the maximum allowed by the Federal Water Power Act. However, the Ford case was aided by a general belief in his good intentions, and by popular antagonism toward the "power trust."

It was the contention of Senator Norris that neither the power companies nor Henry Ford should be entrusted with the Wilson Dam power plant, and his first bill, presented in 1921, had the elements of a public power program in it. The two dams were to be completed by the Secretary of War, and then turned over to the same government corporation that was to operate the nitrate plants. The corporation was to use Wilson Dam power in its fertilizer business, but any surplus power (that is, power not needed in the manufacture of fertilizer or explosives) was to be sold, with preference going to states, counties, and municipalities. If any power was sold to private power companies, the corporation could regulate its resale price.

Senator Norris' 1923 measure, which proposed to turn over the nitrate plants to the Secretary of Agriculture, presented a much more complete plan for the utilization of Muscle Shoals power. The bill went much further toward providing the proposed federal power corporation with adequate distribution facilities and a continuous, marketable supply of power. The corporation was authorized to construct, purchase, or lease its own transmission lines, and to contract with private or public agencies for the joint construction and use of transmission facilities. It was also empowered to enter into interchange agreements with other power systems, thus making it possible to meet unexpected demands for power and insuring against interruption of service due to breakdowns. In short, Senator Norris' plan was that the government should operate from Muscle Shoals a regular wholesale power business, delivering the power over its own lines to municipalities and other public agencies for retail distribution.

Opposed to the Norris conception was the principle embodied in a bill sponsored by Senator Underwood, which the Senate passed in preference to the Norris bill in 1925. The Underwood plan authorized the government to dispose of Muscle Shoals power only at the switchboard, with transmission facilities to be supplied by the purchasers of the power.[17] This arrangement would have confined distribution to the private power companies, which alone had the necessary transmission lines, and would have prevented the use of Muscle Shoals power as a stimulus to public power distribution.

His bills having failed of adoption in three successive Congresses, Senator Norris in 1927 sponsored a compromise measure providing for the temporary disposition of Muscle Shoals power, pending final settlement of the problem. Since 1925 the Secretary of War had been selling power generated at Wilson Dam, but he had no authority to make other than short-term contracts, subject to congressional action and terminable on short notice. Moreover, the Alabama Power Company had the only transmission line to the power plant, so the government was limited to one customer. It was Senator Norris' purpose to put the Secretary of War in a better position to dispose of the power by authorizing him to lease or construct

17. Text in 66 *Cong. Rec.* 1809–11 (1925).

transmission lines from the dam, and to sell surplus power under contracts not exceeding ten years, with preference to public agencies. Re-sale rates on power purchased by private corporations were to be fixed by the Federal Power Commission.[18] The Norris bill was adopted by the Senate on March 13, 1928. However, it was at this time that the House confounded all expectations and produced a comprehensive measure providing for government operation of both nitrate and power plants by a government corporation. Although Senator Norris had opposed this joining of functions, he approved the new House measure, especially after the Senate had modified it to include some of the Norris power provisions.

It was undoubtedly the prospect of government entrance into the power business that led President Coolidge to pocket-veto this measure. When a bill with the same power provisions was again passed three years later, President Hoover made clear his abhorrence for such a public power scheme in a bitter and ill-tempered veto message. He stated that the government could sell Muscle Shoals power only by taking customers away from private utilities, and that the power project would inevitably operate at a loss.[19] He considered that this project entered the field of powers reserved to the states, discouraging any other power developments on the Tennessee River. Primarily, however, his opposition to "government in business" was responsible for the veto, which was sustained by the Senate on March 3, 1931, by a vote of 34 to 49.

This prolonged period of controversy, while it did not produce a legislative solution of the Muscle Shoals problem, did see the development of congressional determination that the Wilson Dam power plant must remain in the hands of the government. The principal question at issue was whether power should be sold at the switchboard, as the Secretary of War was doing from 1925 on, or delivered over the government's own transmission lines. Under the former procedure, Muscle Shoals would simply operate as a pro-

18. S. J. Res. 46, 70th Cong.
19. In this connection he used figures supplied by the War Department based on thoroughly unreliable estimates. See John Bauer, "Muscle Shoals and the President's Veto," 20 National Municipal Review 231–34 (1931).

ducer of cheap power for the private utilities in that area. Under the latter plan, Wilson Dam power could be taken directly to the municipalities and other public agencies of the region, and become the nucleus of a vigorous public power movement. The Muscle Shoals issue was rightly regarded as a contest between private power and public power advocates. The fertilizer plants dropped out of serious consideration after the first few years, and were mentioned only as a camouflage by those who had their eyes on the power potentialities.

Considering the prevailing American antipathy to government participation in business enterprises, congressional acceptance of a public power scheme may seem rather surprising. A number of factors were operative in this connection. Basic was the widespread dislike and distrust of the power companies, or in the familiar phrase, "the power trust." In the case of the Alabama Power Company, which was the company principally affected by Muscle Shoals, there was a special history of antagonism because the corporation was originally foreign-owned (British and Canadian capital). Of more general importance in the public attitude were such factors as high power rates, refusal to undertake rural electrification, swollen and padded rate bases, and various other abuses by the power companies of their monopoly position.

In taking the stand that Muscle Shoals should not be added to the private power empire, public power advocates had a two-fold conception of the role which the Wilson Dam power plant would play if operated by the government. The first was what has since come to be known as the "yardstick" concept. Widespread dissatisfaction with the system of regulation by state utility commissions was felt; the commissions, it was said, were allowing excessive rates to be charged and excessive profits to be earned. Attempts to reduce inflated capital valuations led to interminable legal controversies and conflicts between competing theories of valuation, which could be made to support almost any rate structure. The public power enthusiasts felt that if the Muscle Shoals plant could be organized and administered along the same lines as an ordinary power company, its experience would furnish an example, a "yardstick," by which the rates and service of private companies could be measured.

The second purpose sought in government operation was a demonstration of the social and economic potentialities of cheap electricity. During the period of the 1920's it was generally true, and especially in the South, that in homes which had electricity it was used primarily for lighting. High rates made impossible any substantial use of appliances. Public power supporters had a vision of electricity so cheap that it could be used for a variety of labor-saving and comfort-promoting and income-producing purposes in homes and on farms. Rural electrification, a field in which the private companies had been extremely backward, was a particular concern, and special provision was made for its development in the various Muscle Shoals bills. Up to 1933, however, cheap Muscle Shoals power benefited only the Alabama Power Company.

MUSCLE SHOALS AND UNIFIED RIVER CONTROL

A third influence to be traced through the tedious course of Muscle Shoals history is the conception of the unified development of the Tennessee River by a system of dams which would operate for the multiple purposes of power development, flood control, and provision of a navigable waterway. The Tennessee River and its tributaries constitute one of the more important river systems of the country. Formed by the confluence of the Holston and French Broad rivers a few miles above Knoxville in the Valley of East Tennessee which lies between the Cumberlands and the Great Smokies, the Tennessee River flows 652 miles through three states into the Ohio River at Paducah. Its tributaries extend into four more states, and the total drainage area is 40,569 square miles—four-fifths the size of England. A potentially valuable stream in its unimproved state, it stood in serious need of development and control. Its importance as a navigable highway was severely limited by shoals and reefs, swift currents, and uncertainties of channel depths. Its power sites needed development. Its unregulated flow threatened annually to inundate Chattanooga, and added to the problem of floods on the lower Mississippi.

The notion that a river system might be developed on a planned basis with a view to using all its potentialities was slow in growing. The typical pattern was a channel improvement here, a navigation dam there, a power dam wherever there was a good site —all dictated by local pressures and immediate interests. In 1916 Senator Francis G. Newlands of Nevada attacked this haphazard policy and presented a remarkably far-sighted plan for the unified and coordinated development of all the river systems in the country through a central federal board of river regulation. He contended:

> If we treat the water question comprehensively, we will turn water from a liability into an asset. The flood waters of the country are now destroying about $200,000,000 in value annually. . . . Just to take hold of and control these waters with a view to saving or mitigating that loss would be a profitable undertaking. When, in addition to that, we provide a perfect instrumentality for interstate transportation . . . when we use this water in a compensatory way for the development of water power, for the reclamation of arid lands . . . and direct it and control it . . . we are adding just so much to the great wealth of the country. . . .[20]

The goal of unified development for which Senator Newlands argued so eloquently was achieved some 20 years later on the Tennessee. It was made possible principally by the studies of the Army Corps of Engineers, who are responsible for the development of inland waterways and navigable rivers. However, Senator Norris and others interested in Muscle Shoals legislation also had an important part in the process. From the beginning Norris gave attention to the possibility of storage dams on the upper reaches of the Tennessee River which would equalize the river's flow and prevent extreme fluctuations between flood and drought conditions. His 1921 bill authorized the Secretary of War to make surveys above Muscle Shoals on the Tennessee and its tributaries for the purpose of locating stor-

20. 53 *Cong. Rec.* 3686 (1916).

age reservoirs, and if suitable sites could be found, to secure them and to build dams there, "giving due consideration to the development of hydroelectric power and the necessities of navigation."

The fact that Senator Norris did not mention flood control at this time indicates that even he needed the education on this issue which the Army Engineers were to furnish in their reports on the Tennessee River. Acting under congressional authorization, the Corps of Engineers undertook in 1922 a survey of the Tennessee and its tributaries, and submitted partial reports to Congress in 1926 and 1928.[21] In 1930 the final report was ready, a report of which the Chief of Engineers said that "there has never been presented to Congress a more thorough and exhaustive study." [22] The report outlined the existing status of navigation, water power development, and flood control in the Valley, and pointed out the necessity for all three purposes of "securing regulation of stream flow in order to reduce flood flows and increase low flows." [23] The report then went on to work out in detail a plan for seven high dams on the main stream, plus storage reservoirs on the tributaries, which would provide a nine-foot navigable channel as well as substantial power development and control of floods. An alternative plan calling for 32 low dams, which would give benefits to navigation only, was also presented.

The authors of the report were clearly impressed with the advantages of the plan for combined development, and recommended its adoption as a guide. The difficulty was that it required the participation of private power interests who would be able and willing to build the expensive high dams required. The Engineers' report did not consider the possibility that the government might itself build these dams and undertake to dispose of the power, but tacitly assumed that its interest was limited to the provision of a navigable waterway. Consequently the report was able to recommend only that the government adopt the project of providing a nine-foot waterway in the Tennessee from its mouth to Knoxville by the low

21. House Doc. 463, 69th Cong., 1st sess.; House Doc. 185, 70th Cong., 1st sess.
22. House Doc. 328, 71st Cong., 2d sess., p. 7.
23. *Ibid.*, p. 40.

dam plan. However, the proviso was made that if any private interests, states, or municipalities would undertake to build one of the
recommended high dams under the provisions of the Federal Water
Power Act, it could be substituted for two or more of the low dams,
and the United States would contribute to the cost of such high dam
an amount equal to the estimated cost of the navigation works su-
perseded. Congress accepted the recommendation and adopted the
Tennessee River project by statute in 1930.[24]

The work of the Army Engineers added greatly to the back-
ground of knowledge against which Muscle Shoals legislation was
considered. But in so far as specific provisions for development of
the entire river system were concerned, they were limited largely to
the proposed Cove Creek storage dam on the Clinch River in Tennessee. The Cove Creek site was an exceptionally good one, and the
building of a dam there was generally regarded as the key to further
development of the Tennessee River. Although this dam had played
a part in congressional discussions of Muscle Shoals almost from the
beginning, its first important appearance in proposed legislation was
in the 1928 measure, which would have allotted $2,000,000 for an
immediate start on construction of the dam. The Tennessee representatives in Congress objected bitterly at the time to this federal
"appropriation" of a valuable resource of the state, which they had
hoped might be developed by private enterprise. On the other side,
the need for retaining this important site in federal control, if the
dam there was to be operated in the interests of navigation and
flood control in the lower river, was well stated by Senator Norris
and others, and the argument of the Tennesseeans failed.[25] The case
for government ownership of the Cove Creek dam was so strong,
indeed, that it impressed even President Hoover. In his 1931 veto
message he conceded that the government should build the dam,
but not until power leases had been secured which would guarantee
to the government amortization of its investment with interest.

The unified development of the Tennessee River was thus still

24. 46 Stat. 918, 927–28.
25. 69 Cong. Rec. 9696–9704 (1928).

in the planning and discussion stage in 1933. There were a few
minor navigation dams, locks, and canals, but aside from Wilson
Dam the only major structure on the river was the Hales Bar Dam
below Chattanooga, authorized by act of Congress in 1904 and
owned by the Tennessee Electric Power Company. It should also be
noted that in 1932 the Army Engineers had begun work on the long-
planned Dam No. 3 (Wheeler Dam) at Muscle Shoals, and by 1933
the lock for that dam was well under construction.

A GOVERNMENT CORPORATION
AT MUSCLE SHOALS

A fourth element of interest in the development of Muscle
Shoals legislation was the proposed use of a government owned corporation to operate the properties involved. The suggestion was first
made in the Glasgow bill of 1919, and it was accepted by Senator
Norris and by the drafters of almost all the important Muscle Shoals
measures. Extensive experience with this type of administrative
agency had been secured during the first World War, when such
important emergency agencies as the War Finance Corporation, the
Emergency Fleet Corporation, the U. S. Grain Corporation, and the
U. S. Housing Corporation had been set up. Prior to that time, the
principal example of this form was the Panama Railroad Company,
which had come into the possession of the government in 1904 as
an incident to the building of the Panama Canal, and which the
government continued to operate as a corporation. In the post-war
decade the Inland Waterways Corporation and the Federal Intermediate Credit Banks were added to the list.[26]

In all these cases the corporate form of organization was utilized because the activities to be conducted were not of the traditional type to which government administration had become accustomed, and as corporations it was hoped that these agencies could
find a "freedom of operation, flexibility, business efficiency, and op-

26. See Harold A. Van Dorn, *Government Owned Corporations* (New York,
1926); Marshall E. Dimock, *Government-Operated Enterprises in the Panama Canal
Zone* (Chicago, 1934), and *Developing America's Waterways* (Chicago, 1935); John
Thurston, *Government Proprietary Corporations* (Cambridge, 1937).

portunity for experimentation" which are "not often obtainable under the typical bureau form of organization." [27] The principal administrative advantages which government corporations were expected to possess may be stated briefly.

First, they were customarily financially autonomous units, with a financial structure and financial powers approximating those of private corporations. They thus escaped the strict financial framework within which ordinary government agencies operate. Instead of the time-consuming and restrictive appropriation process, corporations could be financed by subscriptions to stock, and so equipped with capital available for use at the discretion of the corporation's officials. They were expected to be self-supporting enterprises, authorized to use their income for payment of necessary expenses, and to supplement their income if necessary by borrowing on the credit of their own undertakings. Corporations were able to devise their own systems of accounts, suitable for the needs of their enterprises, and thus escape governmental accounting procedures and methods not adapted to commercial ventures. They could issue balance sheets and financial statements which would reflect the efficiency and success of their administration.

Second, incorporation of a government agency could be considered to give it a semi-private status and to confer upon it some degree of freedom from the statutes, regulations, and procedures binding on ordinary government agencies. The expenditure of government funds, the awarding of contracts, the procurement of materials, and the general conduct of government business are controlled by a great number of statutes adopted for the praiseworthy purpose of preventing misuse of public funds but which, because of their strictness and the formalism they impose, too often bind administration in red tape and sacrifice efficiency to scrupulous legality. The Comptroller General, under his authority to settle and adjust accounts, conducts a strict audit which is primarily an examination of each expenditure to determine whether it was made pursuant to

27. President's Committee on Administrative Management, *Report with Special Studies* (Washington, 1937), p. 43.

congressional authorization. Government corporations may escape the Comptroller General's audit entirely, or may be released from compliance with the regulatory statutes ordinarily applicable. Likewise, corporations may be permitted to employ and manage their personnel without regard to civil service regulations and procedure.

Third, the typical pattern of overhead management in a government corporation involves a board of directors-general manager relationship, just as in private corporations. The directors, whose job it is to formulate policies for the organization, are usually appointed for fairly long and over-lapping terms, and are thus in a position to develop expertness, to mark out and carry through well-considered plans and programs, and to resist a certain amount of political pressure. Administration of the corporation's affairs is left to a general manager appointed by the board.

Fourth, the corporate form provides a convenient means for limiting in various degrees the sovereign immunity of the federal government when it undertakes activities of a commercial nature. A corporation can be authorized to pay state taxes, to sue and be sued in the courts, and can be made subject to state laws pertaining to its particular activities. Finally, the government corporation affords considerable opportunity for administrative or regional decentralization and local autonomy. In the familiar departmental set-up all lines of authority must run to the Secretary's office in Washington, but a corporate entity can have its main offices in its area of operations and its center of gravity within the region which it serves.[28]

It should not be supposed that all government corporations exhibit the characteristics described above. Corporations have been utilized by the federal government during the past 35 years for varying purposes, with widely differing charters, and have been sub-

---

28. For a more adequate account of corporate administrative characteristics, see Van Dorn, *op. cit.*; Dimock, *Government-Operated Enterprises in the Panama Canal Zone*, Chap. 9; John McDiarmid, *Government Corporations and Federal Funds* (Chicago, 1938), Chap. 1; C. H. Pritchett, "Government Corporations in the United States," 19 *Southwestern Social Science Quarterly* 189–200 (1938); David E. Lilienthal and R. H. Marquis, "The Conduct of Business Enterprises by the Federal Government," 54 *Harvard Law Review* 545–601 (1941).

jected to no uniform treatment at the hands of federal authorities.[29] But in general, the cluster of attributes indicated could be, and often has been, characteristic of American government corporations.

All of the various proposals for a Muscle Shoals corporation, from 1919 on, attempted in greater or less degree to set up an agency with administrative characteristics similar to those just described. The War Department was familiar with the advantages of corporate administration from its experience with the Panama Railroad Company, and Secretary Baker stated, when presenting the 1919 measure to Congress:

> It will be observed that the bill proposes operation by a corporation in which the Government will be the sole stockholder, rather than through one of the established bureaus of the War Department. The choice of such an instrument is dictated by the greater freedom with which the commercial and scientific undertakings of the plant can be carried on under such circumstances, and the operation of the Panama Canal Railroad is appealed to as illustrating the advantage of that form of operation in a somewhat analogous . . . instance.[30]

The Baker-sponsored bill provided, among other corporate features, for a board of directors of not less than three nor more than eleven members, appointed by the Secretary of War, who was himself to be ex officio chairman of the board. Financial autonomy was recognized as the basic reason for use of the corporate form, and the agency was made a separate financial unit with its own funds and resources. The government was to receive common stock for the properties turned over to the corporation, and preferred stock entitled to five per cent interest for any new capital invested in the business. The government was not to be responsible beyond its stock subscription for the liabilities of the corporation. The agency was released from civil service regulations, and its property and funds were not "deemed to be property and moneys of the United States."

When Norris came to draft his first Muscle Shoals bill, he ap-

29. See C. H. Pritchett, "The Paradox of the Government Corporation," 1 *Public Administration Review* 381–89 (1941).
30. Letter to Senator Wadsworth, 58 *Cong. Rec.* 8055 (1919).

peared to accept the corporation idea unquestioningly, but the corporate provisions he introduced were completely unlike those in the Glasgow bill. There was to be a three-man, full-time board of directors, appointed by the President by and with the advice and consent of the Senate, with no fixed term of office, and removable by a concurrent resolution of the two houses of Congress. Instead of a specific provision exempting employees from civil service, there was a requirement that appointments and promotions be made on the basis of merit and efficiency; board members were subject to punishment by fine or imprisonment if they permitted political considerations to influence their official actions. The corporation was given by Norris no capital stock and no power to issue bonds. The Secretary of War was to make an annual audit of the accounts and financial operations of the corporation, the results to be reported to Congress.

Senator Norris maintained substantially these provisions in his later bills, though there were changes in details. It may be said that on the financial side the corporate schemes worked out by Norris were not satisfactory. Nor had he too clear a conception of the role of a government corporation. When he dropped the corporate form in his 1927 compromise measure, his rather unconvincing explanation was as follows:

> In my opinion, where there is enough work to do, it is more satisfactory that an operation of this kind should be conducted by a governmental corporation than directly by officials of the Government. . . . One of the reasons why . . . a corporation was not provided for was because I thought . . . that the business that would have to be done could be more economically done without having so much overhead.[31]

The House Military Affairs Committee led the way back to utilization of the corporate form in 1928, perhaps the most important new feature in their bill being a definite provision for the post of general manager of the corporation, serving under a part-time board of directors. However, it is unnecessary to trace legislative

31. 69 *Cong. Rec.* 9466 (1928).

development of the corporate feature in any more detail. Enough has been said to show that the corporation idea was inextricably bound up with the Muscle Shoals project, and to indicate in general the reasons why corporate organization was considered desirable.

MUSCLE SHOALS AND PRESIDENT ROOSEVELT

The election of President Franklin D. Roosevelt brought to bear upon the solution of the Muscle Shoals problem an extremely important new force. As Governor of New York, Mr. Roosevelt had taken a strong position on the power question, attempting to increase the effectiveness of state regulation and, more important, developing a program for utilization of the St. Lawrence power potentialities under public auspices. This interest was transferred to the national scene when, in his campaign speech at Portland on September 21, 1932, he discussed the "four great Government power developments" which "will be forever a national yardstick to prevent extortion against the public and to encourage the wider use of that servant of the people—electric power." [32] One of these developments was, of course, Muscle Shoals.

But it was not alone of Muscle Shoals as a producer of electric power that Mr. Roosevelt was thinking. Even in New York he had considered the St. Lawrence project as only a portion of a program "which is far deeper and far more important for the future, in other words, State planning." [33] To a degree unique among public officials, Roosevelt was affected by the mental climate of the time and familiar with the more thoughtful solutions which were being urged for the problems posed so forcibly by the depression. The system which had been built on the assumption that the sum of individual decisions, based on individual self-interests, would total up to a result furthering the best interests of the community as a whole, seemed to have broken down. Its failure resulted in an increasing emphasis on a policy of taking thought in a collective fashion, of developing new social controls, of "planning." This latter term was used widely

32. *The Public Papers and Addresses of Franklin D. Roosevelt* (New York, 1938), Vol. I, p. 740.
33. *Ibid.*, p. 489.

and uncritically, but Roosevelt's program as Governor indicates his interpretation and application of the concept. State planning meant for him an attack on the problem of land utilization, proceeding, on the basis of a detailed soil and land use survey, toward the goal of devoting land to its best use. It meant the withdrawal of sub-marginal land from agriculture and a policy of reforestation, with consequent effects in such diverse fields as the prevention of floods and the reduction of the costs of local government. Planning meant for him the taking of steps which would ensure a better distribution of population, removing an excess from the cities, restoring a balance between industry and agriculture. And planning had for him the challenge of the new, the untried. He said: "I am convinced that one of the greatest values of this total regional planning is the fact that it dares us to make experiments." [34]

It was within this frame of reference that Roosevelt saw the Muscle Shoals problem. In January, 1933, he visited the area in company with Senator Norris and others who had been active and interested in the cause, and in a speech at Montgomery gave a first indication of the larger program which was developing in his mind.

> Muscle Shoals is more today than a mere opportunity for the Federal Government to do a kind turn for the people in one small section of a couple of States. Muscle Shoals gives us the opportunity to accomplish a great purpose for the people of many States and, indeed, for the whole Union. Because there we have an opportunity of setting an example of planning, not just for ourselves but for the generations to come, tying in industry and agriculture and forestry and flood prevention, tying them all into a unified whole over a distance of a thousand miles so that we can afford better opportunities and better places for living for millions of yet unborn in the days to come.[35]

President Roosevelt placed his program for Muscle Shoals before Congress on April 10, 1933. His brief message read, in part:

> It is clear that the Muscle Shoals development is but a small part of the potential public usefulness of the entire Ten-

34. *Ibid.*, p. 498.
35. *Ibid.*, p. 888.

nessee River. Such use, if envisioned in its entirety, transcends mere power development: it enters the wide fields of flood control, soil erosion, afforestation, elimination from agricultural use of marginal lands, and distribution and diversification of industry. In short, this power development of war days leads logically to national planning for a complete river watershed involving many States and the future lives and welfare of millions. It touches and gives life to all forms of human concerns.

I, therefore, suggest to the Congress legislation to create a Tennessee Valley Authority—a corporation clothed with the power of government but possessed of the flexibility and initiative of a private enterprise. It should be charged with the broadest duty of planning for the proper use, conservation, and development of the natural resources of the Tennessee River drainage basin and its adjoining territory for the general social and economic welfare of the Nation. This authority should also be clothed with the necessary power to carry those plans into effect. Its duty should be the rehabilitation of the Muscle Shoals development and the coordination of it with the wider plan.[36]

President Roosevelt thus gave an entirely different direction to the plans for Muscle Shoals development. Instead of a commercial corporation engaged in the power and fertilizer business, there was now contemplated an organization charged with regional planning for an entire river watershed, within which the Muscle Shoals development would be a coordinate part. It might have been expected that an entirely new bill would be drawn up to give effect to the President's expanded conception. He held a conference with the congressmen most interested in the matter and then said, according to Representative John J. McSwain: "You gentlemen draw the bills that you think represent our collective views that we have been expressing here."[37] Consequently, a number of bills were introduced, but all followed the lines of previous Muscle Shoals measures. The statute which finally emerged was the product of compromise.[38]

36. House Doc. 15, 73d Cong., 1st sess. (1933).
37. 77 *Cong. Rec.* 2282 (1933).
38. The Senate and House bills are printed in parallel columns, along with the report agreed to in conference, in House Report 130, 73d Cong., 1st sess. The Act was approved May 18, 1933 (48 Stat. 58).

By the terms of the Act, a corporation was created which was directed to take over the Muscle Shoals properties, to utilize the nitrate plants in a commercial or experimental fertilizer program, and to dispose of the surplus power generated at Wilson Dam over the corporation's own transmission lines. These provisions were largely lifted from previous bills. But, in order to give effect to the expanded role which the President had indicated the Authority should assume, two new provisions were added. First, the corporation was authorized to construct dams, powerhouses, and navigation projects on the Tennessee River and its tributaries. Second, two "planning" sections were included to furnish the basis for a program of regional planning and development; they authorized the President to make surveys of and general plans for the Tennessee basin which might be useful in guiding and controlling its development through the expenditure of public funds or the guidance of public authority, with the general aim of "fostering an orderly and proper physical, economic, and social development" of the area.

It must be admitted, however, that there was little congressional interest in or comprehension of these new powers given the Authority. It was clear that Congress was still planning for a power and fertilizer corporation, and had attempted no serious and thoroughgoing adaptation of the Muscle Shoals plans previously developed to the needs of the unique type of organization which was now contemplated. From the statutory point of view, the Tennessee Valley Authority was merely the Muscle Shoals corporation of previous years, with some additional ill-defined powers and functions.

It is unnecessary to discuss the T.V.A. Act further at this point. Its specific provisions will receive attention when occasion requires throughout the study. Here it is sufficient to have shown how such varied responsibilities as power production, fertilizer experimentation, the unified development of a great river, and the task of planning for the economic and social development of a complete watershed, came to be combined and entrusted to a single corporate administrative agency, the Tennessee Valley Authority.

Program

2: Water Control

"This would be in the main a flood control and navigation proposition; power would be only an incident. I should not advocate the Government building the Cove Creek Dam if there were nothing in it, but the power which may be developed."

—*Senator Norris (1930)*

T O MOST PEOPLE the T.V.A. has seemed primarily a power project. The constitutional contention that power was only a by-product of a plan for rendering the Tennessee River navigable and controlling floods has seemed to them a peculiarly fictitious legal fiction. And yet it is true that the government's concern for an over-all development of the river has been a genuine one. The reports of the Army Engineers represented a clear concentration upon the problems of navigation, and they located dam sites along the river with an eye solely to the development of a navigable waterway. President Roosevelt's interest in the project was also much broader than its power aspects, and the statute finally enacted reflected this expanded conception of the Authority's functions. A failure to see the concern of the T.V.A. as basically for the control and utilization of the water resources of the Tennessee Valley in a true multiple-purpose program will result in completely missing the point of the T.V.A.

The most spectacular instruments of water control are, of course, the large dams which the T.V.A. has built and is building in the Tennessee River and its tributaries. But these dams are really the end, not the beginning of the T.V.A. water control program. The most important water resources are not in the river channel, but are in and on the land. The battle for water control is lost before it is begun if the heavy rains characteristic of the Tennessee Valley fall on hillsides stripped of their forest cover and farms planted in row crops. Land thus exposed does not store water; instead its topsoil is swept into the rivers, there are floods and sheet erosion and gullying, and the region bleeds to death. Water control is consequently an equation to be solved both on the land and in the river.

WATER CONTROL IN THE RIVER CHANNEL

The Act as adopted in 1933 gave the T.V.A. broad authorization "to construct dams, reservoirs, power houses, power structures, transmission lines, navigation projects, and incidental works in the Tennessee River and its tributaries." It did not, however, supply any specific instructions as to the program in which these powers were to be employed. The statute did provide for the construction of the Cove Creek (Norris) Dam, but directed that it be undertaken by the Secretary of War or the Secretary of the Interior. However, a strange alternative provision had been included at the last moment which authorized the President to "place the control of the construction of said dam in the hands of such engineer or engineers taken from private life as he may desire." Under this provision President Roosevelt by executive order placed the construction of the dam "in the hands of Arthur E. Morgan," chairman of the T.V.A., "with the understanding that the work shall be done by and through the Tennessee Valley Authority." [1] The building of this dam was thus the immediate task with which the Authority was confronted upon organization, and it was the only such project authorized at that time.

The T.V.A. was not, however, completely without mandate or guidance in working out a plan for development of the entire river. As already noted, Congress, on the recommendation of the Corps of Engineers, had adopted in the Rivers and Harbors Act of 1930 the project of securing a nine-foot channel in the Tennessee River from Paducah to Knoxville.[2] The low dam plan proposed by the Army

1. Executive Order No. 6162, June 8, 1933.
2. 46 Stat. 918, 927–28.

THE TENNESSEE VALLEY

PROFILE OF THE TENNESSEE RIVER

Engineers was accepted by the statute, but with a proviso that high dams might be substituted for two or more low dams in any part of the project. The Army Engineers began their preliminary work under this statute and in 1932 undertook construction of the lock at Wheeler Dam site, long-planned as Dam No. 3 of the Muscle Shoals project. They also began preliminary investigations in the Cove Creek area.

When the T.V.A. statute was adopted in 1933, it was silent on the subject of the Authority's relationship to the Army Engineers. The T.V.A. was not charged with responsibility for carrying out the nine-foot channel project, thus by implication leaving that task with the Corps of Engineers. In October, 1933, however, President Roosevelt intervened with a request that the T.V.A. take over the immediate construction of Wheeler Dam as a measure to relieve unemployment.[3] The construction program of the five-months old organization was thus doubled.

The Norris and Wheeler dams had both been considered for years as integral parts of the Muscle Shoals development. With these two dams under way, the T.V.A. undertook to consider its role with respect to the development of the entire river. The blue print for this tremendous project had been prepared by the Army Engineers and approved as to its navigation aspects by Congress. An issue which had not been finally determined, however, was whether the plan should be carried out through the building of high dams, serving the multiple purposes of navigation, flood control and power, or low dams, which would serve only to render the river navigable. The report of the Army Engineers had obviously been impressed by the advantages of high dams, but had apparently concluded that it was beyond the power or contrary to the policy of the United States to build them directly. In adopting the project in 1930, Congress left the door open to the high dam plan, and it was this plan which the T.V.A. unhesitatingly adopted. In November, 1934, the T.V.A. board of directors authorized the construction of a high dam at Pickwick Landing on the main river, some 53 miles below Wilson Dam, a project which would solve the most difficult navigation problems in the lower Tennessee. At about the same time the Authority submitted an appropriation request to Congress containing estimates for two additional main-river high dams (Guntersville and Chickamauga) and an additional storage dam on the Hiwassee River.

The case for this adoption of the high dam plan has been stated on many occasions, perhaps in greatest detail before the trial court in the case of *Tennessee Electric Power Co.* v. *T.V.A.*[4] Either plan would have made the river navigable, but the high dams would provide a more satisfactory and efficient waterway. With nine dams instead of 32, the time lost in passing through locks and in breaking up tows at each lock is substantially lessened. High dams, more-

3. See *The Public Papers and Addresses of Franklin D. Roosevelt,* Vol. II, p. 124.
4. 21 F. Supp. 947 (1938).

over, provide a much wider and deeper waterway, flooding out sharp bends and straightening narrow channels.[5] In addition to waterway considerations, high dams provide storage space which can be used effectively for flood control purposes. Finally, high dams make possible the generation of enormous quantities of hydro-electric power, whereas low navigation dams are valueless for this purpose.

On the other hand, the high dam plan was far more expensive than the alternative. High dams as large as those required on the main stream of the Tennessee River are enormously complicated engineering projects. To the cost of the structures, moreover, must be added the expense of acquiring the valuable valley land which they overflow. Fortunately, the Tennessee happened to be one of the few major river valleys in this country which is not the site of important railway and highway arteries, the relocation of which would involve prohibitive cost. The original estimate of the Army Engineers for the 32 low dams was $75,000,000 while for the seven high dams needed the cost was expected to be almost $250,000,000.[6]

In selecting the high dam plan, then, the T.V.A. was undertaking to make the river navigable by the most expensive method. But it was also using the method which offered the economies of multiple-purpose development, which would contribute toward solution of the flood problem on the lower Mississippi, and which presented to the government the opportunity of earning a return on its investment through the sale of power. The choice made seems to call for no apology.

It was a choice, however, which obviously called for congressional review and confirmation. The support and guidance which the 1933 statute gave to such a project was extremely vague, and the commitment to so considerable an expenditure seemed to merit a more thorough consideration than would be given in a mere year-

5. The principal argument against high dams, from the navigation point of view, is that the reservoirs created are in effect inland lakes on which storms and wave action may make navigation hazardous for ordinary river craft. Experienced river men, however, do not seem to attach much weight to this contention.
6. House Doc. 328, 71st Cong., 2d sess., p. 13.

by-year voting of funds in appropriations measures. In amending the T.V.A. Act in 1935, therefore, Congress took care both to buttress the T.V.A.'s statutory authority to undertake this program, and to require it to lay before Congress its complete plans for the unified development of the Tennessee River system. Section 4 (j) of the Act was rewritten to provide that the Authority:

> Shall have power to construct such dams and reservoirs in the Tennessee River and its tributaries, as in conjunction with Wilson Dam, and Norris, Wheeler, and Pickwick Landing Dams, now under construction, will provide a nine-foot channel in the said river and maintain a water supply for the same, from Knoxville to its mouth, and will best serve to promote navigation on the Tennessee River and its tributaries and control destructive flood waters in the Tennessee and Mississippi River drainage basins . . . The directors of the Authority are hereby directed to report to Congress their recommendations not later than April 1, 1936, for the unified development of the Tennessee River system.

In pursuance of this statutory direction, the T.V.A. presented to Congress in March, 1936, a document containing its recommended dam construction program.[7] The report called for the development of the main river from Paducah to Knoxville by nine major dams (including the already existing Wilson and Hales Bar dams), plus three large storage dams on tributaries of the Tennessee. These projects were described in detail, and a time table was presented which called for completion of the entire project and all incidental works by the end of 1943. The report stressed the value of a unified program and an orderly sequence of development, which would permit construction equipment and key men to be passed from one job to the next, thus maintaining a high degree of skill and efficiency.

The ambitious plan which the T.V.A. thus outlined in 1936 has proceeded on schedule and the greater part of it is now an actuality, as a review of the major projects will show. The T.V.A. had completed the following main river dams by 1942: Wheeler (1937),

7. *The Unified Development of the Tennessee River System* (Knoxville, 1936).

Pickwick Landing (1938), Guntersville (1940), and Chickamauga (1941). Still under construction were Watts Bar Dam, scheduled for completion in 1943, Fort Loudoun for 1944, and Kentucky Dam, 22 miles from the mouth of the river, to be completed later in the same year. The T.V.A. had also completed by the middle of 1942 two storage dams, Norris on the Clinch River in 1937, and Hiwassee on the Hiwassee River in 1941.[8]

These projects might well have constituted the complete T.V.A. dam construction program, had it not been for the national defense emergency beginning in 1940. In an effort to meet the demand for power which the vastly increased industrial production program brought, additional projects were hastily approved by Congress.[9] On July 31, 1940, after a favorable report from the National Defense Advisory Commission, Congress authorized the Cherokee storage dam on the Holston River. The construction of this large dam was undertaken with record speed, and the gates were closed in December, 1941, only 16 months after authorization. The dam was scheduled to begin generation of electricity in the summer of 1942.[10]

In July, 1941, four dams were authorized on the Hiwassee River and its tributaries for the purpose of increasing power production; they were the Chatuge, Apalachia, Nottely, and Ocoee No. 3 projects. Then, on August 14, 1941, the T.V.A. signed an agreement with the Aluminum Company of America, one of the features of which was that Alcoa turned over to the T.V.A. its Fontana dam site on the Little Tennessee River. The construction of a storage dam on this site had been one of the projects included in the 1936 T.V.A. report, but attempts made at that time to secure a satisfactory agreement with the Aluminum Company for release of the site had broken down. By the terms of the 1941 arrangement, the company was given no cash compensation for the site, but was to receive the

8. The engineering aspects of the major T.V.A. dams have been fully described in a series of book-length technical reports issued by the engineering staff of the T.V.A. Revised schedules at Fort Loudoun and Kentucky call for completion in 1943.
9. See Theodore B. Parker, "Emergency Program of the TVA," 127 *Engineering News-Record* 866–70 (1941).
10. Because of war conditions, the T.V.A. does not release dates on which power generation started or will start at its emergency power projects.

benefits accruing to two of its existing dams lower down on the same stream. The Fontana Dam is a major structure, estimated to cost $48,000,000, and is expected to begin generating power in the spring of 1945.

The French Broad now remained as the only principal tributary of the Tennessee which was uncontrolled, and in the fall of 1941 the T.V.A. recommended to Congress the construction of the Douglas Dam on that river. The Federal Power Commission and the Office of Production Management supported the plan as the quickest way to get vitally needed electric power. It was contemplated that the dam could be built very rapidly since its design was almost identical with that of the Cherokee Dam, and since the construction equipment used there would be available. However, the Douglas Dam project was strenuously objected to by residents of the area to be affected by the flooding, who felt that East Tennessee should not be called upon to make further sacrifices of valuable valley land unless no other source of power was available. Congress was moved by this plea, and substituted for the Douglas project two dams on the Holston River—the Watauga and the South Holston dams. After Pearl Harbor, however, the situation changed, and Congress was quick to approve the Douglas Dam, which was completed in thirteen months, thus beating the record at Cherokee.

In addition to these dams of its own construction, the T.V.A. acquired in its 1939 purchase of Tennessee Electric Power Co. properties five existing major dams, including the Hales Bar Dam on the main river, three dams on the Ocoee River, and Great Falls Dam on a tributary of the Cumberland River.[11] Finally, to complete the picture, the T.V.A., under the provisions of the agreement with the Aluminum Company previously mentioned, has assumed control over the operation of that company's system of five dams on the Little Tennessee River, in order to integrate their production with

11. Great Falls is the only T.V.A. dam outside the Tennessee watershed. There have been numerous unsuccessful efforts in Congress to add the Cumberland River valley to the T.V.A. area. See Hearings before Senate Committee on Agriculture and Forestry on S. 1539, 77th Cong., 1st sess. (1941). Work was suspended on the Watauga and South Holston dams in 1942 by the War Production Board.

that of the total T.V.A. system. Ownership of the dams remains with the Aluminum Company.

As a result of this amazing program of construction, purchase, and negotiation, the T.V.A. has unprecedented powers of control over the flow of a major river system. Through its 23 dams, built or building, plus the dams it controls, it is in a position to regulate, direct, conserve, and utilize the enormous water resources of the Tennessee River system, and to put into effect a planned and integrated program. Water can be dispatched down the river as trains are dispatched on a railroad system, and managed in such a way as to cause the maximum of benefit and the minimum of harm.

NAVIGATION

Specifically, what do these powers of control mean in the major fields of water resources? For navigation, the T.V.A. development will mean, with the completion of the three remaining main-river dams, the providing of a reliable waterway with a minimum depth of nine feet from Paducah to Knoxville. To traverse this 652-mile stretch, river transportation will pass through the locks of nine dams; at Kentucky and Pickwick they measure 110 by 600 feet, while the standard size of the up-river locks is 60 by 360 feet.[12] All of the dams except Wilson have single lift locks, with lifts ranging from 37 feet at Hales Bar to 80 feet at Fort Loudoun. The double lift at Wilson totals 90 feet.

The questions usually raised about the navigation project do not concern the engineering angles, however, but relate to the use which will be made of the magnificent waterway thus provided. This is not the place to argue the economic aspects of the case for and against inland waterway transportation. The belief that it is a cheap form of transportation has been vigorously attacked by some and defended by others.[13] Here it is sufficient to note that sup-

12. The locks at Wilson are 60 by 300 feet, and the Hales Bar lock is only 60 by 267 feet. In addition to the nine major dams, there is a lock with a 9-foot lift at Wilson Dam No. 1.

13. See Harold G. Moulton, *Waterways versus Railways* (Boston, 1926) and *The American Transportation Problem* (Washington, 1933), for the case against waterway transportation. Cf. Harold Kelso, "Waterways versus Railways," 31 *American Economic Review* 537–44 (1941).

port of and expenditure for navigation projects has been a consistent congressional policy, and the resulting provision of more satisfactory waterways has seen a rebirth of navigation on the Ohio, the Mississippi, and other streams so improved.

There was, prior to the coming of the T.V.A., little navigation of consequence on the Tennessee, nor'could there have been, for channel conditions were unsatisfactory even in the lower river, while in the Knoxville-Chattanooga stretch controlling depths were as shallow as one foot.[14] The 1930 report of the Army Engineers investigated the potentialities of water transportation on the river, and came to the conclusion that of the 27,000,000 tons of traffic moving to, from and across the basin in 1926, one-third could have been more economically transported by water, with an annual saving of $12,000,000. The T.V.A. estimated in 1937 that, had the river been fully open in that year, over 5,000,000 tons of freight would have been carried on the river at a saving of over $7,000,000 to the public.

The actual development of large scale traffic on the Tennessee must await the completion of Kentucky Dam, which will effectively tie in the Tennessee's nine-foot channel with the 5,700 miles of nine-foot channel planned on the Mississippi system. But already the controlling depth in the river as far as Chattanooga has been increased to six feet, and the volume of traffic has increased from 22,000,000 ton-miles in 1933 to 70,000,000 ton-miles in 1939, and to an estimated 100,000,000 ton-miles in 1941.[15] Substantial movements of gasoline, grain, clay, iron and steel have begun to appear on the river, and river excursion steamers have begun to ply again along the Tennessee. As the war production program places an increasing strain upon the country's railroads, there is a proportionately greater use of waterway transportation, particularly for the movement of heavy bulk materials.

In addition to the construction of dams and locks, the T.V.A.'s

14. See *History of Navigation on the Tennessee River System*, House Doc. 254, 75th Cong., 1st sess.

15. *Annual Report, T.V.A., 1940*, p. 3; *ibid., 1941*, p. 3. This document will be cited hereafter simply as *Annual Report*. No report was issued in 1942.

navigation activities include channel dredging operations, preparation of navigation charts, and cooperation with other governmental agencies in the installation of channel markers. The commerce department of the T.V.A. has made traffic estimates and comparative studies of railway and water freight rates. It has studied the problem of navigation terminals along the river in cooperation with the Tennessee Valley Waterways Conference (representing the municipalities on the river), and hopes to see developed a unified system of public-use terminals. The T.V.A. does not, of course, operate any water transportation service, except facilities used in its own program, but it does feel that it is part of its job to foster and encourage the use of the navigation facilities which the improved river will afford.

FLOOD CONTROL

The T.V.A. statute directs the Authority to operate its dams and reservoirs and to regulate stream flow "primarily for the purposes of promoting navigation and controlling floods." The flood situation on the Tennessee owes its seriousness principally to the fact that the city of Chattanooga constitutes a highly vulnerable area. The Army Engineers estimated annual flood damage on the river at $1,780,000. Moreover, the Tennessee is one of the important tributaries of the lower Ohio and Mississippi, and so contributes to the dangerous flood situation on those rivers.

The high T.V.A. dams make available a vast amount of storage space which can be used, under proper management, to control the passage of excess water down the river system. Dams on the tributaries have storage as their primary purpose. Thus the storage volume of Norris reservoir above low pool level is over 2,000,000 acre-feet, and the Cherokee reservoir will provide almost 1,500,000 acre-feet of storage. The main-river dams are also useful for storage, since they are constructed with a five-foot surcharge specially for flood control purposes. The giant Kentucky Dam is the most important in the whole system from this point of view, supplying over 4,500,000 acre-feet of storage space. The completed T.V.A. dam system will provide approximately 10,000,000 acre-feet of controlled storage.[16]

The utilization of this storage capacity so as to give maximum protection from floods requires the adoption of a stream control program based on the fullest possible knowledge concerning the past history of the river system, as well as complete day-to-day information on stream flows and water levels. Because of the fact that reliable information on Tennessee River flows does not go back further than 1867, the Authority has supplemented these data with the historical evidence as to water conditions which dendrochronology can supply, and with studies of the experience of other river systems. From this evidence it has been considered clear that the great Tennessee River floods occur in the winter months of January, February and March, and that by April all danger of large floods is over. Summer floods of high intensity occur in local areas, but do not cover enough territory to constitute a problem on the main river.

In the light of this information it is possible to adopt for storage dams such as Norris a policy which calls for the emptying of the reservoir in advance of the flood season, and the filling of the reservoir after danger from floods has passed. Specifically, from July to December of each year the water in Norris reservoir is drawn down to a low level by releases which help provide a uniform flow in the lower river during the dry season. By January the level of the reservoir is down to between 955 and 965 feet (above sea level). During the flood season one or more floods may be temporarily stored in the space thus made available, and by April 1 the water is at about elevation 1000. From April to June the spring rains are stored until the level is about elevation 1020, which is the level of the spillway at Norris Dam. There is still protection against summer floods, however, for the spillway gates can be raised to provide a reservoir level of 1034 feet.[17]

16. *Annual Report, 1940,* p. 4.
17. Operating diagrams for the Norris and Wheeler reservoirs are shown in 11 *Civil Engineering* 339–40 (1941). See the testimony of Sherman M. Woodward before the Joint Congressional Committee on the Investigation of the T.V.A., 75th Cong., *Hearings,* pp. 5044–45; *Report,* pp. 142–43. For an account of the work of this Com-

On the main river, the opportunity for fluctuating river levels is much less, and storage space is likewise correspondingly less. The principle here is that the main river reservoirs are kept low all winter from December until the end of March, when they are permitted to fill in preparation for the summer dry season. Navigation is the chief controlling factor in the summer, while flood control takes precedence in the winter.

In order to secure the day-to-day information on stream conditions which is a necessary basis for the operation of this system, the T.V.A. receives daily reports from 56 rainfall and river gaging stations, which are supplemented by data from 53 additional stations whenever excessive rainfall or high river stages occur. Daily forecasts are made three days in advance of the probable inflows into the various reservoirs. After the predicted flows have been correlated with current water control operations, predictions are prepared for probable stages at key points on the river. A navigation and flood bulletin is published to provide boat operators and others with current information on river conditions.

The planning of water control operations, and the making of decisions and the giving of orders with respect to release or storage of water at the various dams, are centralized under the T.V.A.'s chief water control planning engineer, who is authorized by the Board to issue such instructions as to release of water as will assure the proper relation of stream flow to navigation, flood control, and power. These instructions take the form of "water control memoranda" which are issued as and when necessary. During the fiscal year 1938, for example, some 63 memoranda of this kind directing release or requiring storage of water were issued. Of these orders, 21 related to flood control, 26 were for controlling the current or providing sufficient depths at shoal points for navigation, 20 were for fluctuation of level to control malaria-breeding mosquitoes, and three were related to power, being issued to provide water for testing power machinery at Wheeler Dam.

mittee, see Chap. VIII, *infra*. Its hearings, conducted during the year 1938, were printed in fourteen volumes, and its final report was filed April 1, 1939, in three volumes. Extensive references will be made to these two sources.

The administrative arrangement for control of these decisions is a matter of great importance, because of the possible conflict between the major purposes of flood control and power. This conflict can be presented baldly by pointing out that for flood control purposes the ideal reservoir is an empty one, always ready to receive flood water, while for purposes of power generation the ideal reservoir is a full one, to provide the maximum of stored water and head. Competent engineering opinion, however, is agreed that a system of reservoirs can be operated so as to serve both purposes effectively.[18] But in such a combined multi-purpose operation, it is inevitable that some water is going to have to be wasted, from a power point of view, in order to provide a margin of safety for flood control operations.

When the T.V.A. first began the operation of its reservoirs, decisions in these matters were entrusted to a joint committee, on which the water control planning department and the power department were both represented. Daily letters went from the committee to the chief system operator at Wilson Dam suggesting the schedule that the operations should follow. There was at least one occasion when these suggestions were ignored by the operating staff at Norris Dam.[19] During February, 1937, instructions to draw down the Norris reservoir were not followed, due presumably to the reluctance of the power personnel to see good water released and, from their point of view, wasted. The situation which made possible such conflict and divided authority was soon remedied, and the power personnel were excluded from this field, decisions as to water control being made solely by the chief water control planning engineer, subject to review by the chief engineer of the T.V.A.

It should be noted, however, that even this arrangement was not satisfactory to the deposed chairman of the T.V.A., Arthur E. Morgan, who made as one of the points in his case against the organization the alleged failure to protect the exercise of flood control

18. See the excellent discussion by Nicholls W. Bowden, "Multiple-Purpose Reservoir Operation," 11 *Civil Engineering* 292–93, 337–40 (1941).

19. See testimony before Joint Committee, *Hearings*, pp. 5053–55.

functions.[20] He considered that a mere departmental separation of this kind was not sufficient, and contended that only by dividing flood control and power functions between two separate organizations could there be adequate insurance against the subversive influence of power considerations on flood control measures.

There can be no question as to the effectiveness of the flood control portion of the T.V.A.'s program. The storage and main-river dams above Chattanooga now completed or under construction will, with local protective works, give that city complete flood protection. Norris Dam alone cut four feet from the crest of the March, 1936, flood at that city. Of wider importance is the contribution of the T.V.A. system to the program of protection for the Mississippi River. The lower river reservoirs, and particularly the enormous Kentucky reservoir, are sufficiently near the Mississippi to permit operation with respect to almost immediate needs at Cairo or below. The water level in the reservoirs may be kept low during the flood season so that flood flows can be halted, with subsequent discharge of surplus waters between flood crests on the Mississippi. During the tremendous Ohio River flood of 1937, storage of water in the Norris and Wheeler reservoirs is believed to have reduced the maximum stages at Cairo by nearly half a foot. The Kentucky reservoir alone is estimated to be capable of reducing flood heights on the Mississippi by at least two feet from Cairo to the mouth of the Arkansas, and by at least one foot between the Arkansas and the Red River.[21]

WATER CONTROL ON THE LAND

The T.V.A. was projected into the water control problem from another angle by reason of its responsibility for custody and operation of the nitrate plants at Muscle Shoals. The long controversy over utilization of these plants has been outlined in the preceding chapter. In final solution of the problem, the T.V.A. statute authorized the organization "to manufacture and sell fixed nitrogen, ferti-

20. *Ibid.*, p. 5067.
21. See "Value of Flood Height Reduction from T.V.A. Reservoirs to the Alluvial Valley of the Lower Mississippi River," House Doc. 455, 76th Cong., 1st sess. (1939); also House Doc. 91, 76th Cong., 1st sess. (1939).

lizer, and fertilizer ingredients at Muscle Shoals by the employment of existing facilities, by modernizing existing plants, or by any other process or processes that in its judgment shall appear wise and profitable for the fixation of atmospheric nitrogen or the cheapening of the production of fertilizer." The Act went on to charge the T.V.A. with responsibility for seeing that the new forms of fertilizer thus produced were tested under conditions of "large-scale practical use," and for this purpose authorized the donation of fertilizer products to state agricultural colleges and county demonstration agents, and cooperation with farmers on demonstration farms.

The development of T.V.A. policy under this statutory authorization was largely influenced by the thinking of Director Harcourt A. Morgan, who had come to the T.V.A. from the presidency of the University of Tennessee with a long experience in the agricultural field. Almost immediately he and his staff found it necessary to make a decision which appeared to depart from the apparent congressional expectation that major attention would be devoted to the production of nitrogenous fertilizers. The Muscle Shoals plants were of course designed for the fixation of nitrogen, but the unsatisfactory nature of the process employed has already been noted. The T.V.A. saw that if nitrogenous fertilizers were to be produced, the plant would have to be modernized, and even then the cost might be excessive. Moreover, the T.V.A. was not interested in becoming simply another producer of mixed fertilizers, which have been traditionally used by farmers of the South to permit them to plant the same crop on the land year after year until the topsoil is mined of its value and the land eroded and destroyed. It is preferable that nitrogen be returned to the land by the planting of leguminous cover crops such as alfalfa and lespedeza, which preserve the structure of the soil.

Consequently, the T.V.A. resolved to leave idle the ammonium nitrate capacity of the Muscle Shoals plant, and to turn instead to experiments with phosphatic fertilizers. Phosphorus is one of the essential plant foods which needs to be supplied to the soil to keep up its fertility, and is one of the ingredients of ordinary mixed fertilizers, constituting on the average about 8 per cent of their content.

Superphosphates, averaging about 18 per cent of phosphoric acid, are also a commercial fertilizer product. In either of these forms, however, the amount of available plant food is comparatively small in relation to the amount of filler and other inert and value-less material included, on which the farmer must pay the cost of bagging and transportation. In undertaking experimentation with phosphates, the T.V.A. had several complementary purposes in view —the production of more highly concentrated forms of phosphatic fertilizer than had previously been possible, the development of improved and cheaper processes and equipment, the securing of a base load for Wilson Dam power by using electric furnaces in fertilizer production, and the utilization of the product in a general program of education for the conservation of the valley's soil resources.

The program thus outlined has been carried along successfully. Two of the electric carbide furnaces in Nitrate Plant No. 2 were converted into phosphate smelting furnaces. Electric furnace processes, which had previously been used mainly for the manufacture of high grade phosphate for baking powder and similar purposes, were utilized for the production of two types of phosphate fertilizers—a triple superphosphate containing about 45 per cent of phosphoric acid, and calcium metaphosphate, with a phosphoric acid content of about 65 per cent. In the production of these fertilizers, improved processes, many of which have been patented by T.V.A. employees, have made it possible to use low-grade phosphate ores which previously were valueless for this purpose. The raw material comes from the beds of phosphate rock in middle Tennessee, where the Authority has purchased the fee title or the mineral rights on some 2,900 acres of phosphate lands, containing an estimated 16,000,000 tons of matrix.[22]

For the testing of its experimental product, the T.V.A. utilized a procedure of cooperation with other government agencies which

22. *Annual Report, 1940*, p. 8. In addition to the two types of phosphate fertilizers described above, the T.V.A. was producing experimentally in 1942 fused-rock phosphate and potassium metaphosphate. Furnaces for the larger-scale production of both products were to be constructed. The combination of two plant nutrients of such importance as phosphate and potash was expected to yield a highly concentrated fertilizer of great value.

has marked so many of its programs. Contracts were entered into with the land-grant colleges of the Valley states under which the T.V.A. furnished them quantities of its fertilizer for testing under varied conditions of soil, climate, and farming systems. The T.V.A. gave the colleges some financial assistance in conducting these experiments.

After the tests had shown the product to be satisfactory, and fertilizer was being produced on a fairly large scale, the T.V.A. was confronted with the major problem of disposing of its output. The statute permitted fertilizer either to be sold or to be given away for demonstration and soil erosion control purposes. The T.V.A. adopted the latter alternative, working out a system of distribution which it felt would give the maximum benefits to its program of water control and erosion prevention. Cooperative agreements were entered into with the land-grant colleges whereby their agricultural extension services would supervise a program of test-demonstration farms throughout the Valley states.[23] On the farms selected for this purpose, the T.V.A. supplied its fertilizer to be used on land growing soil-conserving crops. The farmer in return agreed to a mapping and inventory of his farm, adopted an intensive five-year farm management program conforming with good agricultural practices, kept records of his results, and paid the freight on the fertilizer he used. Each test-demonstration farm became in a sense a community enterprise, for the selection was made by the farmers of the area under the leadership of the county agricultural agent, and the neighboring farmers visited the test farm and watched the results.

In addition to these demonstrations on individual farms, in some cases entire areas or small watersheds were designated for demonstration purposes, and here more extensive programs of crop readjustments to conserve water and control erosion, as well as to build soil fertility and promote better farm management, were instituted. By June 30, 1941, demonstration programs of these two types had been undertaken on 35,713 farms in 27 states. During the

23. The program was later extended to states outside the immediate T.V.A. area.

fiscal year 1941 over 28,000 tons of phosphate were furnished by the T.V.A. for this demonstration work.[24]

In recent years an even larger quantity of T.V.A. fertilizer has been distributed through the Agricultural Adjustment Administration, which has made arrangements to make it available to farmers in lieu of cash payments due them. Some 68,000 tons of T.V.A. triple superphosphate were distributed in this manner during the fiscal year 1941, the A.A.A. paying T.V.A. its cost of production.

The T.V.A. fertilizer program is still in the experimental, or at least developmental, stage. Although accurate cost and accounting records are kept, no attempt is made to operate the program on a commercial basis. The only monetary return which the T.V.A. has received has been through the sales to the A.A.A., which amounted. to $2,125,000 in the fiscal year 1941. These sales reimburse the T.V.A. for much of its actual production cost, but the free distribution of the rest of the product, the farm tests, and the research and development expenses remain uncovered. The net expense of the program to the T.V.A. up through the fiscal year 1941 has been $13,300,000.

Due to the non-commercial nature of the program, it has escaped many of the controversies with private industry which have marked the T.V.A. power program. In recent years, however, the T.V.A. production has become so considerable that commercial fertilizer sales have been affected, particularly in the Valley area, and objections from the industry are increasing.[25] The line taken by spokesmen for the fertilizer industry is that they appreciate the research which the T.V.A. has the money to undertake, though they feel that extravagant claims have been made for some of the new processes developed; and they admit that the T.V.A. educational and promotional work is beneficial to the industry as a whole. They do

24. *Annual Report, 1941*, pp. 4, 84. For an appraisal of this cooperative program, see Carleton R. Ball, *A Study of the Work of the Land-Grant Colleges in the Tennessee Valley Area in Cooperation with the T.V.A.* (1939).

25. See the testimony of Charles J. Brand, representing the National Fertilizer Association, before the Joint Committee, *Hearings*, pp. 4356 ff.

not, however, like the prospect of increasing government competition with their business, and they feel that their emphasis on mixed and balanced fertilizers is better for the farmer than the T.V.A.'s emphasis on a single plant food, phosphorus.

Obviously, a fundamental decision remains to be made as to the future method of conducting the Authority's fertilizer activities. The present quasi-developmental status can hardly be maintained indefinitely. There appears to be no doubt that the T.V.A. is in the field of phosphate production to stay, and after the war it will have available the additional facilities constructed for war purposes.

The agricultural and fertilizer activities of the T.V.A. constitute an important part of its program to secure water control on the land, but there are other aspects as well, of which it is perhaps sufficient to mention only one. More than half of the Tennessee Valley is forested. A proper forest cover is one of the most effective methods of absorbing rainfall and controlling runoff. Moreover, well-managed forests support various forest industries, create recreational opportunities, and shelter wildlife. The T.V.A. thus has a major interest in protecting and developing this renewable resource of the Valley, which has been expressed in various ways. It has undertaken various educational measures for the prevention and control of fires. A forest resources inventory has been made for the Valley, which secures data on the location of various forest types and species, their volume and condition, and the rate of growth and mortality. With a resource which is both exhaustible and renewable, it is essential for effective management to know what the drain is in terms of regrowth. Investigations have been made of forest industries development, which provide employment and income for every eighth family in the Valley.

The T.V.A. has been responsible for the supervision of some 18 to 20 C.C.C. camps, used in protective work on seriously gullied and eroded lands and in reforestation activities. There are in the Valley 1,000,000 or more acres of badly eroded land, abandoned for agriculture, which the T.V.A. by such measures hopes to protect and restore to usefulness. The T.V.A. is itself a proprietor of extensive forest lands, acquired to provide a protective area around the various T.V.A. reservoirs. These forests it has undertaken to manage in such a way as to constitute a demonstration of approved forestry practices. The organization has also undertaken forestry research to discover, develop and test superior strains which will provide quicker food or cash returns when used for erosion control or reforestation.

The program of water control on the land is of coordinate importance with that of water control in the river channel, though it is less spectacular in nature. A proper agricultural and forest cover can do much more toward preventing floods and evening stream flow by storing rainfall and slowing runoff than can a whole system of dams. On the land, the topsoil is the basis of our national existence; in the river, it is simply silt which fills up the reservoirs and gradually decreases their usefulness. In the promotion of soil-conserving practices the T.V.A. has used the devices of education, financial inducement, and cooperation with other governmental agencies. Its goals have ranged from the immediate and comparatively narrow one of protecting its reservoirs to the broader purposes of safeguarding a priceless national heritage.

THE T.V.A. GOES TO WAR

The T.V.A. water control program, having been generated out of a program intended to meet the challenge of the first World War, has now run into its successor. Up to 1940 the national defense angle of the T.V.A. program involved little more than maintaining the Muscle Shoals nitrate plants in standby condition. It was recognized, of course, that the power which the T.V.A. was making available would be valuable in time of war, and the T.V.A. statute did in fact authorize the Authority to allocate a portion of the cost of its dams to national defense. The T.V.A. did not do so, however, limiting the allocation to the three purposes of navigation, flood control, and power.[26] Just what these power resources have meant to the

26. See Chapter IV for a detailed discussion of the allocation problem.

United States in its war preparations and production may be discussed more appropriately in the following chapter.

The Muscle Shoals nitrate plant went to war in October, 1940, when the War Department notified the T.V.A. to recondition and re-open it. Besides modernizing the ammonium nitrate portion of the plant, the T.V.A. was requested by the War Department to construct a new synthetic ammonia plant to supplant the calcium cyanamide process installed in 1918. The modernized plant is reported to be capable of producing daily some 300 tons of ammonium nitrate, an ingredient of high explosives.[27]

The T.V.A. program of phosphorus production also paid dividends in terms of defense and war purposes. Increased demand for this material came from three sources: the War Department required elemental phosphorus for various war uses, while in both Great Britain and the United States there was a greatly increased need for fertilizers in connection with expanded war agricultural programs. The T.V.A. experiments with concentrated phosphatic fertilizers were of particular help to the British, making possible the saving of valuable shipping space.

To meet these added requirements, the T.V.A. built a new phosphate electric furnace capable of increasing capacity from 100,-000 tons annually to 150,000 tons. In addition the construction of a calcium metaphosphate plant at Mobile of 75,000 tons annual capacity was authorized, to be completed by 1944. This location was favored because of easy access by water to the large Florida reserves of phosphate rock. Moreover, after the war cheap water transportation of fertilizer from this plant to agricultural states bordering the Mississippi River would be available.

For the duration of the war the T.V.A. is limiting to a minimum the use of phosphatic fertilizers in its tests and demonstrations program, and is reserving the greater proportion of its plant capacity for the War Department, the Agricultural Adjustment Administration, and Great Britain. By the beginning of 1942 the War Department had placed orders which would require almost one-third of

27. T.V.A. press release, August 1, 1941.

the expanded T.V.A. plant capacity, and their needs were expected to increase.[28]

The war effort was also responsible for stepping up research efforts on emergency needs conducted by or through the T.V.A., particularly with respect to vital defense materials. Late in 1941 the T.V.A. submitted to the Office of Production Management a complete report of a new process for the production of alumina from clay, the result of a five-year research effort.[29] Since then attention has been turned to the perfection of a process for producing magnesium from olivine, of which there are large deposits in or near the Tennessee Valley. The T.V.A. has also taken on other emergency services, such as the construction and management of defense houses in the Muscle Shoals area for the Federal Works Agency.

So it is that the Muscle Shoals development, completed too late to aid in the first World War, had a head start on the job of winning the second World War. The plough-shares created in time of peace —power plants, fertilizer plants, navigable streams—have proved to be useful swords in the war against fascism.

28. Hearings, House Appropriations Committee, "Independent Offices Appropriation Bill for 1943," pp. 864–66.
29. See 105 *New Republic* 456 (October 13, 1941).

3: Power - Finding a Market

> "It is my personal belief that the T.V.A. should
> go out of the power business and confine itself to its
> functions of flood control, navigation, and soil conser-
> vation. I have always been convinced that the power
> activities of the T.V.A. violate the Federal Constitu-
> tion. The soundest solution both for the Government
> and the utilities would be for the T.V.A. to dispose
> of the power generated by it to the utilities at the
> switchboard."—*Wendell Willkie (1938)*

THE DEVELOPMENT of the T.V.A. as a power agency has proceeded, all things considered, at a phenomenal pace. When
the Authority began business in 1933, it had available for purchasers
the power generated by a single hydroelectric plant; today it is one
of the five or six largest power operators in the country, and still
growing. The power generating capacity of the T.V.A. had increased from 184,000 kilowatts to 1,374,500 kilowatts by the middle
of 1942, and its annual power revenues jumped from a low point
of $369,000 in the fiscal year 1935 to $24,000,000 seven years later.
The organization has passed through a period when there was the
gravest doubt whether it could constitutionally sell the surplus power
generated at Wilson Dam, to a time when it operates steam generating plants without any constitutional questions being raised. Once
attacked because of the fantastic amounts of power which it was
proposing to generate, for which it was claimed there could be no
possible market, it has lived to see its planned capacity proving inadequate for national defense needs and having to be supplemented
by hastily authorized additional projects and enlargement of existing facilities. Now that the major power controversies have been

settled and the major power policies formulated, the principal steps in the process by which these results have been achieved may be reviewed.

THE CONSTITUTIONAL ISSUE

As was pointed out in the opening chapter, the T.V.A. Act constituted a victory for the view that the Wilson Dam power plant should be used as the nucleus of a public power program, which the T.V.A. was to foster and encourage. The T.V.A. was authorized "to sell the surplus power not used in its operations . . . and in the sale of such current by the board it shall give preference to States, counties, municipalities, and cooperative organizations of citizens or farmers, not organized or doing business for profit. . . ." Sale of T.V.A. power to industry was to be only "a secondary purpose" to be utilized in securing a sufficiently high load factor, and if power was sold to utility companies for resale at a profit, it was required to be under contracts subject to cancellation upon five years' notice, and at prices not exceeding "a schedule fixed by the board from time to time as reasonable, just, and fair. . . ."

In another extremely important provision the Act authorized the T.V.A. "to construct, lease, purchase, or authorize the construction of transmission lines within transmission distance from the place where generated, and to interconnect with other systems." Such authority, the Act stated, was necessary "to place the board upon a fair basis for making . . . contracts and for receiving bids for the sale of . . . power," thus rejecting the view that the government should limit its activity simply to making the power available at the power house. Statutory authority for the undertaking of a vigorous power program was found in these provisions.

Could such a program be constitutionally undertaken by an agency of the federal government?[1] This question haunted the

---

1. This question has been discussed in numerous law review articles, of which the following are representative: "Constitutionality of the TVA as a Power Development Program," 48 *Harvard Law Review* 806–15 (1935); E. F. Albertsworth, "Constitutional Issues of the Federal Power Program," 29 *Illinois Law Review* 833–66 (1935); H. M. Martell, "Legal Aspects of the T.V.A.," 7 *George Washington Law Review* 983–1012 (1939).

T.V.A. during the first five or six years of its existence, and the ghost was not finally laid until January, 1939.

From the first it was recognized that the constitutional leg on which the T.V.A. might most surely stand was the power of Congress to regulate commerce among the several states. The Supreme Court in the early case of *Gibbons* v. *Ogden* [2] decided that in the exercise of this authority Congress had power to regulate navigation. Throughout the long struggle over the Muscle Shoals problem, all the important bills providing for public operation made some reference to the navigation aspects of the program. The title of the T.V.A. Act as finally adopted began: "To improve the navigability and to provide for the flood control of the Tennessee River. . . ."

A reading of the voluminous congressional debates on the subject reveals that very seldom was the question of constitutionality of power sales by the federal government discussed. [3] This was hardly surprising, for the only power then under consideration was that produced at Wilson Dam, which had been built as a war measure, and so was supported by the government's war power as well as its power to regulate commerce. Perhaps because of this lack of congressional concern on the subject, the T.V.A. Act was not as well buttressed from a constitutional point of view as it might have been. As already noted, the T.V.A. was not made responsible for undertaking the nine-foot navigation project adopted by Congress for the Tennessee River in 1930; moreover, there was in the act no specific statement as to the "incidental" nature of power generation. These deficiencies were remedied in 1935, when the statute was amended to authorize the Authority to construct such dams as would "provide a nine-foot channel in the said river . . . and best serve to promote navigation," and an entire new section was added which provided:

2. 9 Wheat. 1 (1824).
3. However, Senator Bruce on one occasion said: ". . . if this measure shall go into effect attempting to confer upon the Federal Government the authority to produce power at Muscle Shoals, it will be declared in that respect by the Supreme Court of the United States to be an absolutely nugatory, unconstitutional and void thing." (69 *Cong. Rec.* 9724.) On the other hand, Senator Norris on several occasions stated the constitutional basis for the dams.

The board is hereby directed in the operation of any dam or reservoir in its possession and control to regulate the stream flow primarily for the purposes of promoting navigation and controlling floods. So far as may be consistent with such purposes, the board is authorized to provide and operate facilities for the generation of electric energy at any such dam for the use of the Corporation and for the use of the United States or any agency thereof; and the board is further authorized, whenever an opportunity is afforded, to provide and operate facilities for the generation of electric energy in order to avoid the waste of water power, to transmit and market such power as in this act provided, and thereby, so far as may be practicable, to assist in liquidating the cost or aid in the maintenance of the projects of the Authority.[4]

With this statutory basis, the T.V.A. seemed favorably situated to withstand an assault on constitutional grounds. Supreme Court decisions, from 1877 on, had settled that the federal government could, either directly or by grant to the states, provide for the construction of canals, dams, piers, and other works for the improvement of navigation.[5] Then in 1891 the Court had ruled that a state which accepted such a grant and built a dam and canal was entitled as against riparian owners to the "surplus" water power thereby made available. The Court added the warning that the power development must be "a mere incident to the public improvement," and that the power must not be produced by "a wholly unnecessary excess of water." [6] The importance of this limitation was diminished, however, when the Supreme Court in 1913 failed to stress it in deciding that the federal government was entitled to the use and disposal of water power created by a project undertaken directly by it.[7] In 1920 Congress exercised further authority in this field by passing the Federal Water Power Act, creating the Federal Power Commission to license and regulate all dams, hydroelectric develop-

4. Sec. 9a.
5. *Wisconsin* v. *Duluth*, 96 U.S. 379 (1877).
6. *Kaukauna Water Power Co.* v. *Green Bay & Mississippi Canal Co.*, 142 U.S. 254 (1891).
7. *U.S.* v. *Chandler-Dunbar Water Power Co.*, 229 U.S. 53 (1913).

ments, and "other project works necessary or convenient for the development and improvement of navigation," and forbidding the construction of dams in navigable streams except as such licenses were secured.

The most useful precedent for the T.V.A. was, however, the Boulder Canyon Project Act of 1928, providing for the construction by the government of a huge dam and hydroelectric plant on the Colorado River. The purpose of the dam was stated to be to improve navigation, to reclaim public lands, and "for the generation of electric energy as a means of making the project . . . a self-supporting and financially solvent undertaking." The state of Arizona subsequently sued to prevent construction of the dam, alleging that the recital in the act that the purpose was the improvement of navigation was a subterfuge. There was no doubt that the dam's effect on navigation was insignificant in comparison with the irrigation, flood control, and power aspects of the project, but the Court declared:

> As the river is navigable and the means which the act provides are not unrelated to the control of navigation . . . the erection and maintenance of such dam and reservoir are clearly within the powers conferred upon Congress. . . . And the fact that purposes other than navigation will also be served could not invalidate the exercise of the authority conferred, even if those other purposes would not alone have justified an exercise of Congressional power. . . . The possible abuse of the power to regulate navigation is not an argument against its existence.[8]

The first serious test of the constitutionality of the T.V.A. power operations was provided when in September, 1934, holders of a small minority of the preferred stock of the Alabama Power Co. sued to prevent their company from carrying out a contract it had entered into providing for the sale of certain of its properties to the T.V.A.[9] As the case was developed it presented for judicial determination the question whether T.V.A. was acting within the constitutional powers of the United States in selling power generated at Wilson Dam, and in providing its own transmission lines for the pur-

8. *Arizona* v. *California*, 283 U.S. 423, 455–57 (1931).
9. The provisions of this contract are discussed more fully *infra*, p. 66.

pose of facilitating such sales. The plaintiffs enjoyed a sweeping preliminary success, District Judge William I. Grubb holding in February, 1935, that the program of the T.V.A. for the manufacture and
disposal of surplus electric power bore no substantial relation to any
lawful governmental function, but constituted instead an illegal proprietary operation.[10] The court considered that, while the T.V.A.
had the implied right to dispose of any surplus electric power unin-
tentionally created in the exercise of a bona fide effort to make such
power only as was needed for the manufacture of war materials and
for serving the necessities of navigation, it had no constitutional
authority *intentionally* to create and sell any additional surplus.

The court therefore ordered the annulment of the contract in
question because it was in furtherance of "illegal proprietary operations," and enjoined 17 municipalities in the Alabama Power Co.
area, which were under contract to take power from the T.V.A.,
from accepting or spending federal P.W.A. funds for the construction of city plants, on the ground that these contracts were entered
into in aid of the illegal operations of the T.V.A. These same municipalities, plus the city of Athens, Alabama, which owned its distribution system, were further enjoined from purchasing power from the
T.V.A., because it was in illegal competition with the Alabama
Power Co.

On appeal, this judgment was completely reversed.[11] The circuit court of appeals for the fifth circuit held that Wilson Dam had
been built lawfully under the war and commerce powers, and that
the water power which thus became the property of the United
States could be disposed of, under Article IV, section 3, of the Constitution, as freely as any other government property. Judge Grubb
was admonished:

> It never heretofore has been held that the right of disposal
> exists only as to such part as is accidentally produced in excess
> of the amount strictly necessary for purposes of national de-
> fense or of navigation, but always that right has been supposed
> to extend to all the excess or surplus. . . . As a practical mat-

10. 8 F. Supp. 893 (1934); 9 F. Supp. 965 (1935).
11. 78 F. (2d) 578 (1935).

ter there would be no market for the incidental or accidental
surplus created in the honest effort to produce only enough
electricity to supply strictly governmental requirements; for no
user, public or private, of electricity would become a customer
unless assurance could be given of a firm and dependable
supply.

Because of the fact that Wilson Dam alone could adequately serve
the transmission lines involved in the contract, the court considered
discussion of other T.V.A. dams and their constitutional basis to be
immaterial.

The case was finally decided by the Supreme Court in February, 1936, and its decision was a complete victory for the T.V.A.[12]
The Supreme Court followed the circuit court of appeals in limiting
its consideration to Wilson Dam, concerning the constitutionality
of which there could be no question, and in excluding any discussion of the general policies or plans of the T.V.A. for "social experimentation" which the district judge had permitted to be dragged
into the case. With these limitations established, the issue was simply whether the same broad authority which the government had
always enjoyed in disposing of its other forms of property extended
to disposition of electric power. The court found no reason for applying a special rule in this field; Judge Grubb's theory was rejected
as leading to "absurd consequences." The methods used in disposing
of this property, the court indicated, would have to be appropriate
to the nature of the property, adopted in the public interest as distinguished from private or personal ends, and consistent with the
rights of the states under the Constitution. The use by the T.V.A.
of its own transmission lines did not violate any of these principles.
These lines, in the Court's words, simply "furnish a method of reaching a market. The alternative method is to sell the surplus energy
at the dam, and the market there appears to be limited to one pur-
chaser. . . . We know of no constitutional ground upon which the

12. *Ashwander* v. *T.V.A.*, 297 U.S. 288 (1936). Four justices joined in a separate opinion holding that the stockholders were without legal standing to maintain
such a suit. Outvoted on this issue, they concurred in the majority opinion on the
merits of the case.

Federal Government can be denied the right to seek a wider market." In the Tennessee Valley factory whistles were blown and public celebrations of the decision were organized.

Favorable as was the Supreme Court's decision in the *Ashwander* case, it left unanswered several constitutional questions raised by T.V.A. operations. It ruled on the constitutionality only of Wilson Dam, for which there was an exceptionally strong case. The Supreme Court expressed no opinion on the other dams, or on the validity of the T.V.A. Act. It did not pass on the right of the government to acquire or operate local or urban distribution systems. It did not determine whether the T.V.A. could build or operate steam plants. It did not say whether the T.V.A. could purchase power for distribution purposes. In short, the *Ashwander* decision did not clearly indicate where the dividing line was between a constitutional program for the disposition of surplus power and an unconstitutional proprietary enterprise.

The utilities were not slow to take advantage of this uncertainty. In May, 1936, nineteen public utility companies, operating in nine states, brought suit against the T.V.A., alleging that the T.V.A. Act and the actions of the Authority's directors under it were unconstitutional. An injunction was sought against the carrying out of the T.V.A. power program, except "to the extent the production and sale of power at Wilson Dam has been held legal." In practical effect, the injunction asked for would have stopped the power operations of all T.V.A.-built dams, and would have prevented the continued construction of such dams.

After a year and a half of legal maneuvers, which included the granting and subsequent reversal of a temporary injunction against T.V.A. operations, the case was finally brought to trial before a special three-judge district court in November, 1937.[13] The trial lasted two months, and resulted in dismissal of the bill of complaint. In its decision the court first disposed of certain allegations not involving constitutional questions, but charging the T.V.A. with coercion, conspiracy, malice and fraud in its power operations. The court found

13. *Tennessee Electric Power Co.* v. *T.V.A.*, 21 F. Supp. 947 (1938).

no conspiracy between the T.V.A. and the Public Works Administration to finance the construction of duplicating municipal distribution lines, pointing out that "cooperative action by two groups of public officials in administering the provisions of two statutes does not constitute conspiracy." While the court found that none of the utilities had suffered as yet by reason of T.V.A. operations, it did concede that there were prospects of "substantial future damage to these complainants. But such damage constitutes *damnum absque injuria* unless sales of power by the TVA are unlawful."

Thus the court was brought up squarely to a consideration of the legality of T.V.A. power activities and the constitutionality of the statute. The complainants contended that the T.V.A. dams could not and would not be operated within the terms of the provision directing such operation "primarily for the purpose of promoting navigation and controlling floods." Evidence as to the actual operation of the dams convinced the court, however, that navigation and flood control had been given primary consideration, and that the statute had been neither violated nor exceeded.

But was the statute itself constitutional? The utilities contended that it was enacted primarily for power purposes, and that such matters as flood control, navigation, and national defense were "incidental and merely a cloak for the unlawful purpose of permitting the Government to enter the power business." The court, on the other hand, concluded that the effect of the project on navigation and flood control was clear, that the system of dams was "reasonably adapted to use for combined flood control, navigation, power and national defense, and that in actual operation the creation of energy is subordinated to the needs of navigation and flood control. . . . The dams and their power equipment . . . must be taken to have been authorized, constructed and planned in the exercise of the constitutional functions of the Government." The only other constitutional contention was that the T.V.A. Act amounted to an unlawful interference with the police power of the states because the T.V.A. regulated rates and operated within the states without being subject to their control. The court summarily dismissed this objection, noting that the question was not properly before the court and indicating that in any event the T.V.A. Act did not violate either the Ninth or Tenth Amendment.

The opinion of the trial court has been sketched in here because it is the fullest and most authoritative judicial discussion to date of the constitutional aspects of the T.V.A. program. The decision was, of course, appealed to the Supreme Court, but there the case was disposed of by a ruling that the utility companies had no legal standing to bring the suit, thus making unnecessary any holding on the major constitutional questions presented in the T.V.A. Act.[14] Taking up a point which the district court had considered but had not pressed to its logical conclusion, the Supreme Court pointed out that the utilities had no case against the T.V.A. unless it had violated their legal rights. The utilities contended that they did have legal rights by reason of their charters and franchises, which they claimed to be property protected from injury or destruction by competition. The Court's answer was that neither the charters nor the local franchises granted a monopoly or rendered competition illegal. Thus T.V.A. competition was perfectly legal. Damage suffered by the utilities was and could not furnish the basis for legal action.

Consequently this second major test of T.V.A. constitutionality was brought to a conclusion without any final determination of the issues left unsettled by the *Ashwander* decision. However, the decision did have the effect, for all practical purposes, of liquidating the constitutional issue, since it seemed to leave open no legal channels for attacking the T.V.A. power program. There was, moreover, little reason to doubt that had the Supreme Court decided the case on the merits, it would have reached the same conclusion as the lower court. Thus the constitutionality of the T.V.A., once so pressing an issue, was finally established by default.

DEVELOPMENT OF A SERVICE AREA

When the T.V.A. began operations, its only source of power supply was Wilson Dam, and its only customer was the Alabama

14. *Tennessee Electric Power Co.* v. *T.V.A.*, 306 U.S. 118 (1939).

Power Company, which had the sole transmission line to the dam. The T.V.A. immediately took steps to widen its market. A "power policy" was formulated and announced in August, 1933, in which the Authority indicated that it proposed to give service in the regions around Muscle Shoals and Norris Dam and along the transmission line which was to be constructed between those two dams. Later on, the policy indicated, the Authority would expand its service area. Electric service was already being given in these regions, of course, by existing private companies; there were only a few instances of municipal ownership in the area. The T.V.A. policy consequently announced that in marketing power in the selected areas, every effort would be made to avoid construction of duplicate facilities. Instead, a genuine attempt would be made to purchase such facilities from the private utilities on an equitable basis.

It happened that the operating companies in the service areas selected by the T.V.A. were for the most part subsidiaries of the Commonwealth & Southern Corporation or the National Power & Light Company (itself a subsidiary of Electric Bond and Share). Negotiations were undertaken with both companies, and a far-reaching contract was signed with Commonwealth & Southern on January 4, 1934. By its terms the company agreed to sell to the T.V.A. three groups of its properties—the entire system of the Mississippi Power Co. in nine counties in northeastern Mississippi for $850,000; properties (not including municipal distribution systems) of the Alabama Power Co. in seven counties in the immediate Muscle Shoals area for $1,100,000; and properties of the Tennessee Electric Power Co. in five East Tennessee counties for $900,000.

This contract also contained an agreement as to division of territory between the Commonwealth & Southern and the T.V.A. The power company agreed not to sell power in any of the counties involved after the transfer of the properties agreed upon. The T.V.A. in return promised not to sell power outside the stated counties to any customer supplied at the time of the contract by the Commonwealth & Southern companies. This agreement on respective spheres of influence was to be effective for five years, or until three months after completion of the Norris Dam power house, whichever date was earlier. In accepting this arrangement the T.V.A. was not really imposing any limitation on its operations, for so long as Wilson Dam was its sole source of power its output would be insufficient to enable it to go outside the ceded area.

In addition to this contract, the T.V.A. was successful in negotiating, later in 1934, a contract with the National Power & Light Co. for the purchase of the eastern Tennessee electric properties of the Tennessee Public Service Co., which included the distribution system of the city of Knoxville. The T.V.A. thus seemed to have made a handsome beginning in securing an outlet for its power. The appearance was deceptive, however. Of all the properties covered in these two contracts, only those of the Mississippi Power Co. were actually transferred at that time to T.V.A. ownership, delivery being accepted in June, 1934. Various legal obstructions prevented the consummation of the other transactions. Consequently T.V.A. power operations got under way on a much more limited scale than had been anticipated. By the end of its first year of operation the Authority was selling power to only five public agencies, serving a total of 6,500 customers. During that year 98 per cent of the total T.V.A. power output went to the Alabama Power Co., which was almost no improvement on the record of the War Department in disposing of Wilson Dam power.

The development of a market for T.V.A. power is summarized in Table I, which shows the amount of power the T.V.A. has sold, by fiscal years and types of customers, as well as power receipts for the various years.[15] The Authority's attention was directed first to the securing of municipal customers, for cities are obviously the public agencies most likely to be interested in and most able to undertake power distribution. The cities of Tupelo, Miss., and Athens, Ala., which both owned their own distribution systems, were quick to sign T.V.A. contracts. But few other cities in the area were in such a fortunate position, and while there was abundant interest in

15. In addition to the sales shown by Table I, large amounts of power have been continuously used by the T.V.A. itself, in its fertilizer plant and in construction operations.

Table I

T.V.A. POWER SALES, BY CLASSES OF USE,

AND POWER REVENUES, 1934–1942

(000 omitted)

Fiscal Year	Municipalities	Cooperative Associations	Electric Utilities	Industries	Direct Sales	Total Revenues †
1934	2,913*	**	386,964	....	**	$826
1935	12,814	4,251	2,903	....	3,934	369
1936	21,363	12,609	296,038	....	4,497	828
1937	44,724	22,020	514,067	5,548	15,842	1,243
1938	63,914	34,026	62,337	358,075	12,661	2,306
1939	253,028	48,483	192,166	901,509	26,977	4,933
1940	1,539,563	141,930	523,232	1,169,058	27,566	14,517
1941	2,038,211	223,826	626,654	1,809,664	10,325	20,254
1942	2,327,449	282,171	679,489	2,409,931	8,500	24,308

* All figures on power sales are in kilowatt-hours.
** Included under municipal sales.
† Sales within T.V.A. excluded.

securing T.V.A. power, their efforts to buy out the existing private companies or to undertake the construction of competing systems nearly all failed or were delayed by legal action. Consequently the T.V.A. made very slow progress in the municipal field, and by July, 1938, had only 19 municipal contractors; these were all small cities or towns, serving a total of only 19,000 customers. Revenues from municipal sales in the fiscal year 1938 were $342,000.

This record was also attributable to the court actions which were plaguing the T.V.A. itself during this period. Even ice and coal companies brought suits to restrain the Authority's activities. As already noted, performance of the Commonwealth & Southern contract was enjoined by the district court in the *Ashwander* case in February, 1935. This decision was subsequently reversed by the Supreme Court in February, 1936, but in the year intervening the program of the T.V.A. had been seriously delayed and grave doubt had been aroused concerning its chances for continued existence. It might also be mentioned that the pendency of litigation caused the Electric Bond and Share to refuse to convey its Knoxville properties, as it had contracted to do. During this period several municipalities which had been balked in attempts to purchase distribution systems began to talk about, or to undertake, the construction of competing systems, securing P.W.A. grants for this purpose.

The Norris Dam power house was completed in August, 1936, which meant that the contract between the T.V.A. and Commonwealth & Southern would expire 90 days later, thus terminating the agreement on division of territory between the two parties. Some definite limitation of the T.V.A. sphere of activity was regarded as absolutely essential by the Commonwealth & Southern Corporation, because its officials felt that uncertainty as to the future of T.V.A. competition was seriously injuring their operating companies. Utilities in other parts of the country were taking advantage of low interest rates to undertake refinancing operations, but the companies in the T.V.A. area, it was contended, were prevented from making such economies because the T.V.A. threat made their securities unsaleable.

Several times during this period Wendell L. Willkie, president of Commonwealth & Southern, met with David E. Lilienthal, power director of the T.V.A., and presented suggestions for a division of area between the two agencies. Within the proposed "ceded area," which it was suggested might follow the watershed line of the Tennessee Valley, the Commonwealth & Southern would dispose of its properties to the T.V.A. Outside of this area, the T.V.A would agree to sell power not required for its own needs to Commonwealth & Southern, but to no other customer.[16] Such an agreement would have meant that the T.V.A. could not sell power to any city or other public agency outside the ceded area. The proposal was not acceptable to Mr. Lilienthal, who considered it contrary to the provisions of the T.V.A. statute providing preferential treatment for public agencies. Mr. Willkie also discussed the proposal with President Roosevelt on several occasions, and Mr. Roosevelt likewise found it

16. A complete statement of the Commonwealth & Southern position is given in a letter from Mr. Willkie to President Roosevelt, dated September 30, 1936, reprinted in *Hearings*, pp. 870–72.

objectionable.[17] On August 4, 1936, the T.V.A. board adopted, over the dissent of Chairman Morgan, the following resolution: "Resolved, That in future contracts the Authority will not agree to territorial restrictions on the sale of Tennessee Valley Authority power to public agencies." [18]

The approaching termination of the 1934 contract made it imperative, however, that action of some kind be taken. In May, 1936, Mr. Lilienthal had made a tentative suggestion to Mr. Willkie of a southeastern power pool participated in by both private and public agencies, with a "pool gateway rate." Such a pool would, he felt, give the companies the advantage of low T.V.A. wholesale rates, and permit savings resulting from integration of generation and transmission facilities. Although this plan would have virtually eliminated competition between the utilities and the T.V.A., Mr. Willkie opposed it, according to Mr. Lilienthal, because it did not provide certainty for his companies against municipal competition.[19]

Later in the year President Roosevelt undertook to accomplish something along the same line. On September 17, 1936, he invited the T.V.A. and the Commonwealth & Southern, along with representatives of other government agencies and private interests, to participate in a conference to explore the possibilities of a "power pool or grid system" in the Tennessee Valley area, involving the joint use of power transmission facilities. His letter went on: "As the existing contracts between Commonwealth & Southern and the Tennessee Valley Authority for interchange of power and common use of some transmission lines—a rudimentary form of power pool —are due to expire within a few weeks, an early conference appears desirable." [20] The conference was held on September 30, and was, at the request of the President, limited to the subject of the pooling of transmission. The T.V.A., the Federal Power Commission, and the Commonwealth & Southern were asked to make a joint study of the facts on this subject, which was undertaken and completed.

17. See Senate Doc. No. 155, 75th Cong., 3d sess., p. 61.
18. Reprinted in *Hearings*, p. 866.
19. *Hearings*, p. 865.
20. *Hearings*, p. 899.

Nothing came of these plans, however. In May, 1936, the Tennessee Electric Power Co. and 18 other utility companies had filed suit against the T.V.A. in a broad attack on the constitutionality of its power program. On December 22, 1936, a temporary injunction was granted which prevented the T.V.A. from making or negotiating any new contracts or providing any additional facilities for the sale of power within the claimed service area of any of the complainants until final adjudication of the case. The Authority's power activities were thus paralyzed, and the government concluded that any general settlement with the utilities under such conditions could not be considered.[21]

The shadow of this injunction lay over the T.V.A. activities for six months, and the Authority did not finally come into the clear on the constitutional issue until the Supreme Court decision of January, 1939. Even before it had been rendered, however, the log jam of obstruction that had so effectively prevented the T.V.A. from finding municipal outlets was beginning to break up. In January, 1938, the Supreme Court had affirmed the validity of P.W.A. loans and grants to municipalities for the construction of distribution systems, ruling that private power companies were not immune from lawful competition.[22] In September, 1938, the Tennessee Public Service Co., faced with the certainty of municipal competition from a system already under construction, sold out its electric properties to the city of Knoxville and the T.V.A., thus adding 34,000 customers to the T.V.A. system. In November and December the Kentucky-Tennessee Light & Power Co. sold its properties in northwestern Tennessee, serving some 10,000 customers. In January, 1939, the West Tennessee Power & Light Co., with 10,000 customers, took similar action. The city of Memphis had undertaken construction of its own system and was serving some 6,000 customers before the Memphis Power & Light Co. finally agreed, in June, 1939, to sell its system, with 57,000 customers, to the city.

By far the most important purchase, however, was that of the

21. See President Roosevelt's letter of January 25, 1937, in *Hearings,* pp. 867–68.

22. *Alabama Power Co. v. Ickes,* 302 U.S. 464 (1938).

Tennessee Electric Power Co. properties. The Commonwealth & Southern had long maintained that it would not sell any parts of its system, such as the Chattanooga properties, since that would make the rest of the system an uneconomical unit. But it had often indicated that, if T.V.A. competition was to continue, it would look favorably on a sale of the entire T.E.P. system. After the Supreme Court decision in January, 1939, negotiations were renewed and an agreement for the sale of the system for the sum of $78,600,000 was reached. The properties, serving 142,000 customers, were transferred in August of that year, adding Nashville, Chattanooga, and 20 smaller cities to the list of T.V.A. customers. This acquisition program was rounded out with a purchase from the Mississippi Power Co. in December, 1939, of Alabama Power Co. properties in the Huntsville area in July, 1940, and of Kentucky-Tennessee Light and Power Co. systems in five cities and nine counties of western Kentucky in June, 1942.[23]

In all of these major acquisitions the purchases were made jointly by the T.V.A. and the cities affected, the T.V.A. taking possession of the generating plants and the transmission properties, and the cities acquiring the local distribution systems. The T.V.A. share of the Tennessee Electric Power Co. purchase price was approximately $45,000,000, while the city of Nashville paid $14,300,000, Chattanooga $10,850,000, and so on. In the Knoxville purchase the T.V.A. share of the total price of $8,274,000 was $2,549,000, the city paying the rest. With the exception of Memphis, which issued general obligation bonds, the cities purchasing distribution systems under T.V.A. auspices have financed them by the issuance of electric revenue bonds, supported by the revenues of the electric system rather than by the general credit of the respective municipalities. The cities participating in the T.E.P. Co. purchase sold approximately $34,400,000 worth of revenue bonds at interest rates ranging

23. The Kentucky transfer was unusual in that the properties could not be immediately integrated with the T.V.A. system. Integration probably cannot be effected until Kentucky Dam is completed. In the meantime, the T.V.A. will supply power from the steam generating plants acquired in the transfer, and the rates will be higher than the standard rates on the T.V.A. system, though lower than the previously-existing rates in this area.

from 3.6 to 2.3 per cent, these low rates testifying to the general confidence in the soundness of these municipal enterprises.

The T.V.A. had thus by 1942 carried through a program of negotiation and purchase which put practically every city in Tennessee, as well as many in adjacent states, in the power business. In all, 83 municipalities were contracting for T.V.A. power by July, 1942. Over 2,000,000,000 kilowatt-hours of electricity were sold to them in the fiscal year 1942, and revenues from these sales brought $9,556,000 to the T.V.A.

Disposition of T.V.A. power has not been limited, of course, to cities and urban areas. It has already been noted that one of the factors emphasized in the public power case for Muscle Shoals was the need for increased attention to rural electrification. Several sections of the T.V.A. Act specifically referred to the responsibility for bringing power to farms and small villages. From the beginning the principal method which the T.V.A. has employed to meet this obligation has been to encourage and facilitate the formation of rural power cooperatives. It is true that a number of the city systems have undertaken to render service to the rural areas immediately adjacent, but much more important has been the work of the electric membership corporations or electric power associations, to which, as "cooperative organizations of citizens or farmers, not organized or doing business for profit, but primarily for the purpose of supplying electricity to its own citizens or members," the T.V.A. Act directed that preferential treatment be given.

The first organization of this sort for the disposition of T.V.A. power was the Alcorn County Electric Power Association, formed in 1934 as a non-profit membership corporation to buy from the T.V.A. and operate the electric system in and around Corinth, Miss., which the T.V.A. had secured in its Mississippi Power Co. purchase. Membership in the association cost $100, payable by a one dollar a month surcharge on electric bills. The association, with T.V.A. guidance and advice, set up an operating organization, and agreed to pay its debt to the T.V.A. over a period of years out of surplus revenues. The T.V.A. was to construct additional rural lines for the association's system, which would be paid for in the same way. The association was to receive T.V.A. power at regular wholesale rates.

In the fiscal years 1935 and 1936, five more electric power associations were organized in the Mississippi area. In 1935 both the Alabama and Tennessee legislatures adopted statutes authorizing electric cooperatives, and in the fiscal year 1937 five began service in Tennessee, one in Alabama, and one in Georgia. By the end of the 1942 fiscal year, 45 electric cooperatives were contracting for service from the T.V.A. In that year the T.V.A. sold them 282,000,-000 kilowatt-hours of power, receiving revenues of $1,589,000 from these sales. It should be borne in mind that from 1935 on the Rural Electrification Authority was active in this field, and it largely took over from the T.V.A. the responsibility of stimulating and organizing power cooperatives in the T.V.A. area.

In a relatively small number of cases the T.V.A. has found it impossible to secure the formation of an electric cooperative or for some other reason has undertaken to render direct service to a rural or unincorporated area. Where this is the case, the T.V.A. builds the lines, delivers power to residential customers, bills them for service, and so on. These operations are regarded as strictly temporary in character, to be continued only until a municipal or cooperative distributor is ready to take over the service. That this goal is being achieved is shown by the data on direct sales in Table I.

The development of a policy on sales of power to industrial concerns and public utility companies was a matter of some difficulty. The statute permitted, though it did not encourage, such disposition of power, stating that the purpose of these sales should be "principally to secure a sufficiently high load factor and revenue returns which will permit domestic and rural use at the lowest possible rates. . . ." Despite the "secondary purpose" of sales to industrial companies and utilities, these channels have been extremely important to the T.V.A. power program. When the T.V.A. was organized, the one customer it inherited was the Alabama Power Co. Sales to this company continued, and in the 1934 Commonwealth & Southern contract a basis was provided for the continued purchase of power from, and interchange of power with, the T.V.A. Extremely heavy purchases of power were made by the company in the fiscal year 1934, but they dropped off to practically nothing the following year. T.V.A. officials considered that this failure to purchase power reflected a definite intent to keep the T.V.A. plant idle.

Power company purchases picked up, however, late in 1935, but even so the failure to secure municipal outlets, noted above, meant that the T.V.A. was disposing of only a fraction of its potential output. This situation became more serious as the Norris and Wheeler dams neared completion, with their addition to the system's capacity. Under these circumstances, the T.V.A. decided that it would be in the public interest, and not contrary to the provisions of the act requiring preference to be given to public agencies, to dispose of some of the power, which would otherwise be wasted, to industries and utility companies. In May, 1936, a 20-year contract was entered into with the Monsanto Chemical Co. providing 50,000 kilowatts of firm and interruptible power for its plant at Columbia, Tenn., then under construction. The second important industrial customer was the Aluminum Company of America, which contracted in 1936 for 40,000 kilowatts of secondary power, and in 1937 for an additional 60,000 kilowatts, half primary and half secondary. The Aluminum Co. and the T.V.A. likewise agreed to provide standby service for each other. Contracts were also signed with the Arkansas Power & Light Co. and other important industrial users.

These industrial and utility contracts were subjected to irresponsible attacks on the ground that the T.V.A. was forsaking the interests of the municipal and rural user, and diverting the advantages of cheap power to huge corporations. When the defense program got under way in 1940, however, and the necessity for a vast increase in aluminum production was realized, the availability of T.V.A. power proved providential in the highest degree. Almost overnight the opponents of the T.V.A. turned from bemoaning its great surplus of power capacity to allegations that the T.V.A. had flunked its defense test by having insufficient power available.

Table II

T.V.A. POWER REVENUES FROM DIFFERENT
CLASSES OF SALES, FISCAL YEARS 1939–1942 *
(000 omitted)

Classes	1939	1940	1941	1942
Municipalities............	$1,228	$6,678	$8,633	$9,556
Cooperatives............	288	836	1,300	1,589
Electric Utilities........	561	2,184	2,361	2,739
Industries.............	2,508	4,423	7,780	10,249
Direct Sales............	348	396	180	159
Other Federal Agencies..	...	...	...	16
Total..............	$4,933	$14,517	$20,254	$24,308

* Interdepartmental sales within the T.V.A. excluded.

During the severe drought of 1941 the T.V.A. played a major part in keeping the Alcoa aluminum plant in full production, supplying it 140,000 to 150,000 kilowatts of emergency power over and above the 30,000 kilowatts of firm power for which the contract called. The Aluminum Company subsequently contracted with the T.V.A. for the enormous additional amount of 120,000 kilowatts of firm power, required for the company's new reduction plant and rolling mill. The T.V.A. also supplied power directly to several other large chemical and metals plants, ordnance works, and munitions plants, as well as to its own expanded war plants at Muscle Shoals. To meet this tremendous war production load, the T.V.A. had to press into service all available generation facilities in the area. Sales to industries and utilities amounted in the fiscal year 1942 to more than half of the total T.V.A. power sold, and brought in well over half of total T.V.A. power revenues.

GENERATION AND TRANSMISSION

Thus far attention has been concentrated on the development of the power disposition program, and no notice has been taken of the growth of T.V.A. generation facilities and its transmission system. For over two years all T.V.A. power came from the Wilson

Dam power plant, with its installed capacity of 184,000 kilowatts. Since 1936, new T.V.A. dams have been completed almost yearly, adding steadily to the capacity of the system. In practically all of the dams, space has been provided for more generating units than were originally to be installed, but the rapid growth of power needs, especially under the impetus of the national defense program, has meant that additional power generating units have had to be added faster than was ever contemplated. The Kentucky Dam, at first planned without initial power installation, is now scheduled for five 32,000 kilowatt generators. Doubling of the Pickwick capacity was authorized in 1940, six new generators added 150,000 kilowatts to the Wilson Dam capacity, and the doubling of the capacity at Wheeler Dam was completed in 1941. Wilson Dam remained the most important generating plant, with an installed capacity in 1942 of 335,200 kilowatts. Generating capacity at other major dams (actual or planned, 1942) was as follows: Fontana, 201,000; Kentucky, 160,000; Watts Bar, 150,000; Pickwick Landing, 144,000; Wheeler, 129,600; and Norris, 100,800.

In addition to its dams, it must not be forgotten that the T.V.A. acquired among its Muscle Shoals properties a 60,000 kilowatt steam generating plant. The importance of steam plants to a hydro system has been well stated by Melvin G. de Chazeau:

> Because of their complementary technical traits, interconnection of steam and hydro plants is particularly desirable. Water turbines may be raised from no-load to full-load almost immediately whereas steam turbines require from 10 to 12 hours of warming up. This inflexibility of the latter means substantial out-of-pocket expense in banking furnaces and maintaining steam pressure while, in a hydro plant, it is often possible to conserve water by storage during short periods of light load without additional expense. Finally, available water in most hydro systems is subject to seasonality which makes steam plant necessary if a substantial proportion of the power is not to be sold as secondary power. Interconnection of steam and hydro power, therefore, permits the maximum utilization of both—steam being employed at the optimum load when

used at all with hydro taking shortrun load fluctuations. Over long periods, on the other hand, water is used at its maximum economic power-generating rate while steam power supplements seasonal deficiencies in hydro capacity relative to load.[24]

In spite of the great advantage of integrating steam and hydro production in this fashion, it was not clear in the early days whether the constitutional position of the T.V.A. would permit it. For in legal theory the T.V.A. was simply selling surplus power generated by dams built for water control purposes, whereas a steam generating plant is a naked power proposition. The operation of such a plant to firm up hydro power would seem to indicate a planned intent to produce power incompatible with the "incidentalness" required by the official theory.[25] Actually, the question was an academic one for the first several years, since hydro power was more than sufficient to meet T.V.A. power requirements during that period, and the steam plant was seldom operated. As late as the fiscal year 1939, over 99½ per cent of all T.V.A. power was hydro generated.

When the T.E.P. Co. properties were purchased in 1939, the T.V.A. acquired several additional large steam plants. By this time, however, the Supreme Court had made it clear that there was no practicable method of attacking the constitutionality of the T.V.A. power operations, and since there was pressing need for all the power that could be generated, the steam plants were operated without question. In 1940 Congress authorized the T.V.A. to build a new 180,000 kilowatt steam plant at the Watts Bar dam site to provide power for defense needs. In the fiscal years 1940 and 1941, steam generated power supplied more than one-fifth of T.V.A. gross generation.

All sources combined, the total T.V.A. generating capacity stood at over 1,000,000 kilowatts by the end of 1941, and was sched-

24. "Electric Power as a Regional Problem," 7 *Southern Economic Journal* 494, 502 (1941).

25. As one commentator concluded, "the Authority can probably not construct steam stand-by capacity, since the contribution of such facilities to navigation and flood control is dubious." Edward S. Mason, "Power Aspects of the Tennessee Valley Authority's Program," 50 *Quarterly Journal of Economics* 377,387 (1936).

uled to increase 50 per cent in the following year and to reach the 2,000,000 figure by the middle of 1944.

Along with this power generation program has gone the building of the T.V.A. transmission system, tying together all of the T.V.A. generating plants and interconnecting with the major private utility companies in that area, with all of which the T.V.A. has agreements for the sale and interchange of power. These agreements create what is essentially an interconnected grid system in the southeastern area. For example, the T.V.A. agreement with the southern operating companies of the Commonwealth & Southern enables both sides to achieve economies in operation whenever one party can reduce generation at its plants and obtain energy from a more economical plant of the other party.[26] While Hiwassee Dam was under construction, an agreement with the Aluminum Co. of America permitted the T.V.A., which had no transmission line near the construction site, to turn over power to the Aluminum Co. in Tennessee and to take the power back from a company line in North Carolina close to the site, thus saving the T.V.A. the cost of building a transmission line or buying the necessary power. During the dry months of 1940 the T.V.A. brought power from Arkansas and North Carolina over its lines and delivered it to the drouth-stricken Aluminum Co. and Commonwealth & Southern companies. To meet the power famine of 1941 some additional interconnections were ordered by the Federal Power Commission in this area in order that all available power might be drawn in and utilized.

The T.V.A. power program has yet to experience any period of normality. The stormy developmental stage of 1933 to 1939 has been followed by the hectic times of defense preparation and war, with their accompanying responsibilities. However, the pattern of T.V.A. power service has been definitely established. The Authority

26. The T.V.A. has reduced its waste of power due to unused capacity during off-peak hours to 20 per cent, in comparison with the average utility figure of 50 per cent. During slack hours .T.V.A. reduces its own production and borrows surplus steam-generated power from private utilities, thus saving its water. When demand revives, T.V.A. releases the stored water and returns the borrowed power. T.V.A. exchanges power with utilities as far away as Chicago.

has become almost solely responsible for the generation and transmission of power in Tennessee and in substantial portions of Mississippi, Alabama, Georgia, and Kentucky. Relations between the T.V.A. and the private utility companies have become stabilized, although further expansion of T.V.A. service in Kentucky may well be expected when power from Kentucky Dam becomes available.

Fortunately for all concerned, the T.V.A. succeeded in carving out its service area with a minimum of wasteful and uneconomic duplication of existing systems. An effort to buy out privately owned utilities was made in every case by the T.V.A. or the municipalities concerned. Because these efforts failed at first, some competing systems were begun, but in most cases the decision to sell came before they were very far advanced. Moreover, the sales were not at sacrifice prices. It is generally conceded that Mr. Willkie drove a good bargain for the Tennessee Electric Power Co. properties.[27] As another example, the city of Knoxville paid an estimated $1,000,000 more for the existing system than it would have cost to duplicate it.

For the future, the T.V.A. can look forward to the operation of one of the most efficient power systems in the world. With nine dams on the main stream, and 14 dams at present built or under construction on the tributaries, water passing down the river system can be used from 10 to 12 times for the generation of power. In so far as the requirements of navigation and flood control permit, the flow of the river can be perfectly controlled for the maximum production of power. Moreover, the extensive steam generation facilities which the T.V.A. now operates greatly increase the amount of firm power available. The resulting 2,000,000 kilowatt capacity of the T.V.A. system is typical of the enormous resources which the post-war world will be challenged to put to wise and productive use.

27. The actual original cost of the properties concerned, less accrued depreciation, was $60,000,000, according to T.V.A. calculations, whereas the purchase price was $78,600,000. The T.V.A. justified this excess payment as representing "the importance of judgment factors in depreciation estimates and the value to the Authority and the local distributing agencies of eliminating competition in electric service." *Annual Report, 1939*, p. 52.

4: Power - Operating Problems

> "I hesitate to contemplate the future of our institutions, of our Government, and of our country if the preoccupation of its officials is to be no longer the promotion of Justice and equal opportunity but is to be devoted to barter in the markets. That is not liberalism, it is degeneration."—*Herbert Hoover (1931)*

WHEN THE federal government undertakes to operate a power system, it runs into problems which a private power company never encounters. A government corporation charged with the administration of such a program is a denizen of two worlds, and must balance the claims and techniques of a business enterprise against the requirements and practices of traditional tax-supported agencies. It must reconcile benevolence with revenues, and seek both within reason. In achieving this middle way, the T.V.A. has had to move largely without the benefit (or handicap) of precedents. There were other and earlier federal power projects, of course, such as the dams built by the Reclamation Service, but their methods of operation were quite dissimilar. It is the purpose of the present chapter to discuss some of the most important operating problems which the T.V.A. power program, as a government-operated commercial venture, has had to face.

SETTING THE RATES

Perhaps the basic problem confronting the Authority when it began power operations was that of determining the price at which it proposed to offer its product for sale. This decision was one of the most important which the T.V.A. had to make, and it was also one of the most difficult, because it had to be based so largely on estimates and assumptions. Why this was so needs some explanation.

In determining the price of a product, the cost of producing it is normally the most important factor to be considered. But the T.V.A. did not know what it was going to cost to produce power at Wilson Dam. Actual operating costs, it is true, were available from past experience. But almost every other factor entering into cost calculations depended upon judgment factors or estimates of some sort. No definite valuation had ever been established for Wilson Dam. It had been built under extremely unfavorable conditions, and in part during a period of high prices. Construction work had been halted on several occasions while additional appropriations were being secured from Congress. The hydro power units were seven years old when acquired by the Authority, and the steam plant considerably older. Altogether, it was recognized that it would be quite unfair to require the dam and plant to be carried on the books of the T.V.A. at their original cost. Consequently, section 14 of the T.V.A. Act authorized the board to "make a thorough investigation as to the present value" of the properties which, after approval by the President, should be considered as their book value.

Once a valuation was established, however, there still remained the task of determining how much of that value was allocable to power. For section 14 of the Act recognized the multiple-purpose character of the T.V.A. dams, and provided that their value or cost should be allocated and charged up to the various purposes served, namely, flood control, navigation, fertilizer production, national defense, and the development of power. The reasonableness of some such plan of allocation was generally admitted. Even those who felt that the emphasis on navigation and flood control was simply a method of putting a constitutional gloss on an unconstitutional power program had to admit that the T.V.A. multiple-purpose dams were more expensive than they would be if they were simply power dams. However, the making of such an allocation proved to be an extremely difficult task, involving difficult and basic decisions on policy. There were also policy questions involved in deciding whether taxes and interest, though not actually paid, should be considered as costs of T.V.A. power generation.

The T.V.A. officials felt that they had a mandate to get T.V.A. power into use as quickly as possible, without waiting for final answers to these questions. Consequently short-cuts were taken. As Mr. Lilienthal subsequently explained, the capital investment was determined by estimating "what a prudent businessman would pay for the Wilson Dam property as a going concern for the production of electricity," based primarily on cost per kilowatt of installed capacity. This "businessman's price" or "horseback appraisal" was checked in various ways and found satisfactory. As for other cost factors, the actual operating costs at Wilson Dam under War Department operation were taken, plus interest on the power investment at 3½ per cent, an allowance of 12½ per cent of estimated gross revenues as an equivalent for taxes, and depreciation charges based on data as to the life of the property. On the basis of these calculations, and after consultation with outside experts, the T.V.A. came to the conclusion that its wholesale power rate should be set at the level of $22.50 per horse-power-year, or as Mr. Lilienthal put it in layman's language in his announcement of September 14, 1933: "Any municipality, in the area we plan to serve initially, which owns its distribution system, assuming half-time use, may secure wholesale power from the Authority at an average cost to it of seven mills a kilowatt-hour." [1]

Even more important than the wholesale rates were the retail rates at which T.V.A. power would be passed on to the ultimate consumer. The T.V.A. concluded that there was only one way to insure that its municipal contractors would fix retail rates low enough to furnish a real test of the possibility of stimulating increased consumption, and that was for the T.V.A. itself to specify those rates. Consequently Mr. Lilienthal's announcement also covered the retail rate schedule for residential service, which was to be three

1. Printed in *Hearings*, p. 761.

cents, two cents, one cent, and four mills per kilowatt-hour for successive blocks of power.[2] These rates were much lower than those prevailing in the United States generally at that time. In adopting them the T.V.A. was definitely counting on their stimulative effect to increase the use of electricity by the ordinary household, which at that time stood at an average figure of about 55 kilowatt-hours per month. It was calculated that T.V.A. rates ought to increase that figure to 100 kilowatt-hours a month, and at that level of consumption sales at the new rates would be profitable. In other words, the T.V.A. was proceeding on the same theory in reducing the price of its product that Henry Ford and other industrialists had followed and proved sound.

Our concern here is not, however, with these promotional retail rates,[3] but with the wholesale rates, for it is on these rates that the T.V.A. power revenues and financial position depend. Mr. Lilienthal's rough seven mills per kilowatt-hour figure was subjected to revisions and refinement in the course of negotiations with the first prospective customers of the Authority, and a standard wholesale rate soon evolved. It takes the familiar form of a two-part tariff, with a demand charge of 90 cents per kilowatt of demand per month (measured by the maximum integrated load for 60 minutes), and an energy charge ranging from four mills for the first 100,000 kilowatt-hours consumed per month to two mills for the excess over 1,000,000 kilowatt-hours. In the fiscal year 1941, the four large cities of Memphis, Nashville, Chattanooga, and Knoxville paid an average rate of 3.9 mills per kilowatt-hour for their power. The average rate for all other T.V.A. municipal contractors was just over 5 mills, and for the cooperatives, 5.8 mills.[4]

Contracts with industrial concerns and public utilities for the sale of power can of course take no such standard form as that developed for municipalities and cooperatives. In so far as these con-

2. Three cents was the rate for the first 50 kilowatt-hours, two cents for the next 150, one cent for the next 200, and four mills for all the remainder of the power taken during one month up to 1400 kilowatt-hours, after which the rate rose to three-fourths of a cent.
3. See the discussion *infra*, pp. 101–3.
4. *Annual Report, 1941*, pp. 91–92.

tracts call for the sale of firm power, the ordinary wholesale rate applies. But normally they also provide for the delivery of various amounts of interruptible and secondary power, the price for which is fixed by negotiation. The announced policy of the T.V.A., in selling power to industries and utility companies, is to get what the traffic will bear, since the statute states that such sales are "secondary" and for the purpose of building load and reducing costs to public agencies. Large industrial interests are in a strong bargaining position in such negotiations, for if they do not like the T.V.A. price they can threaten to build or enlarge their own generating plants. During fiscal 1941 the average rate on T.V.A. power sales to industries was 4.3 mills, and to electric utilities 3.8 mills. These averages cover sales of both primary and secondary power.

ALLOCATING JOINT COSTS

The original T.V.A. rates were fixed, as we have seen, without benefit of a definite rate base. There was, in fact, no such rate base until 1938, due principally to the difficulties encountered in working out a satisfactory allocation of value for the T.V.A. multiple-purpose dams. A power house is obviously to be allocated entirely to power, and locks are a navigation charge. But the dam itself is a joint structure, useful for navigation, flood control, and power, and the same thing applies to the storage reservoir. The problem is to find a satisfactory formula for distributing the joint costs among these purposes.[5]

In August, 1933, the T.V.A. board delegated to Mr. Lilienthal the responsibility of preparing a valuation and allocation of value for the Muscle Shoals properties. The importance of this job was recognized by everyone. The relationship of such data to the fixing of rates has already been mentioned. Its importance for accounting purposes was equally great. In December, 1933, a report of the T.V.A. finance division pointed out: "The need for fixed capital data in properly accounting for the program of the Authority makes it

5. One of the most interesting theoretical discussions of this problem is that by Horace M. Gray, "The Allocation of Joint Costs in Multiple-Purpose Hydro-Electric Projects," 25 *American Economic Review* 224–35 (1935).

imperative that an early decision be made on the matter of securing valuations. Until this work is completed, only arbitrary estimates can be made on such things as fixed charges to be made against power." The finance division tried to prepare balance sheets for the Authority's power operations, but they were meaningless without any valuations for the most important capital items. Profit and loss statements could not be prepared, since there was no basis for determining many of the charges which should be made. Interest on investment could not be figured, and an amortization plan could not be adopted. It was difficult to depreciate power properties. At first, merely as a temporary measure and for internal operating purposes, 10 per cent of gross power revenues was charged to operations as depreciation. This method was soon dropped, but with no valuation basis, no other could be substituted.

In spite of the recognized necessity for allocations to be made, the work did not proceed very rapidly. After lengthy study and consultation with outside experts, a preliminary draft of a report on Muscle Shoals valuation and allocation was ready late in 1934, and was used at that time by the T.V.A. in hearings before the Alabama Public Service Commission.[6] This plan allocated to power the powerhouse section of Wilson Dam and all power machinery, plus half the value of the spillway section, the other half being charged to navigation. This 50-50 division was a purely arbitrary one, and made no pretense of relying upon any elaborate allocation theory.

The T.V.A. board was ready early in 1935 to approve a report on the subject of valuation and allocation. But there were objections from its consultants, and then Congress began to discuss amendments to the T.V.A. Act which would affect this problem, so action was held up. The amendments were passed in August, 1935, and one of them required the T.V.A. to file with Congress by January 1, 1937, a statement of its allocation of the value of its properties. With this deadline, the T.V.A. board decided to ask three of its consultants to form a valuation committee which would guide and review

6. See E. B. Whitman, "Rate Making by the TVA," 3 *Edison Electric Institute Bulletin* 209 (1935).

the Authority's work.[7] As Mr. Lilienthal said in a letter at that time, "it is the first case of such apportionment, so far as I know, among the Federal power projects and to that extent may become a settled part of the national power policy."[8] Consequently the T.V.A. desired that the allocation be made on as sound a basis as possible.

Unfortunately the work of this committee was hampered by the growing antagonism of Chairman Morgan toward Mr. Lilienthal, with whom the committee members were rather closely identified. This connection apparently caused Chairman Morgan to distrust them, and in March, 1936, he attempted first to place the job in the hands of a commercial appraisal firm, and then to have it turned over to the T.V.A. engineering and construction staff, which he himself headed. Two of the members of the committee concluded that they did not enjoy the chairman's confidence, and offered to retire. However, a procedure was finally worked out for the continuance of the committee's work. Chairman Morgan subsequently insisted that a board of consulting engineers be employed as well, and there were thus two reports to be reconciled and approved by the board. The report on Muscle Shoals valuation was not ready for the President until April, 1937, some four months after the deadline fixed by Congress.

The problem of allocation still remained. This task had been assigned to Professor Glaeser in the summer of 1936, but the arrangement again proved unsatisfactory to Chairman Morgan who, without notifying the other board members, directed his engineering staff to prepare their own allocation. This he presented to the board on December 24, 1936, asking its immediate adoption to meet the statutory deadline. The other two board members refused. A short time later Chairman Morgan presented this allocation to a congressional appropriation committee, although the board majority had disapproved of the principles on which it was based. An impasse was reached as Mr. Glaeser found his efforts to secure data from the

7. The committee was composed of Prof. Martin Glaeser, University of Wisconsin; Prof. James C. Bonbright, Columbia University; and Edward Morehouse, Wisconsin Public Service Commission.
8. *Hearings*, p. 713.

engineering staff under Chairman Morgan were futile. It was not broken until a financial policy committee of T.V.A. officials [9] was formed in July, 1937. The necessary decisions on principles were made by this committee, and a final report, covering the three dams completed at that time (Wilson, Wheeler, and Norris), was submitted to the President in June, 1938.[10]

The principles on which this allocation, and that of the dams subsequently completed, is based need brief explanation. The problem of allocation applies, of course, only to a part of the total investment in the T.V.A. dam system, that part which is represented by facilities useful for more than one major purpose. Direct investments for one purpose only, such as expenditure for a power house, must be deducted from the total investment as the first step in the allocation process. For example, the total cost of Pickwick Landing Dam was $29,793,000. Of this amount $5,813,000 was for the lock and for channel improvements, thus clearly a direct navigation expense. One qualification must be made, however. The lock serves as part of the dam, and if it had not been built, the space it occupies would have had to be filled by a non-overflow section forming part of the dam. Such a section in the Pickwick Dam would have cost $406,000. To that extent, then, the lock serves not merely a navigation function but a multiple-purpose function, and consequently $406,000 must be deducted from the navigation charge, leaving a direct navigation cost of $5,407,000. The power house, turbines, generators, and other electrical equipment at this dam cost $10,-345,000, but again a deduction (in this case $593,000) must be made to cover the cost of replacing the power intake section of the dam with an ordinary non-overflow section. Direct power investment is thus $9,752,000. Finally, it was estimated that $1,021,000 of the total Pickwick cost was incurred purely for flood control purposes. Deducting these three classes of direct costs from the total

9. The committee included the T.V.A. comptroller, chief engineer, chief water-control planning engineer, solicitor, chief budget officer, and chief power planning engineer.
10. House Doc. 709, 75th Cong., 3d sess. (1938).

investment in the dam leaves the sum of $13,613,000 which was spent to serve all three purposes in combination.

It is here that the problem of allocation is reached, and it is here that a second point needs to be made clear. The T.V.A. dams operate as a system. Each dam is necessary to the navigation of the entire river. Each storage dam and up-river dam increases the power capacity of all the dams below it. Consequently, allocation of value must be made on a system basis, if it is to be realistic. The allocation made in 1938, as noted above, was for the three dam system then operating. As additional dams are completed and added to the system, the allocations are revised to take account of the resulting changes in the operation and characteristics of the entire system.

On what basis is this system allocation to be made? It was this problem with which T.V.A. officials and outside consultants wrestled for two years, and for the solution of which there were almost no relevant precedents.[11] On the surface the task might seem similar to that of pricing commodities or services produced at a joint cost, such as cotton fiber and cottonseed, or to that of allocating administrative overhead among the operating divisions of an organization. For various reasons, however, such situations were not comparable with the allocation dilemma facing the T.V.A.

Several theories of allocation were considered. One of these called for the allocation of joint costs on the basis of the estimated benefits which the dams would render to each of the various uses served. This method was favored by Mr. Arthur Morgan, and was opposed by Mr. Lilienthal on the ground that calculation of these benefits would necessarily be a purely speculative process. Another theory would have distributed joint costs upon the basis of the comparative use of joint facilities, figured in terms, presumably, of acre-feet of water or reservoir capacity. A third theory was that the several functions served by the dams should share costs on the basis of

11. A most complete account of the T.V.A. allocation problem is given in Ransmeier, *op. cit.*, Part II; see also Martin Glaeser, "Those Joint TVA Costs," 24 *Public Utilities Fortnightly* 259–69 (1939).

equality, in this case power, navigation, and flood control each bearing one-third of the joint costs.[12] The T.V.A. finally rejected these and other suggestions, and relied primarily upon a so-called "alternative justifiable expenditure" theory.

This theory is based on the obvious proposition that the T.V.A. dams permit the achieving of several purposes on a more economical basis than would prevail if the same purposes were sought independently. In the case of the original three-dam system, it was estimated that navigation benefits equal to those supplied by the three multiple-purpose dams could have been secured by spending about $48,000,000 on low dams and navigation works. Similarly, a flood control system providing the same protection could have been built for $33,000,000, and the same amount of power could have been generated by dams operated only for power costing $79,-000,000. In other words, the benefits achieved by an expenditure of $94,000,000 on the multiple-purpose system would have cost $160,-000,000 to secure separately.

The alternative justifiable expenditure theory called for the distribution of common costs among the three purposes in proportion to the costs of obtaining the equivalent results by three single-use projects. Therefore the ratio which the cost of each of these theoretical single-use projects (less actual direct costs for each purpose in the multiple-purpose system) bore to the total of the three projects (again less actual direct costs) would be the ratio to be used in allocating common costs in the multiple-purpose system.[13]

12. A fourth theory, the "by-product theory," was apparently not seriously considered, although Mr. A. E. Morgan accused Mr. Lilienthal of favoring it. The by-product theory, as stated by H. M. Gray, *op. cit.*, holds that power should be charged only with direct power costs, and with none of the joint costs, on the ground that the joint costs are incurred for the general good, and so should be paid out of the general public revenue like other social services.

13. The calculations involved in this process are given in the following table, taken from House Doc. No. 709, 75th Cong., 3d sess., p. 40:

	Total Alternative Cost	Direct Investment	Remaining Alternative Costs	Per cent
Navigation	$48,334,000	$4,408,807	$43,925,193	34.4
Flood Control.....	33,210,000	2,600,000	30,610,000	24.0
Power	79,230,000	26,059,335	53,170,665	41.6
Total.........	$160,774,000	$33,068,142	$127,705,858	100.0

For the original three-dam system the division was roughly 25 per cent for flood control, 35 per cent for navigation, and 40 per cent for power, and these were the ratios adopted by the board. When the direct costs were added to this allocation of the common costs, the total expenditure on the three-dam system was divided 52 per cent to power, 28 per cent to navigation, and 20 per cent to flood control.

As additional dams have been completed and brought into the system, some modification in the percentages first established has been necessary, since the calculations are made on a system basis. In November, 1940, the T.V.A. reported to the President its allocation for the seven dams then completed, but the changes in percentages were slight (navigation 36 per cent, flood control 24 per cent, power unchanged).[14] On this basis the entire $210,000,000 cost of the seven-dam system was distributed 52 per cent to power, 31 per cent to navigation, and 17 per cent to flood control. If to the cost of the dams proper there is added the cost of the transmission lines and other power properties, the allocation of the total T.V.A. investment (as of November, 1940) was 66 per cent to power, 22 per cent to navigation, and 12 per cent to flood control. In terms of dollars, the power investment was placed at $195,000,000.

The allocation of only 40 per cent of the joint costs to power has been attacked by critics of the T.V.A., on the ground that power charges are thus unfairly minimized.[15] There is no point in arguing the question, for the answer depends upon what theory of allocation is used. All that can be said is that the theory used by the T.V.A. was not an unreasonable one, and that the allocation was approved by the President and the congressional investigating committee. It might be noted that the 40 per cent charge to power was heavier than the allocation worked out for Bonneville Dam by the Federal Power Commission.

14. *Annual Report, 1940*, pp. 412–14.
15. See E. R. Abrams, *Power in Transition* (New York, 1940), pp. 189–238. Ransmeier, whose recent book is by far the best study of this problem, concludes that there is no sound allocation theory, that joint costs are by definition insusceptible of apportionment, and that charging direct costs only is the sole satisfactory solution.

POWER ACCOUNTING AND REPORTING

With the adoption of its allocation principles in 1938, the T.V.A. had for the first time a definite figure for its power investment, and it became possible to do many things in the way of power accounting and reporting that could not be done so long as no value data on the most important capital items were available. Most important, it became possible to calculate what return the T.V.A. was earning on its power investment—whether its power operations were making or losing money.

The answer to this question is by no means as simple as it sounds, however. For it involves the making of a number of major accounting decisions, all of which are based on judgment considerations and give full opportunity for reflecting personal biases. Thus the congressional investigating committee heard evidence from a T.V.A. witness to the effect that power sales from a completed 11-dam system would yield estimated annual surpluses of $4,500,000, while a power company witness testified that the annual deficit from the same system would be over $10,000,000. The majority and minority reports of the committee showed a similar variance in viewpoint.

Such widely differing conclusions result from disagreement as to what costs a government-operated power system may legitimately be called on to bear. The principal items involved, and the controversy concerning them, may be discussed briefly.

1. *Operating expenses.*—These are of course a proper charge. In the T.V.A. accounts, the following power expenses are included: production, transmission, distribution, in-lieu tax payments,[16] customers' accounting, sales promotion, and power department administrative expenses, plus a pro rata share of the general T.V.A. administrative overhead.

2. *Depreciation.*—Here also there is full agreement that depreciation of power properties, as well as such portion of joint use properties as has been allocated to power, is a necessary charge on

16. See discussion of these tax payments, *infra*, pp. 111–15.

power revenues. There is disagreement, however, as to the methods to be employed in calculating depreciation and the rates to be used. The two principal methods of depreciating public utility property are the "straight-line" and the "sinking fund," either of which can yield satisfactory results if properly used, though the former is generally regarded as preferable. Under either system it is necessary to make age life calculations with reference to the property involved to determine the rate of depreciation to be applied, and substantial differences of opinion are possible here. Before the congressional investigating committee, the utility witness referred to above assumed a 30-year life for the power houses and power facilities, and a 50-year life for the remaining power investment. The T.V.A. on the other hand estimated an average life of 35 years for all machinery and equipment, 85 years for dams and mass concrete structures, and 75 years for superstructures and buildings, with investment in transmission facilities divided into six life classifications ranging from 15 to 50 years. A longer estimated service life, of course, means a smaller annual depreciation charge against revenues.

3. *Amortization.*—Privately owned utilities do not, and in fact, theoretically cannot, amortize their bonded indebtedness. Publicly owned utilities can and often do undertake to pay off their indebtedness. The engineers of the congressional investigating committee concluded that a charge for amortization of the entire power investment over a 50 year period was proper. The T.V.A., however, presented to the committee an amortization plan covering only the non-depreciable property with an indefinite life, such as reservoir lands and rights, the investment in which it proposed to amortize over a period of 85 years.

4. *Interest.*—The T.V.A. does not pay interest on funds appropriated to it by Congress for its construction program. But it can be argued that when the government conducts a commercial power program, interest on the investment in that business is a proper charge, and that the taxpayers are paying a subsidy to the power users if the capital for the system is furnished free. The force of this

argument is generally granted, but the question remains as to what interest rate should be charged. In calculations for the investigating committee the utilities used 3½ per cent as the rate, while the T.V.A., relying on the fact that the interest rate on long-term Treasury bonds from 1933 to 1937 was 2.899 per cent, used a 3 per cent figure. Raising this rate ½ of one per cent results in a great increase in the annual interest charge.

5. *Taxes.*—Under the original T.V.A. Act, the Authority was required to pay 5 per cent of gross power proceeds to the states of Alabama and Tennessee, which was generally considered as in lieu of taxes. However, privately operated utilities were paying around 12½ per cent of their gross revenues in taxes during that period. Consequently it was argued that this difference should be wiped out by entering an appropriate charge against T.V.A. power revenues for taxes it would have paid had it been in private hands. In 1940, the amount of the in-lieu payments was increased to a basis roughly comparable with the local and state taxes on utilities generally.

6. *Other non-incurred costs.*—There are other relatively minor costs which the T.V.A. escapes because of its governmental status. One is interest during construction. Another is workmen's compensation charges, which are paid directly by the United States in accordance with regular federal practice. Still another is free use of the mails. It has been contended that charges should be made against power revenues to cover these and other non-incurred costs.

It was difference of opinion on the above points, plus disagreement as to whether the T.V.A. allocation of capital investment to power was sufficient, which led the majority and the minority of the investigating committee to reach such widely varying conclusions. The former, relying on the report of the committee's engineers, concluded that on the basis of the T.V.A. rates and forecasts of power sales, "the total cost charged to power, together with a reasonable interest thereon, will be recoverable to the Treasury of the United States within a period of 50 years." [17] The minority concluded that

17. *Report of the Joint Committee,* p. 7.

the T.V.A. rates would not yield revenue sufficient to pay operating expenses and fixed charges, let alone liquidate the investment, and consequently that the rates were in violation of the T.V.A. Act.[18] However, both these conclusions were based on forecasts of future power sales, and it is wiser to forget about them and to examine the actual record.

Table III presents the financial experience of the T.V.A. power program for the fiscal years 1939 to 1941. That is the period since the allocation was made, and since there have been substantial power revenues. The statement is prepared on a commercial basis in that power revenues are charged with all relevant costs which are actually incurred by the T.V.A. It does not make any allowance for hypothetical, non-incurred costs of the type previously discussed. However, depreciation is charged, and at a rate substantially

Table III

FINANCIAL RESULTS OF T.V.A. POWER
OPERATIONS ON COMMERCIAL BASIS,
FISCAL YEARS 1939–1941 *

	1939	*1940*	*1941*
Gross power revenues. . .	$5,507,077	$15,285,074	$21,137,371
Power operating expense.	2,089,548	6,554,142	7,764,848
In-lieu tax payments. . . .	243,056	527,593	1,499,394
Depreciation (straight-line).	1,731,593	3,615,623	4,546,547
Interest on T.V.A. bonds.	60,479	432,082	484,602
Net return on power investment.	1,382,401	4,155,634	6,841,980
Power investment (depreciated) at close of year.	86,471,629	179,032,687	186,961,334
Return on power investment.	1.6%	2.3%	3.7%

* Source: *Annual Reports.*

18. *Ibid.*, p. 294.

higher than has been customary in the public utility field.[19] The table reveals a net return in all three years, reaching the figure of 3.7 per cent on power investment in fiscal 1941. Prior to 1939, the power program operated at a deficit.

Table III, while compiled from T.V.A. annual reports, does not correspond exactly with any presentation which the T.V.A. has made of the commercial results of its power operations. In fact, the Authority has not considered it desirable or necessary to prepare separate commercial reports on its power business. The general T.V.A. practice has been to account for power operations in the same way as for its other programs. Thus the annual financial statements present a single balance sheet, in which the investment in power properties is lumped with all other assets. Net power income is shown on the liabilities side of the balance sheet, deducted from the net expense of operating the other T.V.A. programs.[20] Exhibits and schedules subsidiary to the balance sheet carry full data on power assets and power revenues and expense.

While the financial reports thus include the information necessary to the preparation of commercial power reports, the T.V.A. policy from the beginning was against their issuance. The question whether this was the proper attitude to take was raised by the congressional investigating committee in 1938. The committee commended the Authority's "attempt to conform to commercial-accounting practices to an extent unusual in Government agencies," [21] but felt that the attempt had not been carried far enough. Since the T.V.A. power business was of a character so different from its other operations, the majority report of the committee recommended the "separation of power operations from noncommercial operations for balance sheet purposes, treating the one on a profit-

19. The calculations in Table III minimize the T.V.A. rate of return also because the year-end figure on power investment is used, thus including properties purchased or brought into operation during the year, from which a full year's earnings have not been secured.

20. For a discussion of the problems involved in preparation of the T.V.A. balance sheet, see Chap. VIII.

21. *Report*, p. 101.

and-loss and the other on an expense basis," as a measure to avoid possible misunderstandings.[22]

T.V.A. Comptroller Kohler indicated to the committee, however, that he did not consider it proper to prepare a profit-and-loss statement for T.V.A. power operations, because ". . . this is not a commercial venture, it is not one that is run for profit, and consequently any figure that remains after deducting expenses and costs must be regarded either as a return of the original appropriation, as an off-set against a previous net expense, or must be covered back into the Treasury or disposed of according to the ways that are provided for by the act or some other measure set up by Congress."[23] This view is of course technically correct, but it remains true that revenues are expected and secured as a result of the T.V.A. power investment, and that the public is accustomed to judge the validity of such investments in terms of the return received.

The T.V.A. was not moved by the committee's suggestion to change the form of its regular annual financial statements. However, beginning with the fiscal year 1939, each T.V.A. annual report has carried, apart from the regular financial report, a brief statement or table relating power revenues to power investment.[24] Unfortunately, these "commercial statements" have not been prepared on the basis of a consistent accounting policy, as is illustrated by the handling of interest payments. The T.V.A. has secured some of its funds by selling bonds to the Treasury and the R.F.C., and on these obligations it pays interest. It also receives interest from municipalities and cooperatives which are indebted to the T.V.A. on account of the purchase of power systems. In the 1939 report the T.V.A. counted the excess of interest receipts over interest payments as power income. In 1940, however, interest payments exceeded interest receipts; surprisingly enough, credit was taken for the receipts, but the payments were omitted in calculating return on investment. In the 1941 report, both interest receipts and payments were ex-

22. *Ibid.*, p. 109.
23. *Hearings*, p. 6061.
24. The references to the reports are: *1939*, p. 59; *1940*, pp. 19–20; *1941*, p. 39.

cluded in the special commercial computation. No explanation was given in the reports of these varying practices. The view of the author is that all three were wrong. Bond interest payments should be charged against power revenues, since the funds were borrowed for power purposes, while interest receipts from municipalities and cooperatives should not be considered power receipts.[25] This is the practice followed in Table III.

Practice in handling depreciation has also been confused in the special commercial statements issued thus far. In 1939 depreciation was charged to the power investment on the basis of the regular straight-line calculations used in T.V.A. accounting. In 1940, however, the commercial report used depreciation figures derived by the sinking fund method (which results in a lower charge and gives a higher earnings rate), although the straight-line method was used for all other accounting calculations. In 1941 the report sought to please everyone by using both methods, thus giving two sets of results. In Table III, the straight-line method has been used, since the T.V.A. has accepted it for regular accounting purposes.

It would seem preferable for the T.V.A. to have stuck consistently to its policy of no separate power reports, rather than to have issued the half-hearted and ill-considered commercial statements just described.[26] By way of comparison, attention may be called to the example of the British Post Office, which since 1912 has been preparing annually a remarkable set of "commercial accounts" somewhat comparable to what the T.V.A. would seem to require. The purpose of the accounts is "to show the financial results on a commercial basis of the operation of the Post Office services . . . they are, in effect, profit and loss accounts exhibiting the financial results of the trading relations between the Post Office and its customers."[27] Balance sheets are prepared on a commercial basis

25. However, interest receipts might be used to offset interest payments to the extent that the T.V.A. used borrowed funds to purchase power properties subsequently sold on credit to municipalities and cooperatives.

26. It should be emphasized that the author is not referring to the general financial statements of the T.V.A., which are impeccable.

27. *British Parliamentary Papers*, 1938–39, Vol. 16, "Post Office Commercial Accounts, 1938," p. 4.

for the Post Office and its principal operating services. Income and expenditure accounts are submitted in which the Post Office is charged with all expenditures attributable to its operations, including interest on invested capital, pensions for its staff, and services rendered for it by other government departments; in the same way the Post Office is given credit, not only for its regular receipts, but for the services it renders to other government departments without payment. Thus each of the principal Post Office services—postal, telephone, and telegraph—is transformed into a self-contained commercial undertaking, which can be judged by the public on a true profit-and-loss basis.

In this discussion of commercial reporting of T.V.A. power operations, there has been no suggestion that reports could or should be prepared which would permit the comparison of T.V.A. financial results with those of private power systems. A discussion of the problem of making such comparisons may be more appropriately presented in a consideration of the so-called "yardstick" issue.

EXIT THE YARDSTICK

The belief that government distribution of Wilson Dam power would furnish a standard for measuring the service and rates of private power companies had been of considerable influence in the Muscle Shoals controversy. President Roosevelt gave widest circulation to the "yardstick" concept in his 1932 campaign, when at Portland, Oregon, he referred to Muscle Shoals as one of four national power projects that "will be forever a national yardstick to prevent extortion against the public and to encourage the wider use of that servant of the people—electric power." [28]

Just what acting as a yardstick was supposed to involve was never made clear in an official way. The T.V.A. Act contained no reference to the idea. In the popularly accepted sense of the term, the yardstick was expected to function by permitting a comparison between the Authority's rates for electricity and those of private utilities. But such a comparison immediately involved complica-

28. *The Public Papers and Addresses of Franklin D. Roosevelt*, Vol. I, p. 740.

tions, because the T.V.A. as a public agency enjoyed certain advantages which its private competitors did not. Unless these advantages were cancelled out in some way, it seemed obvious that T.V.A. rates would be an unfair yardstick, and the utility companies would have to make their showing against subsidized competition.

One of the immediate problems facing the T.V.A. as its power program got under way was whether it would accept this role of serving as a "yardstick" in the power field, and if so, whether it would adopt the popular conception of the yardstick and attempt to solve the difficulty just pointed out. The initial reaction of T.V.A. officials appears to have been a rather uncritical acceptance of the yardstick concept. The power policy which was worked out by Mr. Arthur Morgan and Mr. Lilienthal and announced in August, 1933, carried as one of its eleven points the following: "Accounting should show detail of costs, and permit a comparison of operations with privately owned plants, to supply a 'yardstick' and an incentive to both private and public managers." [29] When the T.V.A. wholesale rates were announced a few weeks later, the T.V.A. press release stated: "These wholesale rates have been computed on a conservative basis to cover all the costs of furnishing the service, including operation, maintenance, depreciation, and taxes. In addition to these costs, we have made provision for interest and retirement, although such provision is not required by the Tennessee Valley Authority Act. The power project is designed to be strictly self-supporting and self-liquidating." [30] The inclusion of charges not actually incurred by the T.V.A., such as taxes and interest, was rather widely taken as meaning that T.V.A. rates could legitimately be compared with the rates of private utility companies.

As time passed, however, it became apparent to everyone that T.V.A. wholesale rates could not possibly serve yardstick purposes. For the T.V.A. setup for power generation was unique, and its costs could not furnish a basis for comparison with any other hydroelectric plant or system, and certainly not with steam generation.

29. *Annual Report, 1934*, p. 24.
30. Printed in *Hearings*, p. 761.

Some features in the T.V.A. system tended to lower its costs, such as the efficiency in the use of water made possible by a controlled river system, and its ability to charge off a part of its capital costs to purposes other than power. Other features tended to increase its power costs, particularly the necessity of operating the dams primarily for navigation and flood control purposes.[31] T.V.A. costs consequently had little value for comparative purposes, and they could not be made to serve as a yardstick for other power operators simply by including allowances for such items as interest and taxes.

So far as T.V.A. generating costs and wholesale rates are concerned, then, talk of a yardstick is meaningless. There has been, however, an attempt in some quarters, notably by the majority report of the congressional investigating committee,[32] to rehabilitate the yardstick by discussing it in terms of the T.V.A. *retail* rates and the experience of T.V.A. municipal and cooperative contractors. The operation of these public or quasi-public agencies in selling power at the low T.V.A. retail rates has certainly yielded interesting results in testing the stimulative effect of low rates. Moreover, the conditions imposed by the T.V.A. in its power contracts ensure that the financial experience of the contractors is accumulated under conditions which do make possible a measure of comparison with the experience of private distribution agencies.

What are these conditions? First, the T.V.A. sells power to cities and cooperatives at regular wholesale rates, and the contractor agrees to retail this power at standard T.V.A. resale rates.[33] To provide an element of flexibility, the contract may provide for adding

31. The T.V.A. has estimated that at least 28 per cent more power could be generated by its system if flood control and navigation considerations were ignored. See *Hearings*, p. 5293.

32. See *Report of the Joint Committee*, pp. 190–98. The majority concludes: "The yardstick is not in the Authority's wholesale rates, but in the retail rates of the various municipalities and other local organizations that have purchased Authority power and distributed it at unusually low rates. If their operations are shown to be of a kind that may be substantially duplicated in other parts of the country, their rates may be considered a Nation-wide yardstick, or measure of results to be expected."

33. These rates are fixed for four classes of use—standard residential rate, basic small lighting and power rate, basic large lighting and power rate, and standard street-lighting rate.

to the basic resale rates a special amortization charge of between $0.25 and $1.00 per customer per month, for the purpose of paying long-term indebtedness on the distribution system. The contract may also permit a surcharge, usually a flat 10 per cent of individual bills, to be collected during the developmental period of a system in order to insure sufficient revenues.

The contractor agrees to administer its electric system as a separate department, with its funds separate from those of its other operations, and to keep its accounts according to the standard system prescribed by the Federal Power Commission. Finally, the contractor agrees to apply its power revenues in the following order: first, payment of current operating expenses; second, payment of interest on indebtedness, amortization charges, and sinking fund obligations; third, reasonable reserves for replacements, new construction, and contingencies, plus a reasonable amount of cash working capital; fourth, payment into the general fund of the city of a return on its investment in the system, if any, and a tax equivalent on the system properties; [34] and fifth, all remaining revenues to be considered surplus revenues and devoted to retirement of system indebtedness before maturity or to reduction or elimination of surcharges, and thereafter to the reduction of rates.

What have been the results of operations under these contracts? In terms of power consumption, the low T.V.A. resale rates have brought phenomenal increases in the use of power. In the "guinea pig" town of Tupelo, Miss., average residential consumption, which prior to T.V.A. rates was 49 kilowatt-hours per month at an average rate of 7.4 cents per kilowatt-hour, reached in the fifth year of T.V.A. rates the high point of 164 kilowatt-hours per month, for which the average charge was 1.67 cents per kilowatt-hour. In Athens, Ala., five years of T.V.A. rates saw an increase in residential use from an average of 51 to 150 kilowatt-hours per month.[35] In the case of some of the T.V.A. contractors, particularly in the cooperatives where service has not been available for so long a period, the

34. In the contracts with cooperatives, these provisions are somewhat different than for municipal contractors.
35. *Annual Report, 1940*, pp. 93–94.

results are not so spectacular. But the powerful effect of lower rates in increasing use of electricity has been abundantly demonstrated. The average use per residential customer of T.V.A. power in 1941 was 120 kilowatt-hours per month, compared with the national figure of 81 kilowatt-hours. The explanation is found in the average payment of 2.06 cents per kilowatt-hour by T.V.A. customers, as compared with the national average of 3.79 cents.[36]

The financial experience of T.V.A. contractors has likewise been excellent. In the fiscal year 1941 gross operating revenues of all T.V.A. municipal and cooperative distributors were over $27,372,-000. After deducting operating expenses, depreciation, taxes and interest, the combined net income was $4,166,000, or slightly more than 15 per cent of gross revenues. Of the 76 municipal distributors reporting in the fiscal year 1941, only three systems showed a net loss; in two cases the loss resulted from writing off substantial acquisition adjustments against current income. The cooperatives have a more difficult problem, since they serve widely-scattered customers and in many cases have built up their systems from scratch. The combined net income of the 38 cooperative systems in the fiscal year 1941 was only $33,000, and a number showed net losses.[37]

It has been contended by some that the financial experience of these T.V.A. contractors furnishes no basis for yardstick comparisons because of certain subsidies or other advantages which they receive. Arthur E. Morgan made such charges as part of his campaign against his co-director Mr. Lilienthal, but they were rather thoroughly disproved by the engineering report of the congressional investigating committee, as well as by an investigation conducted by the Federal Power Commission. On the question of taxes, the municipal systems, though tax exempt, make tax payments on the regu-

36. *Annual Report, 1941*, p. 34. It is ironic that the T.V.A., which has come to symbolize low power rates, has recently had to ask some of its contractors not to make further reductions in retail rates, even though cash surpluses were piling up, because such reductions would increase civilian use of power needed for war industries. The T.V.A. has suggested to municipalities in these circumstances that they turn part of the surplus back to their customers in the form of war bonds, rather than reduce rates.

37. *Ibid.*, p. 33.

lar basis for utility property. Thus when the city of Knoxville took over the electric system which had previously been contributing some $210,000 annually in city, county, and state property taxes, the city continued these payments at the same rate.[38] As for the co-operatives, they are subject to local and state taxation in all of the T.V.A. states except Mississippi. The principal advantage which T.V.A. contractors enjoy is the low T.V.A. wholesale rate.

There is little point, however, in analyzing comparative advantages and disadvantages of T.V.A. contractors for the purpose of salvaging the yardstick concept. Professor Glaeser has rightly pointed out the "naive" sense in which the uninformed are sure to understand the idea, and the folly of attempting overall comparisons of rates. "Long ago," says Mr. Glaeser, "I had concluded that the yardstick idea is a will-o'-the-wisp which lends itself admirably to propaganda purposes, but the pursuit of which could end only in a bog of discussion, of claim and counterclaim." [39] He does feel that T.V.A. operations can provide a number of scientific yardsticks, particularly of unit costs of operation, which could be "useful instruments of regulation in the hands of unbiased and scientific practitioners." However, the difficulty of securing an understanding of the yardstick in this sense makes it preferable for the term to be "stricken once and for all from the T.V.A. vocabulary," as the minority on the congressional investigating committee recommended.[40]

INTERGOVERNMENTAL RELATIONSHIPS

As the first federal agency to undertake a large-scale program of wholesale power distribution, the T.V.A. has found itself involved in a variety of novel relationships with other governmental agencies.

38. The Knoxville Electric Power Board had a net operating income of $875,000 for the year ending May 31, 1942, after deducting depreciation and taxes. This was a return of over 12 per cent on the city's investment. The Board had retired bonds in the sum of $441,000 and had a total earned surplus of $1,600,000 as a result of four years' operation.

39. Martin G. Glaeser, "The Yardstick Once More," 24 *Public Utilities Fortnightly* 733, 737 (1939).

40. *Report of the Joint Committee*, p. 273. For another discussion of this subject, see M. Fainsod and L. Gordon, *Government and the American Economy* (New York, 1941), pp. 357-61.

On the federal level T.V.A. power activities brought it into contact with the Public Works Administration, which granted funds for the construction of distribution systems to a number of municipalities desiring to take T.V.A. power, and the Rural Electrification Administration, which financed and assisted many of the rural power cooperatives in the T.V.A. area. Of more interest, however, are the Authority's relations with the Federal Power Commission, which has since 1920 controlled the licensing of dams in navigable streams, also exercising some degree of authority over the operations of the licensed undertakings. Since 1935 it has had full regulatory powers over all electric utilities engaged in interstate transmission of power. Should a public agency such as the T.V.A. be subjected to regulatory control of this type? The same problem has of course been faced by states in which publicly owned utilities operate; in most cases these public systems have been freed from state regulatory supervision, or at least subjected to less stringent controls than those exercised over private utilities.[41]

A similar policy of autonomy has developed in the case of the T.V.A., and in most respects its power operations are completely free from regulation by the Federal Power Commission. One of the important exceptions to this rule is in the field of power accounting. When the T.V.A. statute was first adopted there was no provision on this subject, but in 1935 the congressional desire to insure that T.V.A. accounts would be comparable to those of private utilities was responsible for the addition to section 14 of the following language:

> . . . the board shall keep complete accounts of its costs of generation, transmission, and distribution of electric energy and shall keep a complete account of the total cost of generating and transmission facilities constructed or otherwise acquired by the Corporation, . . . and a description of the major components of such costs according to such uniform system of accounting for public utilities as the Federal Power Commission has, and if it have none, then it is hereby empowered and directed to prescribe such uniform system of accounting, together

41. S. P. Reese, "State Regulation of Municipally Owned Electric Utilities," 7 *George Washington Law Review* 557–94 (1939).

with records of such other physical data and operating statistics of the Authority as may be helpful in determining the actual cost and value of services. . . .

A similar obligation was imposed by the Public Utility Holding Company Act of 1935, which was passed at about the same time. It subjected utilities and licensees to accounting control by the Commission, and extended such control also to "all agencies of the United States engaged in the generation and sale of electric energy for ultimate distribution to the public . . . so far as may be practicable. . . ." The Federal Power Commission, which did not have a uniform system of accounts for public utilities, prepared one to meet the needs of this statute. When promulgated in 1937, this system was adopted by the T.V.A., which also required its municipal and cooperative contractors to use the Power Commission's standard accounting system for distributing agencies.

The Commission has not attempted to exercise any supervision over the Authority's accounting practices. In 1938, however, the congressional investigating committee asked the Power Commission to review T.V.A. power accounting methods, and the resulting report pointed out numerous respects in which T.V.A. practices were not in accord with the Commission's system of accounts. The general conclusion of the Commission's accountants was that "the accounting records do not permit the prompt preparation of an income statement or account as called for by the system of accounts, and, in addition, they lack the completeness, definiteness, and finality which they should have if the system of accounts were accorded full effect." [42] E. L. Kohler, then newly-appointed comptroller of the T.V.A., agreed before the committee that many of the objections were justified, but pointed out that the revisions in accounting policy and practice he was introducing had already remedied the most serious defects. [43] It is also important to note that the Federal Power Commission system of accounts, intended primarily for privately owned utilities, was in several respects inapplicable to a multi-pur-

42. *Hearings*, p. 5508.
43. *Ibid.*, pp. 5984–94.

pose public power program, and this fact called for some variations from the standard system.

The Federal Power Commission, in time of war or other emergency, has the power to order temporary interconnections between power systems for the interchange of electric energy. Such an emergency was presented by the drought in the southeastern United States during the spring and summer of 1941, at which time the Commission ordered a number of interconnections, some of which affected the T.V.A. The Authority was a major participant in conferences called by the Power Commission to work out methods of supplying national defense power needs in the southeastern area. Other contacts between the Commission and the T.V.A. are of less significance. For example, section 15 (a) of the T.V.A. Act provides that credit contracts entered into by the T.V.A. with public agencies and nonprofit organizations for the purpose of assisting them in acquiring distribution systems, must be approved by the Federal Power Commission, but no problems have been raised by this relationship.[44]

In some fields where the T.V.A. might have been subjected to Power Commission control, it has retained its autonomy. The Commission, for example, was authorized by Congress to prepare the allocation of value at Bonneville Dam, and the rates set by the Bonneville Administration, an agency responsible to the Secretary of the Interior, are subject to the approval of the Commission. The T.V.A. has escaped such controls. The only limitation on rate-making imposed by the T.V.A. statute is found in an amendment adopted in 1935, which reads: "It is hereby declared to be the policy of this Act that, in order, as soon as practicable, to make the power projects self-supporting and self-liquidating, the surplus power shall be sold at rates which, in the opinion of the Board, when applied to the normal capacity of the Authority's power facilities, will produce gross revenues in excess of the cost of production of said power. . . ."[45]
In 1936 an administration-sponsored bill relating to Bonneville Dam

44. See Federal Power Commission, *Annual Report, 1940*, p. 98.
45. Sec. 14.

carried a provision which would have given the Federal Power Commission authority to fix the rates to be charged by any federal agency selling water power or surplus electric energy, but this bill was defeated.[46] The allocations of power costs at T.V.A. dams, as noted above, are subject only to the approval of the President. The T.V.A. is thus for the most part free from regulatory control by the Federal Power Commission.

The T.V.A., by reason of its status as a federal agency, is exempt from state regulation in the conduct of its power business, although there was some controversy on this point at first.[47] In all of the Tennessee Valley states except Mississippi, there are regulatory bodies with the usual powers of control over public service corporations with respect to rates, service, accounting, and acquisition or sale of properties. The question of the Authority's relationship to these state agencies was first raised in Alabama, when the Alabama Power Co. presented to the Alabama Public Service Commission for approval the proposed sale of some of its properties to the T.V.A.[48] Certain coal and ice companies intervened in these proceedings, contending that the transfer should not be approved because the T.V.A. had no right to engage in the public utility business in Alabama except in subordination to state laws, and that the T.V.A. had no intention of seeking a certificate of convenience and public necessity or otherwise subjecting itself to the laws of Alabama as a utility. The Commission approved the sale, but it did hold that the T.V.A. was "a utility as defined by the statutes of Alabama, engaged in a proprietary business and not a governmental function, and is therefore subject to regulation as a utility under the laws of Alabama." [49] The commission indicated that the T.V.A. would be required to file with it a copy of its rates and service regulations, and that it could be required to extend its lines and service by the commission. In short,

46. S. 4695, 74th Cong.

47. See "State Taxation and Regulation of the Tennessee Valley Authority," 44 *Yale Law Journal* 326 (1934); Hal T. Gibson, "Tennessee Valley Authority—Conflict between States and Federal Jurisdiction over Utility Rates," 3 *Federal Bar Association Journal* 295–302 (1939).

48. *Re Alabama Power Co.*, 4 P.U.R. (N.S.) 225.

49. *Re Alabama Power Co.*, 4 P.U.R. (N.S.) 233, 259.

the Authority was to be subject to the same controls as would apply to a privately owned utility.

The commission's action in this case was set aside by court order on another ground, and consequently it was necessary to bring the sale before the commission again. On this occasion, however, the T.V.A. agreed to appear only on condition that its presence be not construed as acquiescence in the jurisdictional claim asserted by the commission, so this matter was left open in the final approval of the sale.[50] The 1935 session of the Alabama legislature settled the question by enacting a statute defining federal agencies such as the T.V.A. as "non-utilities," over which the Alabama Public Service Commission should have no jurisdiction, and to which utilities could sell their property without securing the approval of the commission.[51]

In Tennessee the experience was somewhat the same. The Authority's contract to purchase the Knoxville power system was presented to the Tennessee Railroad and Public Utilities Commission for approval. In the face of Mr. Lilienthal's statement to the commission that the T.V.A. would probably hold itself accountable only to the United States and resist any exercise of state control, the commission merely approved the sale and left the jurisdictional questions to the courts, saying: "The Commission reserves for the courts the adjudication of the question as to whether or not the approval of this contract by the Commission has the effect to relinquish the jurisdiction, authority, and control of the state of Tennessee generally over the properties here involved and particularly the right of the state to regulate rates, service, etc., and to tax said properties and said operation."[52] The next session of the legislature, however, took the matter in its own hands and passed a statute to the same general effect as the Alabama law, removing the T.V.A. from the control of the state commission.[53]

The Authority is not only exempt from the control of the state utility commissions. In effect, it takes the place of these commissions

50. *Re Alabama Power Co.*, 4 P.U.R. (N.S.) 813–14.
51. Alabama, *Laws*, 1935, ch. 1.
52. *Re Tennessee Public Service Co.*, 5 P.U.R. (N.S.) 449, 456.
53. Tennessee, *Acts*, 1935, Chap. 42.

to the extent that its power contracts with municipalities and co-operatives fix electric rates, prescribe accounting procedures, and regulate other features of their power service.[54] The states in the area have for the most part succeeded in setting at rest any doubts which might be felt about the legality of this relationship by enacting legislation specifically authorizing their municipalities to enter into such contracts. When an Alabama statute to this effect was tested in the courts, the Alabama supreme court ruled that it did not involve an abandonment of the state's regulatory powers, as charged, but was merely an exercise of such powers.[55] In Tennessee the state supreme court upheld similar legislation against the charge that it unconstitutionally delegated state regulatory powers to the T.V.A. The court considered that in selling power a city was acting in a proprietary capacity and carrying on a quasi-private activity, so that the question of delegation was not relevant. But even if that were not the case, the court held that there would be no question of unconstitutional delegation; rather, the T.V.A. was simply acting in a supervisory capacity. The T.V.A. requirements as to accounting and disposition of revenues were reasonable and commendable stipulations, the court felt.[56]

The only important set-back encountered by the T.V.A. in the state courts on this issue came in Kentucky. There the court of last resort held that the standard T.V.A. contract gave the Authority such a complete measure of control over municipal power operations as to reduce a city to a condition "of complete subjectivity to the domination and control of the federal government. . . ." The contract was therefore held to be ultra vires, but the court indicated that it could be validated by proper state legislative action.[57]

54. See O. C. Hormell, "State Legislation on Public Utilities in 1934–35," 30 *American Political Science Review* 522, 528–31 (1936), and 32 *ibid.* 1123–26 (1938). Hormell notes that "the legal department of the TVA does not consider the contracts an important part of any regulatory process."

55. *Oppenheim* v. *City of Florence*, 155 So. 859 (1934).

56. *Memphis Power & Light Co.* v. *Memphis*, 112 S.W. (2d) 817 (1937).

57. *City of Middlesboro* v. *Kentucky Utilities Co.*, 146 S.W. (2d) 48 (1940). In 1942 the Kentucky legislature remedied this situation by adopting what John Bauer calls "the most comprehensive statutory provision in the country for the establishment of municipal ownership." (31 *National Municipal Review* 277–78 [1942].) Contracts with the T.V.A. for the purchase of bulk power were specifically authorized.

Substantially the same issue has been raised in the federal courts, although in a different guise. Thus in the *Tennessee Electric Power Co.* case, the contention was pressed upon the Supreme Court that "the acts of the Authority cannot be upheld without permitting federal regulation of purely local matters reserved to the states or the people by the Tenth Amendment. . . ." The Supreme Court found it unnecessary to consider this contention, however, because it held that only the states involved or their officers would have a standing to raise any question under the Tenth Amendment.[58]

The greatest problem in intergovernmental relationships which the T.V.A. has had to face has arisen because of its tax exempt status.[59] Even before the T.V.A. was set up, the state of Alabama was concerned over its inability to tax the power operations and properties at Muscle Shoals. The state had never become reconciled to the loss of this valuable resource to the federal government, and had made various efforts to secure some reimbursement. One of the state's contentions was that the United States owed it a privilege tax on its Wilson Dam operations, payable at the same rate charged other hydroelectric plants operating in the state. An effort was made to enforce this demand in the United States Court of Claims, but it was unsuccessful.[60]

While the Muscle Shoals legislation was before Congress, Alabama legislators, later joined by those of Tennessee, pressed for some payment for their states from the power operations at Wilson Dam and at the prospective Cove Creek Dam. Senator Norris resisted these demands at first, but later included a provision to this effect in his 1929 measure. As finally adopted in section 13 of the T.V.A. Act, it required the Authority to pay to the state of Alabama 5 per cent of the gross proceeds from sale of power generated at any dams in Alabama, and a similar amount to Tennessee from dams in that state. In addition, power made available at dams in Alabama

58. *Tennessee Electric Power Co.* v. *T.V.A.*, 306 U.S. 118 (1939).
59. For a discussion of the problem of state taxation of federal corporations, see Ruth G. Weintraub, *Government Corporations and State Law* (New York, 1939), Chap. 2.
60. *Alabama* v. *United States*, 38 F. (2d) 897 (1930), 282 U.S. 502 (1931).

by the operation of storage dams in Tennessee was to be the basis of further payments, 2½ per cent of the gross proceeds of such power to go to each of the two states. These percentages were subject to change by the T.V.A. board, with the approval of the President, but not more often than once in five years.

These payments were generally considered as *in lieu* of taxes, which the states could not charge against the T.V.A. They were not, however, equivalent to the amount that state and local governments would have collected from the Authority in taxes had it been a private concern. According to studies made by the T.V.A., tax payments of utilities throughout the country averaged about 12½ per cent of gross utility revenues. The payments also failed of their *in lieu* function in that the money went only to the state governments, which passed none of it on to the local governments in which the T.V.A. properties were located. Yet it was the local governments that were hardest hit by T.V.A. purchases of reservoir land and power systems and their consequent removal from the tax rolls. Another objection to this plan of payments was that it was limited to Alabama and Tennessee, ignoring adjoining states which also had claims.

It was the purchase by the T.V.A. of the Tennessee Electric Power Co. generation and transmission properties which finally made revision of the existing system of payments imperative.[61] By this transaction, plants and systems for which the T.V.A. paid $45,000,000 were removed from the tax base of the region, leaving several counties in an impossible financial situation. Under the pressure of prospective revenue shrinkages, various proposals for taxing the T.V.A. were put forward by local government representatives, and though they were known to be unconstitutional they were adopted in at least two cases. The Georgia legislature passed two laws subjecting federal agencies engaged in the generation and distribution

61. See L. L. Durisch and H. Macon, "Payments in Lieu of Taxes by the T.V.A.," 3 *Journal of Politics* 318–34 (1941); A. T. Edelmann, "Public Ownership and Tax Replacement by the T.V.A.," 35 *American Political Science Review* 727–37 (1941). For a general consideration of the problem, see H. L. Macon, "Payments in Lieu of State and Local Taxes," 8 *Southern Economic Journal* 493–503 (1942).

of electricity to state and local taxation.[62] Hamilton County, Tennessee, which contains the city of Chattanooga, made a forced assessment of $2,000,000 on personal property of the T.V.A. located within the county.[63] In neither of these two cases was any effort made to enforce the measure.

The T.V.A. had been watching the situation which its power program had created, and had decided by 1939 that it should assume the responsibility of replacing the ad valorem tax losses caused by its purchases. The Authority had prepared data showing the exact amount of this liability, and it was not so large as might have been supposed. For while the T.V.A. program had resulted in the transfer from private to public ownership of power properties formerly responsible for the payment of over $3,000,000 in taxes, not all of this sum was lost, nor was the loss attributable solely to the T.V.A. Distribution properties paying almost $1,500,000 in taxes had been purchased by municipalities and cooperatives; the T.V.A. contracts required the cities to continue to pay tax equivalents, while the cooperatives were actually taxed on their property in all states except Mississippi. On these distribution properties, then, there was no tax loss, except to the extent that in most cases the cities did not pass on to the county and state the amounts collected as the equivalent of county and state property taxes. The real tax "loss" was occasioned on the power properties and reservoir land purchased and retained by the T.V.A., taxes on which had averaged $1,120,000 for the last two years this property was in private ownership. There was also a loss, principally by the state governments, from business taxes which could no longer be levied, such as those on corporate income, franchise, gross receipts, hydro-generation, and so on.

It was the property tax loss resulting from its purchases that the T.V.A. felt an obligation to replace. T.V.A. officials approved and assisted in drafting the Norris-Sparkman amendment, which was passed in June, 1940, setting up a new system of payments to the states and affected counties.[64] The rate of payment was fixed at

62. Georgia, *Acts*, 1939, part I, title III, nos. 202 and 203.
63. Edelmann, *op. cit.*, p. 733.
64. 54 Stat. 626 (1940).

10 per cent of T.V.A. gross power receipts for the fiscal year 1941, and then was to drop each succeeding year until it reached the figure of five per cent in 1949 and thereafter.[65] These payments, which were "to constitute a charge against the power operations of the Corporation," were to be distributed according to a prescribed formula. One half of the total sum was to be apportioned among the states in the same ratio as the book value of T.V.A. power property located in each state bore to the total value of such property, and the other half in proportion to the gross proceeds of T.V.A. power sales in the various states. Payments were to be made not only to the states, but also directly to counties and tax districts which had suffered tax losses from T.V.A. purchases. The minimum total annual payments to each state and to the individual counties were required to equal the two-year average of former property taxes on power property purchased and held by the T.V.A. and on the portion of the reservoir lands allocable to power.

For the fiscal year 1941, 10 per cent of gross power revenues amounted to $1,500,000. Of this sum, $882,000 went to some 111 counties in six states, and the remaining $618,000 to the states of Tennessee, Georgia, Mississippi, Alabama, Kentucky, and North Carolina. During the same fiscal year, taxes and tax equivalents provided by municipalities and cooperatives distributing T.V.A. power were in excess of $1,800,000, so that the combined payments totalled $3,300,000. Since the actual property taxes lost or displaced by the entire T.V.A. public power program amounted to only $2,600,000, a substantial excess remained to be applied against the loss from business taxes.

Objections may be urged against this method of solving a perplexing problem. Those who felt that the T.V.A. had already proved itself to be a channel for the distribution of federal largess to the Tennessee Valley region considered that the requirement of additional federal payments was "almost as bad as charging Santa Claus for the privilege of coming down the chimney." [66] It is certainly true

65. Increases in power revenues during the period were expected to offset the decline in rate of payment, so as to yield substantially the same amount each year.
66. Edelmann, *op. cit.*, p. 733.

that the advantages resulting from the T.V.A. program, including the providing of jobs, the reduction of power rates, the creation of recreation resources, and so on, far outweighed the comparatively small tax losses. The difficulty was that these losses were not distributed evenly, but usually fell on small and poor units of government unable to bear them. The use of this financial dilemma to encourage the consolidation of these governmental units was apparently considered outside the realm of political possibility. Tax replacement was thus adopted as the best method of meeting the immediate problems of financial adjustment.

The public power program which the statute directed the T.V.A. to undertake has, for good or evil, succeeded on a scale few would ever have considered possible. Its failures are minor in comparison. The T.V.A. has built an efficiently functioning power system in the midst of great difficulties. In time of peace it has supplied an important demonstration of the stimulative effect of low rates on power consumption, and of the contribution toward a fuller life which cheap electricity can bring. In war time it has had the great responsibility of supplying power for war production purposes, and its magnificent construction organization has made it possible for new dams and power plants to be erected with amazing speed. Both in peace and war the experience of the T.V.A. has shown that an instrument of the people can operate with competence, integrity, and imagination in a relatively new field. It is good to have this example, for the world into which we are moving will have increasing tasks for such agencies to perform.

5: Regional Planning and Development

> "The public of America quite generally has the impression that the Tennessee Valley Authority was given a charter with far-reaching powers to plan and to work out the social and economic reconstruction of a great region. That is far from being the case."—*Arthur E. Morgan*

IN THE preceding chapters a picture has been presented of the T.V.A. in action—vigorous, dramatic action. But from the beginning the Authority was expected to be something more than a dam building, power generating, fertilizer producing organization. It was to "plan." This was the point to which President Roosevelt devoted the bulk of his short message to Congress on April 10, 1933. "It is time," he said, "to extend planning to a wider field, in this instance comprehending in one great project many States directly concerned with the basin of one of our greatest rivers." He proposed that the T.V.A. "be charged with the broadest duty of planning for the proper use, conservation and development of the natural resources of the Tennessee River drainage basin and its adjoining territory for the general social and economic welfare of the Nation." While this statement seemed to stress the angle of natural resources, it was clear that broader goals were in mind. As President Roosevelt later said: "The original legislation . . . was intended . . . to raise the standards of life by increasing social and economic advantages in a given area." [1]

1. House Doc. 565, 76th Cong., 3d sess. (1940), p. iii.

T.V.A. AS PLANNER

Planning was a magic word in 1933. To many it smelled of collectivism, but the Hoover philosophy had led only to Hoovervilles, and there was a general willingness to do some experimenting with new social controls. Thus there was extraordinary interest in the work of an agency called into being with a task understood to involve bringing purpose and plan into the development of an area that seemed to have been isolated from the main stream of American life.

There was no prototype for the T.V.A. as planner. The city planning movement had given birth to such agencies as plan commissions and zoning boards, but their purposes, jurisdictions, and powers were altogether dissimilar to those of the T.V.A. It is true that there had developed before 1933 a "regional planning" concept, but it had never assumed the meaning or form that regional planning took in the T.V.A. Regional planning was originally an extension of city planning, an extension made necessary by reason of the growth of metropolitan centers which sprawled across city and county and state lines, so that their problems could not be attacked, let alone solved, through any existing governmental machinery. Regional planning resolved to disregard artificial boundaries, and to concentrate on the unity of the metropolis and its environs. The typical problem of regional planners of this metropolitan school was transportation.[2]

The region for which the T.V.A. was to plan was not a metropolitan area, but a watershed. In so far as its problem was to secure the most effective use of water resources, this was a logical operating area. In so far as the T.V.A. was supposed "to raise the standards of life by increasing social and economic advantages in a given area," the river valley set a purely arbitrary boundary. In either case, the planning problem was unlike any ever before bequeathed to a governmental agency in the United States.

2. See Charles A. Beard, "Some Aspects of Regional Planning," 20 *American Political Science Review* 273–83 (1926); Charles E. Merriam, "Planning Agencies in America," 29 *American Political Science Review* 197–211 (1935).

The social and economic problems of the Tennessee Valley, toward the solution of which a planning approach would look, can only be sketched in here in the barest fashion. Generalizations must be qualified by recognition of the fact that the river is the region's only unity, and that all else is diversity. People, climate, soil, type of farming, degree of industrialization—all vary greatly from one end of the valley to the other.

There were in 1930 slightly over 2,800,000 people in this area of 40,000 square miles. It was a region of large families and a high fertility rate. Roughly 10 per cent of the population was Negro, though this was largely a meaningless average, for some areas were predominantly colored while in others it was boasted that a Negro had never stayed over night. The white population was extraordinarily homogeneous, its ancestors being typically North European in origin, and the foreign-born inconsequential in number. The Valley was largely non-industrial, and the people typically lived in small towns or on farms. The two largest cities, Chattanooga and Knoxville, were only slightly over 100,000 population in 1930. Type of farming varied from the hill patch of East Tennessee to the cotton plantation of northern Alabama. There were 13,000,000 acres of woodlands.[3]

The climate was kindly, the rainfall abundant, natural resources were many and varied, including coal and water power, and the people came from good stock. Yet the area was characterized by backwardness and sub-normal living standards, by fundamentalism and poverty, by Dayton and Scottsboro. It was a region curiously "left by the wayside . . . caught halfway between an agricultural economy which has always been its main source of livelihood . . . and an industrial economy which was still in relatively early stages of growth when it was attacked by the same malady affecting the industry of the entire nation."[4] The general pattern was that of an

3. See Howard W. Odum, *Southern Regions of the United States* (Chapel Hill, 1936), pp. 163–73; W. E. Cole and S. E. T. Lund, "The Tennessee River Valley, Its People, Resources, and Institutions," 15 *Journal of Educational Psychology* 130–36 (1941).

4. Edwin Lamke, "Planning Under the TVA," 1 *Plan Age* 3 (December, 1935).

exploitative and an exploited community. The soil had been mined, not cultivated, and was being destroyed by erosion. The forests had been wantonly slaughtered. According to the pattern of a raw material, colonial economy, resources were shipped out with little margin to the people who did the work, and were bought back in fabricated form. Such manufacturing as was done in the Valley tended to give low-wage employment, as in the textile mills. A visitor from Britain said to A. E. Morgan: "I am surprised to find a place solidly settled with Englishmen that have not made good." [5]

This was the area in which the T.V.A. was "to raise the standards of life." In so far as the goal was to be sought by a general planning approach, the T.V.A. had to rely on the powers given it by the two so-called "planning sections" of the T.V.A. Act which, strangely enough, did not even mention the Authority. Section 22 authorized the President to make "surveys of and general plans for" the Tennessee basin area which would be useful to Congress and the states "in guiding and controlling the extent, sequence, and nature of development that may be equitably and economically advanced through the expenditure of public funds, or through the guidance or control of public authority, all for the general purpose of fostering an orderly and proper physical, economic, and social development of said areas. . . ." Section 23 directed the President to recommend to Congress from time to time legislation to carry out the purposes of the preceding section, and these purposes were specified to include "the economic and social well-being of the people living in said river basin."

President Roosevelt immediately delegated to the T.V.A. the authority to make general plans granted by section 22. But the fact is that the planning reputation of the T.V.A. does not rest on its accomplishments under section 22. Paradoxically enough, the best planning work of the T.V.A. has been done in connection with its action program. There has been much loose talk about the T.V.A. as a planning agency which has failed to recognize this fact. The situation has been stated correctly by Earle S. Draper, first director

5. 172 *Annals* 53 (1934).

of the T.V.A. land planning and housing division, in these words: "TVA is not primarily a regional planning agency. Essentially it is an administrative agency acting under delegated authority, both broad and specific, to accomplish regional development. As such it is primarily an action agency." [6]

With even more emphasis, Arthur E. Morgan has pointed out how the work of the T.V.A. for social and economic development of the area is linked much more directly with the T.V.A. action program than with any vague planning power. He wrote, in 1937:

> Except for provisions for studies, demonstrations, and experiments . . . the sociological aspects of the TVA do not come from any broad charter to do sociological work. They arise rather out of the fact that in any important undertaking sociological components are as real and important and as deserving of analysis and treatment as the engineering or financial or legal components, all of which should be treated so as to result in an integrated program, from which no important elements are omitted. If the TVA seems to have more sociological implications than certain other large development projects, it is only because we have endeavored to recognize their existence and to make orderly provisions for their proper consideration. [7]

In other words, planning in the T.V.A. has manifested itself principally in guiding and controlling the construction program and other developmental activities. Planning has been in consequence not something external and superimposed; it could not afford to be utopian or impractical. It has become part of the daily routine, essential to the job to be done. The T.V.A. has never set up a staff of planners, divorced from day-to-day participation in the work of the organization, with no responsibilities except to dream dreams and see visions of a better world. There is a regional planning council and a regional studies department, but they do not fit this description. The T.V.A. practice has been described by Gordon Clapp, general manager of the Authority, in these words:

6. In George B. Galloway and associates, *Planning for America* (New York, 1941), pp. 517–18.
7. "Sociology in the TVA," 2 *American Sociological Review* 159–60 (1937).

We have found it necessary to discard a number of assumptions generally entertained when the subject of planning is under discussion. For example, we have made a persistent effort in all phases of this program to couple administrative responsibility for execution with the function of formulating plans for action. We find that the distinction between those who plan and those who execute is by no means as sharply drawn as would appear on the printed page—it is a line which is vague and always shifting. We have undertaken to bring about the widest possible diffusion of competence and responsibility for both functions among all of the departments in our organization. In practice this means that the same individual, staff, or department may frequently participate at several stages in the planning, formulation, and execution of the same project.[8]

This is the sense, then, in which the T.V.A. is most truly a regional planning agency—that it has attempted to think through the policies on which its actions should be based, to secure the best and most complete information obtainable, to weigh its program in terms of effect upon the over-all development of the region, and to act accordingly.

PLANNING IN ACTION

In 1933 the T.V.A. was not too clear as to what the role of regional planning agency required. Water control planning in the river and on the land, the approach to which has already been described, was certainly an important part of the job, but not the whole of it. The T.V.A. assumed that its responsibility included social and economic planning as well as physical planning, and that its concern was with human as well as natural resources. At first there were some fantastic plans for remodeling the life of the Valley, and for "doing good" to its inhabitants. In part this approach came from well-meaning idealists within the Authority. In larger part it existed as a popular misconception created by "writers, amateur sociologists, professors, newspaper columnists from New York who, after a hurried trip to Knoxville, with perhaps a few side trips to Muscle Shoals

8. "Some Administrative Aspects of Regional Planning in the Tennessee Valley," a paper presented at a joint meeting of the American Political Science Association and the American Society for Public Administration, Chicago, December 30, 1940.

and the Norris Dam site, went home and solemnly analyzed the Valley experiment for the benefit of the outside world." [9] In their enthusiasm they called the T.V.A. "a prevision of Utopia" and wrote such things as: "There is to be a new civilization in the Valley and the customs of the countryside must be made over, not by imposition but by adaptation to the new realities." [10]

Whatever there was of this missionary approach within the T.V.A. soon faded, particularly as the extremely limited scope of the Authority's powers in this field was realized. The two major policies which have marked the social and economic planning work of the T.V.A. were not long in developing. The first of these was to work wherever possible through established local governments and organizations so as to strengthen those agencies and minimize the resentment likely to be felt against the intervention of an outside organization. The Authority did not repeat its early mistakes, which had led the valley people to feel that they were being treated as "the untutored inhabitants of some island colony . . . incapable of handling their own destinies." The second policy adopted was to limit planning projects and activities to those areas which were clearly within the special jurisdiction and competence of the T.V.A.

Much of the social and economic planning of the Authority has been incidental to, or necessitated by, its dam construction program. The building of the "model town" of Norris, for example, was incidental to the construction of Norris Dam.[12] It was sponsored by the then chairman, A. E. Morgan, who reasoned that the cost of a temporary construction camp, which would have only a salvage value after the dam was completed and which might well constitute an unwholesome environment for the workers, should be put into a permanent town demonstrating town-planning principles and furnishing an opportunity for housing experimentation. Unfortunately the

9. James R. McCarthy, "The New Deal in Tennessee," 42 *Sewanee Review* 411 (1934).

10. Joseph K. Hart, "The Building of the City," 8 *Journal of Educational Sociology* 306 (1935).

11. J. R. McCarthy, *op. cit.*, pp. 411–12.

12. See Tracy B. Augur, "The Planning of the Town of Norris," 148 *American Architect* 18–26 (April 1936), for a discussion of the architectural features.

execution of the project failed to live up to its original promise in some respects. There was no consistent idea as to the economic basis of the town, its ultimate size, or the kinds of facilities required. At first it was presented as a subsistence homesteads project, but later this angle was dropped completely. The homes constructed exceeded estimated costs, and Lewis Mumford has stated: ". . . little of the order and imagination expressed in the Tennessee Valley Project itself or in the dams, reservoirs, construction works, and power plants, has been embodied in either the plan of the town or the architectural elements. . . . These houses affect the weakly traditional—and in fact betray the living tradition." [13]

The town of Norris is nonetheless an extremely attractive community. Its residents are largely, though not entirely, T.V.A. employees who work in Knoxville, some 20 miles away, or in the town itself, where several T.V.A. departments maintain their offices. Norris is completely a "company town," the residents renting their homes from the Authority. The town manager is appointed by the T.V.A., and is thus only indirectly responsible to the elected council. The T.V.A. has not been too happy about the undemocratic aspects of this arrangement, but there has seemed no feasible alternative. [14] No such elaborate community as Norris has been established at any of the other T.V.A. construction sites.

The building of huge dams and the flooding of thousands of acres of valley land disturbs many an equilibrium established by man or nature, and creates the need for planned action to meet the new situations. When a problem of this sort has arisen, the Authority's policy has been not to patch up a solution, but to use the crisis as an opportunity for developing a permanent improvement. Concretely, a large T.V.A. construction operation creates in the area where it is located the health and sanitation problems of any boom town situation. The T.V.A. has sought not merely to meet this problem, but to meet it in such a way that after the construction is com-

13. *The Culture of Cities* (New York, 1938), p. 325. But compare the favorable comments of Willson Whitman, *God's Valley* (New York, 1939), pp. 90–2.
14. See M. H. Satterfield, "Government of Norris, Tennessee, Studied," 28 *National Municipal Review* 799–800 (1939).

pleted there will be a more effective health organization in that area than there was previously. The method of operation has been described as follows:

> When construction of a dam is authorized, representatives of the Authority meet with representatives of the State health department in the State where the dam is to be built to appraise the increase in public-health problems that will result. . . . Such a conference is guided by the point of view that a permanent benefit may come to the county or district in question if the burden of supplying health services is thrown upon the local community, rather than being carried by the Authority. If no organized public-health department exists in the county at the time, it may be possible to create one; if the organization already exists, it may be possible to strengthen it. With this in mind the Authority provides funds for this "co-operative public health" work, the local community also providing funds as well as administration of the actual services. Thus the educational advantage which comes to a community from the execution of any public service is earned by the local people. The people in the area become accustomed to using the services supplied, and so carry over into the postconstruction period an understanding of and desire for these services.[15]

To take another type of situation, T.V.A. reservoirs have backed water up to the doorsteps of a number of Tennessee Valley towns, seriously affecting their economic basis and way of life. The T.V.A. has endeavored to assist such communities in planning adjustments to meet the new conditions. One of the most interesting cases of this sort is the town of Guntersville, Alabama, a small agricultural trading center of some 3,000 population. The Guntersville Dam flooded its rich bottom lands and left it on a peninsula thrust out into the reservoir. The town expected catastrophe, but instead it soon appeared that its new site had recreational and navigation possibilities that could more than replace lost sources of income. But planning of the new developments was required, and so, with

15. E. L. Bishop, R. F. Leonard, and M. G. Little, "Community Education Improvement under the Impact of the Construction Program," 15 *Journal of Educational Sociology* 154 (1941).

the cooperation of the T.V.A. and the Alabama Planning Commission, the city set up an official planning board. A zoning ordinance was adopted to facilitate orderly municipal development, a public park and boat harbor were developed on the tip of the peninsula, and a major street plan was adopted.[16]

In some 20 other reservoir-affected communities, municipal planning commissions have been created. The T.V.A. has cooperative agreements with the state planning commissions of Alabama and Tennessee which make it possible for the state agencies to employ resident planning technicians and to aid the local commissions in initiating and guiding their planning programs.[17] In this way the T.V.A. meets its obligation to assist the reservoir towns in solving their adjustment problems, secures the establishment of planning as a recognized function of local government, and leaves the communities with stronger, rather than weaker, administrative resources as a consequence of federal intervention.

T.V.A. activities create problems not only for humans. The impounding of huge reservoirs disturbs the established living conditions and food supply of both fish and land animals in the area. Since they are an important source of income and recreation for the people of the Valley, the T.V.A. has met its responsibility for their protection and readjustment by the establishment of fish hatcheries and wild-life refuges, operated by the T.V.A. itself or by other federal or state agencies. The reservoirs have also created a serious problem in the breeding of malaria-bearing mosquitoes. The T.V.A. has adopted various control measures, including the fluctuation of reservoir levels, and cooperates with the local public health organizations in meeting this danger.

In some fields where planned action might advantageously be applied, it has been impossible or inadvisable for the T.V.A. to do all that the situation seemed to require. Nowhere did the Authority's program have more direct and disturbing effects than upon the hundreds of families who had to abandon their homes and farms

16. Gordon R. Clapp and H. K. Menhinick, "The Approach of the TVA to the Solution of Regional Problems," 15 *Journal of Educational Sociology* 146 (1941).
17. See discussion by Bishop, Leonard, and Little, *op. cit.*, pp. 156–59.

to the waters of a T.V.A. reservoir. The Authority did what it could to alleviate this process of tearing up roots which quite often went down through several generations. Generous payments for land and buildings were made. Where cemeteries were flooded, the T.V.A. moved the graves as directed by relatives. The living created a more difficult problem. The possibility of a planned relocation of reservoir families was considered, but there was doubt as to the Authority's legal powers in this field and also as to the feasibility of any such scheme. Relocation assistance therefore was limited to the securing of complete information on the problems of the families involved, assistance to individual families in search of new farms, and cooperation with local welfare agencies in handling cases of distress.[18]

The work of the T.V.A. has brought it into contact with the local governments of the area at almost every turn. The question was early considered as to whether the T.V.A. could not use its influence toward modernizing the machinery and raising the general level of local government in the Valley. In an article published in 1934 Chairman A. E. Morgan speculated as to the possibility of doing something about counties which were unchanged from horse and buggy days, with the idea of making them larger and more efficient administrative areas.[19] T.V.A. purchases of reservoir land and of utility properties, with the consequent derangement of local government finances, might have seemed to create the kind of crisis which the T.V.A. has so often used for effecting permanent improvements. But fundamental changes are not easily made in local government structure. A Tennessee county may be small, and usually is, but there are many who love it. Thus, even a county which saw almost half of its land and tax base swallowed up by Norris Lake, and which was divided by the lake into two mutually inaccessible segments, preferred to go on living in its mutilated condition rather than effect a consolidation with adjoining counties.

18. See M. H. Satterfield, "Removal of Families from T.V.A. Reservoir Areas," 16 *Social Forces* 258–61 (1937); Willson Whitman, *op. cit.*, pp. 79–90.
19. "Purposes and Methods of the Tennessee Valley Authority," 172 *Annals* 50–57 (1934).

Some influence may be exerted, however, by such examples in intercounty cooperation as the tri-county service of the Huntsville, Alabama, public library under a plan inaugurated for the benefit of T.V.A. construction workers on the Guntersville Dam, or by the eight-county health district which the T.V.A. has assisted in northern Alabama. Other activities of the T.V.A., including a fairly elaborate research program in the problems of local government, are likewise having their effect. Studies in this field have been made not only by T.V.A. staff members, but also by state universities in the area with T.V.A. financial assistance, again with the goal of strengthening local resources.[20]

The T.V.A. has an opportunity to influence local educational arrangements in several ways. The school set-up in a local area is certain to be vitally affected by a T.V.A. reservoir, which may flood out existing schools or radically change the location of the school population. During the construction period educational facilities must be furnished for children of T.V.A. workers. These problems are handled by cooperative action of T.V.A., state, and local officials, and the entire situation is considered as a unit. Thus at Gilbertsville, Kentucky, a new consolidated elementary school was built by the county with funds obtained from the sale of a school on land needed by the T.V.A. for building the Kentucky Dam. Then the T.V.A. entered into a contract with the county permitting children from the T.V.A. construction village to attend the new school, tuition payments on a per-pupil basis being made by the Authority. After the construction period ends and T.V.A. pupils are withdrawn, additional consolidations can be made on the new school.[21]

In its concern for a coordinated approach toward its educa-

20. See discussion by Lawrence L. Durisch, "Local Government and the T.V.A. Program," 1 *Public Administration Review* 326, 331–34 (1941). An excellent intimate view of local government in the area is given in Karl Bosworth, *Tennessee Valley County* (University of Alabama, 1941). For examples of T.V.A. local government studies, see M. H. Satterfield and C. H. Pritchett, *County Government and Administration in the Tennessee Valley States* (Washington, 1940), and L. E. Abbott and Lee Greene, *Municipal Government and Administration in Tennessee* (Knoxville, 1939).

21. Bishop, Leonard, and Little, *op. cit.*, p. 152.

tional responsibilities, the T.V.A. has entered into agreements with the state departments of education in both Kentucky and Tennessee defining mutual interests of the departments and the Authority in dam and reservoir areas. The purpose of the agreements has been described as follows:

> The Authority has provided an education officer for appropriate areas; the State department has agreed to undertake to establish a coordinating committee for the area, on which the various educational agencies of that area will be represented. Using the impact of the construction program as a point of departure, the joint efforts will be directed toward developing a pattern of cooperation and coordination, under which the contributions of the various educational agencies will be welded into an integrated attack on the area's educational problems.[22]

Other examples could be given demonstrating how the T.V.A. has endeavored to plan the effects of its water control activities so as to secure the maximum advantages for regional development and the maximum utilization of new resources. Because of the broad ramifications of the program, the effects of this attitude have been felt in many areas of Valley life, of which those just described are representative. All of the Authority's development activities have not been channeled through the water control program, however. The T.V.A. has accepted a general responsibility for improving the status of the region which has led it to use whatever methods are available and useful. While the fantastic expectations of the early days have not been met, still its achievements in general regional development have been of considerable importance.

In this role the T.V.A. has acted as fact-gatherer, press agent, and even special pleader for the Valley region. It has undertaken directly and has encouraged other government agencies in the accumulation of data of all kinds on the area.[23] A Valley-wide program

22. *Ibid.*, p. 153.
23. Earle Draper has described the result of this work as "the most valuable collection of basic data that has ever been gathered for an area of equal size—air photos and air mosaics, planimetric maps showing the culture of the country in greater or less detail and at various scales, land classification maps of unusual sim-

REGIONAL PLANNING AND DEVELOPMENT

of topographic mapping has been carried on with the cooperation
of the U.S. Geological Survey, which had never previously mapped
the entire Valley area. The T.V.A. has conducted surveys of the
mineral resources of the Valley, to one of which, clay, it has devoted special attention in ceramic experiments intended to prove the
value of this resource and the possibilities of electric kiln firing.

The Authority has considered that one of the most promising
avenues for regional development lay in the recreational opportunities offered by the Valley. The Great Smoky Mountains with their
streams and virgin forests form the largest remaining wilderness
in the eastern United States. The chain of lakes created by the
T.V.A. dams has opened up new recreational possibilities. The
Authority has considerably enhanced the drawing power of the
area by the beautiful settings given to its dams and the thoughtful
arrangements made for the convenience of visitors, as well as by
demonstration park projects such as are maintained at Norris Dam.
A volume on *The Scenic Resources of the Tennessee Valley* has
been published by the T.V.A., and in 1940 a report was submitted
to the President and Congress making recommendations for the
further recreation development of the Tennessee River system.[24]

The extent to which the T.V.A. can effect an improvement in
the basic economic situation of the Valley is obviously limited by
many factors. It has, however, selected certain sectors where it has
sought to make its influence felt. Chairman A. E. Morgan brought
to the Authority the conception of making the area into a more self-
sufficient economy through the increased utilization of producers'
cooperatives. The principal measure taken in this direction was the
formation in 1934 of the Tennessee Valley Associated Cooperatives,
Inc., by the directors of the T.V.A. under the laws of Tennessee.
The purpose of this organization was to give assistance to the development of cooperative enterprises in the Valley through organi-

plicity and value, maps of natural resources such as forests, a complete compendium
of scenic resources. . . ." ("Land Planning in the Tennessee Valley," 1 *Plan Age* 9
[December, 1935]). See also G. Donald Hudson and others, "Studies of River
Development in the Knoxville-Chattanooga Area," 15 *Economic Geography* 235–70
(1939).

24. House Doc. 565, 76th Cong., 3d sess.

zational, promotional, and financial assistance. It secured funds for this purpose by a grant of $300,000 from the Federal Emergency Relief Administration. The relationship of the T.V.A.C. to the T.V.A. was rather anomalous. The fiction of a distinction between the two agencies was maintained, though the directors of both corporations were the same and regular T.V.A. officers and employees acted as officers and employees of the T.V.A.C., so that the latter organization was in the happy position of having no administrative expenses.[25] The Authority's connection with the T.V.A.C. was eventually severed, however, and the encouragement of cooperatives became of lesser importance.

Another approach which the T.V.A. has followed with somewhat greater persistence is to call attention to alleged discrimination against the South in the country's freight rate structure. It has been the contention of Mr. Lilienthal and others in the T.V.A. that the southern region is handicapped in escaping from a low-income raw material economy by freight rates which encourage the shipment of raw materials to the north while discouraging the shipment of finished products. The T.V.A. undertook an elaborate survey of this problem, and in 1937 presented to the President and Congress a report on the interterritorial freight rate problem of the United States.[26] Officials of the T.V.A. have continued to study and to speak out on this question.[27]

Any measurement of the total effect of the Authority's activities on the social and economic status of the Valley would require a general appraisal of the land and power programs which is beyond the scope of this study. Here it is enough to recognize that the influences the T.V.A. has brought to bear on the land and the people and their way of life, though they will not create a "new civilization," will be, and already have been, responsible for noticeable changes. Two million kilowatts cannot be turned loose in a

25. See John Thurston, *Government Proprietary Corporations,* p. 39. For the status of T.V.A.C. in 1940, see "Financial Statements of Certain Government Agencies," Senate Doc. 172, 76th Cong., 3d sess., Part I, pp. 267–68.

✓ 26. House Doc. 264, 75th Cong., 1st sess. (1937).

27. For a recent statement of Mr. Lilienthal's views on the subject, see 87 *Cong. Rec.* A1665–68 (1941).

Valley without some shocks being felt. Edward A. Woods was not writing wholly fancifully when he said in 1935:

> You of the Tennessee Valley region are living today as you are not going to be living twenty-five years hence. Your lives are going to be changed, first of all by electricity. Then you will be changed by the responsibilities of operating the institution which brings you this electricity. This will make you co-operative where you are now competitive; forward-looking where you now stand upon the traditions of a musty past; free where you are now enslaved by a brutal land economy; hopeful of your future in this world where now your only hope lies in an unknown, unseen beyond.[28]

THE REGIONAL APPROACH

In some ways the most novel feature of the entire T.V.A. development is its status as a federal agency organized on the basis of a geographical region. The major subdivisions of our federal government have traditionally been arrived at by the process of departmentalization according to major purpose or function, resulting in units like the Treasury Department or the Department of the Interior.[29] It is true that since these departments function over the entire country, they must arrange for internal subdivision on the basis of geographical areas, utilizing various regional or district schemes. But these are purely administrative regions, for field office purposes. Officers of the departments are stationed in these regions as extensions of the central office for administrative convenience in furthering the major purpose with which that department is charged.

The T.V.A., on the other hand, was established directly upon a regional or geographical basis. It was not given a major function to perform for the entire country, but was assigned general developmental responsibility for a certain section of the coun-

28. "TVA and the Three R's," 8 *Journal of Educational Sociology* 292–93 (1935).

29. For a discussion of the principles involved in the subdivision of the work of government, see Luther Gulick and L. Urwick (eds.), *Papers on the Science of Administration* (New York, 1937), Chap. 1; also Schuyler C. Wallace, *Federal Departmentalization* (New York, 1941).

try. What it was to do in this region on a unified basis, was being done throughout the rest of the country, in part at least, by numerous separate and independent departments, bureaus, and agencies of the federal government. The T.V.A. was given a responsibility for the Valley's soil and agriculture, which the Department of Agriculture had for the country generally. It was to plan and build dams and sell power and assist navigation, as did the Reclamation Service and the Corps of Engineers elsewhere in the nation. It proposed to conserve and develop the Valley's forests, which was also part of the larger job of the U.S. Forest Service and the Civilian Conservation Corps.

The unique position of the T.V.A. begins to emerge from a consideration of these facts. It was based on the conception that there was something to be gained by accepting a particular region, rather than a particular function, as the basis for organization. It assumed that single-purpose departments operating on a nation-wide basis were likely to impinge upon a particular area in a rather segmented and uncoordinated fashion, and that a corrective could be supplied by setting up a unified multi-purpose federal agency with jurisdiction limited to a single region. As David E. Lilienthal put it:

> For the first time a President and Congress viewed the problems of a region as Maitland saw "the unity of all history": as a "seamless web," recognizing that one strand cannot be torn without affecting every other strand. The problems of the Tennessee Valley were viewed as a *single problem* of many integrated parts, rather than dissected into separate bits in order to fit the pigeonholes of existing governmental instrumentalities. This thesis of unity led Congress to vest no single function of the Federal Government in the TVA, but rather an integrated group of Federal functions related to the regional conservation of natural resources of water and land and to promote the interests of the people of a region.[30]

This is a challenging conception, but one which raises a number of questions for examination. First of all, is the regional concept

30. Address before the University of California, November 29, 1940.

a real and valid one? Disregarding the various senses in which the term "region" may be used, it is sufficient to point out here the existence of natural resources areas, geographical areas, other areas of all sorts within the nation which are not contained within and do not conform to any existing political boundaries. As the National Resources Committee noted in 1935: "The qualities, resources, and problems of the natural environment occur in particular combinations locally and are distributed unevenly over the earth; and the existing areas of government are rarely coterminous with either the areas of human and natural resources, or with the 'problem areas' which demand treatment." [31] The Committee concluded that because of these facts, "no coordinated handling of resources and problem areas can be hoped for unless new and appropriate governmental devices be developed." And so it went on to make its notable study of such devices of a regional character as had been effective in national planning and development.

When the problem becomes one of determining the regions into which the nation is or should be divided, however, difficulties are encountered. The regions discovered will depend upon the criteria used—culture, geography, natural resources, agriculture, and many other factors are relevant. One of the most careful considerations of the regional question was that made by the Southern Regional Study, and the conclusion reached there was that "the regions should be few enough, and therefore large enough, for general composite use, yet not too large or heterogeneous to preclude quantitative and qualitative analysis of important factors." [32] On the basis of this test the Tennessee Valley was classified as a "subregion."

Whether a watershed is a significant unit at all for anything except drainage purposes has been questioned. One of the geographers polled on the subject by the National Resources Committee declared it "almost obviously absurd to take a river basin as a funda-

31. *Regional Factors in National Planning and Development* (Washington, 1935), p. 2; see also Part IV of this report for a general consideration of the regional idea.

32. Howard W. Odum, *Southern Regions of the United States*, p. 165.

mental regional basis." [33] However, as was pointed out elsewhere in the same report: "In neither theory nor practice has the sphere of authority of the T.V.A. been definitely set at the watershed boundary." [34] Section 22 of the T.V.A. Act refers not only to the Valley but also to "such adjoining territory as may be related to or materially affected by the development consequent to this Act. . . ." Actually, the T.V.A. has demonstration farms in more than half the states, it sells power outside the confines of the watershed, its plea for lower freight rates makes out a case for the entire South and the West as well, and in other ways the T.V.A. steps over the relatively narrow confines of the Valley boundaries.

Is there a danger in the regional approach? Does it not lend itself to the taking of a partial rather than a national view, to a sharpening of sectional consciousness and jealousy? There are certainly possibilities of this sort to be watched. A feeling of resentment against the distribution of favors to the Tennessee Valley through the T.V.A. was reflected in the riddle, widely propounded a few years ago, asking what river flowed through seven states and drained all forty-eight. There is, however, a distinct difference between the spirit of regionalism and the spirit of sectionalism. As Howard Odum has said:

> . . . regionalism envisages the nation first, making the total national culture the final arbiter, while sectionalism sees the region first and the nation afterward. In the second place, sectionalism emphasizes political boundaries and state sovereignty, technical legislation, and local loyalties. Where sectionalism features partisan separateness, regionalism connotes component and constituent parts of the national culture. [35]

What is to be the relationship of a compendious regional authority to the regular federal departments? Obviously there are real possibilities of conflict or duplication when the T.V.A. and the

33. *Op. cit.*, p. 148.
34. *Ibid.*, p. 113. Lewis Mumford considers it a mistake to attempt to assign definite boundaries to a region, since it is a system of inter-relationships that overflow and become shadowy at the margins. He would define regions by their centers rather than by their peripheries. See *The Culture of Cities*, p. 315.
35. *The Regional Approach to National Social Planning* (1935), p. 19.

Department of Agriculture are both carrying on agricultural activities within the Tennessee Valley. This is a problem which can be solved, however, and the T.V.A. has been extremely successful in working out harmonious relations with other federal agencies operating in its area. The T.V.A. agricultural program has been built on the firm basis provided by a three-way memorandum of understanding signed by the U.S. Department of Agriculture, the land-grant colleges of the Valley states, and the T.V.A. Locks in T.V.A. dams are designed and operated by the Army Engineers. Channel markings are planned, constructed and maintained in conjunction with the Coast Guard. The Authority produces ammonium nitrate and pure elemental phosphorus for the War Department. It has made available to the U.S. Fish and Wildlife Service a 40,000 acre tract of land and water in the Wheeler reservoir for development as a wildfowl refuge, and has turned over two fish hatcheries to the same Service for operation. In 1939 T.V.A. transferred the title of its Electrotechnical Laboratory at Norris to the U.S. Bureau of Mines, which is continuing research started by the T.V.A. on nonmetallic minerals of the Valley. The Authority has financed a complete program of planimetric and topographic mapping of the Tennessee Valley by the U.S. Geological Survey. With this kind of approach, the T.V.A. has not only been able to avoid for the most part interference with, or duplication of, the work of other federal agencies, but has even fostered, encouraged, and sometimes subsidized the programs of those departments where they were related to the Tennessee Valley area.[36]

Is not a federal regional agency undemocratic to the extent that, while it presumes to a local status, the local residents have no direct control over it or responsibility for it? It is obviously true that the primary responsibility of such an agency must be to the President, who appoints the directors, and the Congress, which supplies

36. For an analysis of methods used by the T.V.A. in cooperating with federal and local agencies, see Clarence L. Hodge, *The Tennessee Valley Authority: A National Experiment in Regionalism* (Washington, 1938), Chap. 7. A complete list of T.V.A. cooperative relationships is found in a 54-page statement issued by the Authority on June 9, 1942 (mimeographed).

the funds. It is possible to provide formally for regional representation on the board of directors, although this was not done in the T.V.A. Act.[37] However, even such representation would inevitably leave such a regional authority an essentially external, superimposed agency, which could carry on its benevolent role in the region without ever becoming really a part of the region.

Because the T.V.A. recognized these inevitable limitations on the regional character of a federal agency, it has developed the consistent policy that wherever possible those parts of its program which require direct relationship with the people of the area must be carried out by the agencies which those people support and control. How this principle has been applied in the agricultural demonstration program, in local public health and community planning activities, and in the distribution of power has already been indicated. The evolution of the T.V.A. program for training and education of its employees and their families furnishes another useful example of this cooperative approach.

At the Authority's first project, Norris Dam, an elaborate training program was set up without any outside assistance or relationship to other institutions in the area. A school was built and run by the T.V.A. Trade classes were set up, agricultural training was provided, a Norris house was used as a center of demonstration in homemaking. These activities, as the T.V.A. has recognized with commendable candor in appraising this early experience, "overlapped the work of the agricultural extension service, the State division of trade and industrial education, and that of other established educational agencies." [38]

The T.V.A. policy was soon revised to take account of these weaknesses. At Hiwassee Dam the Authority contracted with the

37. This has been attempted by two recent bills for the establishment of an Arkansas Valley Authority. One measure would set up an advisory board of five members appointed by the President from five different sections of the Arkansas Valley area, who would meet with the administrator of the Authority at least once each month to confer on policies. The second plan would set up the Authority with a five-man board of directors, three of the directors to be residents of the area. See S. 280, S. 2226, 77th Cong.

38. Management Services Report No. 1, "Personnel Administration in the T.V.A.," p. 17.

county in which the dam was located to operate an elementary school built by the T.V.A. in the construction village. How such contacts can be used to improve local services is shown by the fact that after construction of the dam was completed, the county leased the vacant T.V.A. buildings and consolidated a number of scattered rural schools into these improved facilities. At Guntersville Dam there was an even more complete utilization of local educational services. The T.V.A. entered into a contract with the school boards of the three surrounding counties, with subcontracts involving the Huntsville public library and a nearby Negro college, under which these local agencies provided a complete training program for T.V.A. employees: craft training, library service, general adult education, recreation, and school facilities for children living on T.V.A. property. The Authority furnished financial assistance, in no case greater than the cost of administering these services on its own account, together with guidance based on its earlier experience. Here again the arrangement had a stimulating effect on the local agencies. The Negro college set up extension facilities and adjusted its curriculum to the needs of Negroes living off the campus, while the Huntsville library began to give rural service throughout the three counties. In 1941 the T.V.A. turned over operation of the Norris school to the University of Tennessee. Thus the T.V.A. relies almost wholly on contractual arrangements with local agencies for educational and library services to its employees and communities.

The most serious questions raised by the use of this kind of regional machinery can be answered, then. But there still remains the task of demonstrating what virtues, if any, flow from this combining of functions in the hands of a regional authority. The minority of the T.V.A. investigating committee could see none. They recommended the complete disestablishment of the T.V.A. as a regional organization. Its agricultural activities they proposed to transfer to the Department of Agriculture. "There is no need," they said, "to try to build up a new regional Department of Agriculture in the Tennessee Valley. To return these agricultural functions to the Department of Agriculture where they belong would avoid duplication and waste. . . ." [39] The whole function of river control, including the construction and operation of dams, they would have turned over to the War Department, which has jurisdiction of such matters in the rest of the country, and which even under the present arrangement operates the locks in the T.V.A. dams. The T.V.A. would thus have been left simply with the job of operating its power system, and its regional function would have been liquidated.

These recommendations were properly ignored by the majority of the congressional committee. The proposal to wreck the Authority's magnificent engineering design and construction organization by turning the whole job over to the War Department was a piece of utter folly. If it had been adopted, many of the generators now producing power for vitally-needed aluminum would still be on the drawing boards. But if for no other reason the recommendations were unsound because they proposed to end what was admittedly an experiment before the demonstration was completed.

When will the experiment have proceeded far enough so that its merits can be judged? If the war had not intervened, one might have suggested a ten-year period as adequate for the purpose. Experience up to the present time, however, has been more than sufficient to convince the writer that the establishment of a regional authority with broad developmental responsibilities and with the job of seeing a given region as a whole has tremendous potentialities for good. The Tennessee Valley has profited immeasurably from the fact that the T.V.A. brought together specialists in various fields —agriculture, power, engineering, law, economics, land planning, and so on—to examine its problems in a coordinated and unified fashion. The process has been, incidentally, a liberal education for the specialists themselves.

Is the T.V.A. idea to be extended, then, to the rest of the country? Other regional agencies may well be established, but exact imitation of the T.V.A. is unlikely and would probably not be desirable. To cover the country with regional authorities each charged

39. *Report of the Joint Committee*, p. 276.

REGIONAL PLANNING AND DEVELOPMENT

with carrying on an action program as broad as that of the T.V.A. would be to create very difficult problems of coordination with the regular functional departments of the federal government. The endowment of the T.V.A. with its extensive activities was largely the result of accidents, such as custodianship of the Muscle Shoals nitrate plants, and it has required hard work and consistent effort to mesh these regional programs in with the national efforts of other federal agencies. There is just enough truth in the charge that the T.V.A. has created a "regional Department of Agriculture" to illustrate the dangers in repeating the process all over the country.

It is noteworthy that all the numerous legislative efforts that have been made to duplicate the T.V.A. in other watersheds have so far come to nothing. The most substantial program of this sort was the one outlined in 1937 by President Roosevelt in his proposal for a country-wide system of conservation authorities. These were referred to at the time as "little TVA's," but actually President Roosevelt envisaged for them a much less extensive action program than the T.V.A. has carried on. He indicated that

> the work of these regional bodies, at least in their early years, would consist chiefly in developing integrated plans to conserve and safeguard the prudent use of waters, water power, soils, forests, and other resources of the areas. . . . Projected programs would be reported by the regional bodies annually to the Congress through the President after he has had the projects checked and revised in light of national budgetary considerations and of national planning policies. . . . Projects authorized to be undertaken by the Congress could then be carried out in whole or in part by those departments of the Government best equipped for the purpose, or if desirable in any particular case by one of the regional bodies.[40]

The establishment of water conservation authorities in the western part of the country is complicated by the fact that the Bureau of Reclamation is already well-established and doing good work in this field. This is one of the factors which has prevented the

40. "Creation of Conservation Authorities," Hearings before the Senate Committee on Agriculture and Forestry on S. 2555, 75th Cong., 1st sess. (1937), p. 2.

setting up of a true regional agency for the Columbia Valley; the result is that the Army Engineers run Bonneville Dam, the Bureau of Reclamation operates Grand Coulee, and the Bonneville Power Administration sells the power which the dams generate. It is true that the T.V.A. has inspired several proposals for establishment of an Arkansas Valley Authority, but they follow the T.V.A. pattern only in part. Thus the most recent bill would give the proposed agency rather complete control over the rivers of the area, including the power to construct dams, but would limit the Authority's activities in connection with soil conservation to the making of plans to be carried out by the Department of Agriculture.[41]

Exciting and illuminating as the T.V.A. regional experiment has been, then, its usefulness as a precedent appears somewhat limited. Certainly this experience justifies no vision of a day when the Department of Agriculture and the Department of the Interior will be abolished and their duties taken over by regional authorities operating from regional sub-capitals. Decentralization of federal administration is an obvious necessity in a country as large as this, but it seems likely to come for the most part through less spectacular means.

THE BALANCE SHEET OF REGIONAL DEVELOPMENT

The entire T.V.A. program of regional development must be judged partly in terms of its cost. Cost figures have meaning, however, only as related to accomplishments. If the accomplishments can be expressed in financial terms, the judgment is relatively easy to make. If the T.V.A. power system pays its way, no other justification is needed. But other activities of the Authority do not, and are not intended to, bring in revenues to the government, and so cannot be appraised so readily. Is the 650-mile navigable highway of the Tennessee worth what it is costing? What is the value of T.V.A. flood control? How do the gains from T.V.A. fertilizer experimentation and agricultural education compare with the losses and dislo-

41. S. 2430, 77th Cong. (1942).

cations resulting from permanent flooding of thousands of the best farms in the Tennessee Valley? Even in the power program there are intangibles that cannot be listed on a balance sheet, such as the bombers we would not have without the aluminum created by T.V.A. power.

An appraisal of the T.V.A. program in financial terms, then, cannot be a very satisfactory one, but a sketching in of the basic data on program costs will serve to round out this account of the Authority's activities. By far the greatest part of the money which the federal government has put into the T.V.A. has been invested in its flood control, navigation, and power programs. In other words, it has gone into multiple-purpose dams and reservoirs, and power generation and transmission facilities. At the close of the fiscal year 1941, when the T.V.A. had received approximately $435,000,000 from the government, the asset accounts of its navigation, flood control, and power programs totalled $410,000,000. It is estimated that by the end of the fiscal year 1943 there will be an investment of $722,000,000 in these programs, with another $50,000,000 needed thereafter to complete the projects now planned.[42]

What is this three quarters of a billion dollars buying? First of all, it is creating one of the largest and best power systems in the country, with a 2,000,000 kilowatt capacity, which sold $21,000,000 worth of electricity in 1941, $25,000,000 in 1942, and will sell an estimated $37,000,000 in 1943. The investment ultimately charged to power will depend upon allocations which have not yet been made, but if present averages hold the T.V.A. power system will be entered on the books at close to $500,000,000.[43]

There is good reason, on the basis of present experience, to expect that power revenues will be sufficient to make this a sound investment. It has already been noted that net power income for

42. House Appropriations Committee Hearings, "Independent Offices Appropriation Bill for 1943," 77th Cong., 2d sess., pp. 849–50.
43. For the 7-dam system on which allocations were announced in 1940, 65.8 per cent of the total investment in dams and electric plant was charged to power. *Annual Report, 1940,* p. 414.

the fiscal year 1941, after generous depreciation charges, was 3.7 per cent on the power investment, quite sufficient to cover interest and amortization. Assuming the demand for power continues after the war, the T.V.A. system should have no difficulty in continuing to earn these charges. The half billion dollars of power investment in T.V.A., then, has a commercial justification, and need not call for support upon its other services, such as furthering regional development or aiding national defense.

Through the fiscal year 1941, T.V.A. expenditures on making the Tennessee River navigable were charged as $64,000,000, or 21.8 per cent of the 7-dam system then existing. If present averages prevail for the completed system, the capital charge to navigation will be something around $175,000,000.[44] Unless the government changes its policy and begins charging tolls on inland waterways, there will be no monetary return on this investment. The worthiness of the expenditure must be judged in terms of government projects on other streams, the national defense value of navigable rivers, the cost of waterway transport as compared with that of other modes, and the proper place of waterways in a coordinated transportation system. These are obviously not questions to be answered here.

The third partner in this multiple-purpose program of river development is flood control. Like navigation, it is not a paying partner. On the basis of present averages, flood control investment in the completed dam system will be around $100,000,000. The reasonableness of this expenditure and the precise effectiveness of the system are matters for the experts.

The remainder of the T.V.A. program does not bulk large in financial terms. The fertilizer and agricultural development activities of the Authority had involved an investment in plant and phosphate reserves of $6,500,000 by the fiscal year 1941, a figure which was expected to increase to $15,000,000 by the time the new

44. It should be understood that these are the author's own estimates, not T.V.A. figures. They are based on T.V.A. data as to cost of the completed program, presented to the House appropriations committee in January, 1942.

calcium metaphosphate plant was completed in 1944.[45] Operation of the fertilizer experimentation, production, and demonstration program required a net expenditure of $2,250,000 during fiscal 1941.[46] During that period T.V.A. sold three-fourths of its production of superphosphate to the Agricultural Adjustment Administration for over $2,000,000, but that was its only important source of outside income. The Authority distributed free almost $1,000,000 worth of superphosphate and calcium metaphosphate in its demonstration program. The T.V.A. could undoubtedly make its fertilizer activities very nearly self-supporting if it turned to commercial production, but that would be a fundamental change in approach of which there has been no indication.

The remaining T.V.A. activities fall under the general headings of development activities and operation of reservoir properties and villages. The development program, which required almost $1,400,000 during the fiscal year 1941, and which brings in no revenues to the Authority, included expenditures for the following purposes:

General mapping	$247,000
Forestry development and erosion control	267,000
Development of mineral resources	182,000
Public health work	127,000
Agricultural industries development	177,000
Freight rate studies	12,000
General development studies (community planning, local government, etc.)	100,000

In operating its reservoir agricultural and forest lands, recreational facilities, and five villages, and in maintaining the unused portion of the nitrate plants at Muscle Shoals, the T.V.A. incurred a net expense of $950,000 during fiscal 1941.[47]

It is important to keep in mind the fact that the T.V.A. will be

45. These figures do not include the two nitrate plants which T.V.A. took over at Muscle Shoals; they were given no value on the books. The ammonium nitrate plant which the T.V.A. has constructed at Muscle Shoals recently for production of explosives was financed by the War Department.

46. The total net expense of the fertilizer program from 1933 through fiscal 1941 was $13,293,000.

47. From 1933 through fiscal 1941, net expense on development activities was $10,540,000, and for property operations the figure was $4,950,000.

entering an entirely new phase within two or three years. From the beginning its energies have been so centered on its construction program that it is difficult to conceive of the Authority without any dams to build. Yet, barring unexpected additions to the present schedule, the T.V.A. will have completed its construction phase by about 1945, and will be settling down to the management and operation of its $800,000,000 investment (estimated) in dams, power system, fertilizer plants, parks, and other properties. The annual operating expenses of the T.V.A. when that stage is reached will be comparatively small. The power system will pay its own way. Net operating expenses of the other programs during fiscal 1941 were:

Navigation (including depreciation)	$993,000
Flood control (" ")	594,000
Fertilizer and agricultural development	2,250,000
Related property operations	953,000
Development activities	1,398,000
Total	$6,188,000

Allowing for an increase in navigation and flood control costs as the remaining dams are completed and brought into the system, it appears that an annual appropriation of around $10,000,000 should be ample for operation of the Authority's regional development program along its present lines. It is in terms of an annual expenditure of these proportions that the continuing operations of the Authority should be appraised.

In these four chapters an attempt has been made to discuss the principal activities of the T.V.A., with some indication of accomplishments achieved, but with more attention to the problems encountered in the course of these novel governmental efforts and the implications of such a multiple-purpose regional program. In the chapters which follow attention is shifted from the program to its administration. Particular attention will be given to the Authority's internal organization, its position and responsibility in the federal structure, the administrative consequences of its corporate form, and its outstandingly successful personnel program.

Administration

6: Administrative Organization

> "For the object of organization is control, or
> one might say that organization is control."—
> *Mary P. Follett*

THE TASK of organizing, controlling, and coordinating the operations of an agency the size of the T.V.A., with functions varying so widely in nature and characteristics, was one to challenge the courage and resourcefulness of the most gifted group of administrators. It was a job which would have been difficult under the best conditions, but which had nonetheless to be performed at first in an emergency situation and later under conditions of acute dissension among the heads of the organization. It is consequently not to be wondered at that the organization and administration of the T.V.A. was marked by some false starts and mistakes. The wonder is rather that the end result was so good, and that the T.V.A. was able to plow through these obstacles to earn its reputation as one of the best administered federal agencies.

THE BOARD OF DIRECTORS

The T.V.A. Act provided for control of the corporation by a three-man board of directors, appointed by the President by and with the advice and consent of the Senate. The chairman of the board was to be designated by the President. The directors were given nine-year terms regularly, but two of the first three directors were to be appointed for shorter terms, one for six years and the other for three years. The directors were subject to removal at any time by a concurrent resolution of the Senate and House of Representatives. Their salaries were set at $10,000, they were forbidden to engage in any other business while on the board, and they were required to believe in the "feasibility and wisdom" of the T.V.A. Act.

The responsible heads of the T.V.A. were styled a board of directors because the organization had been established in the form of a corporation. However, the T.V.A. board bore little resemblance to the type of board normally encountered in business corporations. Regular corporate practice calls for a fairly large board of directors, representing the stockholders and controlling the policy of the corporation by actions taken at periodical meetings. Such a board does not attempt to administer the affairs of the organization for which it is responsible. Rather, administrative control is entrusted to a president or general manager, selected by the board and responsible to it.[1] In providing for a small, full-time board of directors, the T.V.A. Act seemed to be more in the tradition of the ordinary government board or commission. The directors were thus placed in a somewhat ambiguous position, and their efforts to work out a proper relationship to the administration of the corporation's activities constitute one of the most interesting and important chapters in the administrative history of the organization.

President Roosevelt selected as his first appointee to the T.V.A. board Arthur E. Morgan, president of Antioch College. Mr. Morgan was a man of rare gifts and possessed of an unusual combination of qualities. He was an engineer with a rather wide reputation and experience in the field of water control projects, having served as chief engineer of the Miami Conservancy District which was organized to prevent a recurrence of the disastrous Dayton flood. In all he planned and superintended the construction of some 75 water control projects, and assisted in drafting drainage codes for a number of states. He was also endowed with an active social conscience and was particularly interested in educational problems, an interest which expressed itself in such forms as the Antioch experiment in combining formal education and work experience. His activities and views had brought him to the attention of President Roosevelt, and

1. This is of course the legal theory of corporate control. The actuality may be quite different, with the administrative management effectively dominating the board of directors.

during the period when the T.V.A. Act was under consideration it was known that he was to be appointed to the new agency, and he in fact drafted a few of the provisions which found their way into the Act as finally adopted.

The influence of Mr. Morgan, who was designated chairman of the board of directors, was very great during the formative period of the T.V.A. He was consulted by President Roosevelt in the selection of the other two directors. He made on his own responsibility a number of appointments of key officials, filling positions not only in the field of engineering, but also in finance, personnel, land planning, and so on. It was his decision to build the town of Norris, and it was his interests which were responsible for the adoption of an elaborate employee training program there. It was he who bluntly told Postmaster General Farley and Senator McKellar that they would have no hand in the appointment of T.V.A. personnel. It was an engineering staff of his selection which began the construction of Norris Dam.

While the appointment of Mr. Morgan seemed an exceptionally good one on the surface, a shrewd student of men and administration might have predicted difficulties for the future. For the chairmanship of the T.V.A. was not an office carrying full powers of control over the organization. On the contrary, the statute, by failing to assign any special authority to the chairman of the board, seemed to contemplate that he would be no more than *primus inter pares.* Mr. Morgan had been accustomed to run the organizations with which he had been connected. As president of his own engineering firm, and as president of Antioch College, the sole responsibility for leadership had been his. On the T.V.A. board, if the other two members were also men of strength and initiative, he would be placed in a situation requiring compromise, conciliation, adjustment, adaptability, and a willingness to admit that one's own judgment might on occasion be wrong.

Unfortunately, these were characteristics which it appeared that Mr. Morgan's nature might lack. For there was intensity, rigidity, puritanism, and domination in his personality. He had made his own way over many obstacles with little assistance, even his engineering knowledge being self-taught. He was much given to introspection, to measurement of his conduct in terms of moral principles, unwilling to make compromises. As Willson Whitman says:

> Dr. Morgan is a remarkable man with a keen and original mind, although it is not a mind adapted to effective dealing with people of the present era. . . . As an administrator he was always for going right ahead in a straight line. This brought him into conflict with other people, and he seemed to have some trouble understanding ordinary folks. He himself could always see what should be done, and in theory at least he was always right, so it was odd that people should oppose him.[2]

He was a serious and somewhat diffident person, often appearing ill at ease in social relationships, with little lightness or humor apparent in his make-up, yet with the capacity to inspire extraordinary degrees of loyalty in his subordinates. Strong-willed, earnest and determined, convinced that there was a moral basis in his judgments, he was marked for trouble on the kind of board set up by the T.V.A. Act.

For the three-year term on the board, President Roosevelt selected David E. Lilienthal, a completely different type. An outstanding graduate of the Harvard Law School, Mr. Lilienthal was for several years after his graduation a member of Donald Richberg's law firm in Chicago. His interest in utility regulation and his reputation as a liberal led to his appointment, at the age of 32, to the Wisconsin Public Service Commission. Here his active participation in the efforts of that agency to make the regulatory process more effective attracted national attention, and two years later he was appointed to the T.V.A. He brought to the board an aggressive and whole-hearted belief in the public side of the power issue, which was presumably his major interest in the T.V.A.

Harcourt A. Morgan, president of the University of Tennessee, was chosen for the six-year term on the board. His eligibility grew

---

2. *Op. cit.*, p. 137. See particularly the biographical sketch by his wife, Lucy G. Morgan, *Finding His World* (Yellow Springs, 1928).

out of the fact that he was a representative of the region immediately affected, and that his specialty was agriculture. Originally trained as an entomologist, he had been connected with the University of Tennessee since 1905, first as director of the agricultural experiment station, then as dean of the college of agriculture, and finally, from 1919 on, as president. He seemed well-qualified to interpret the T.V.A. to the region and the region to the T.V.A., and thus to insure that the Authority's projects and program would remain within the realm of feasibility and acceptability.

These were the three men who were to develop the policy, and direct the administration, of this unique and many-sided venture. The composition of the board remained unchanged during the first five years of the Authority's history.[3] Then came the removal of Arthur E. Morgan in 1938, and his replacement by James P. Pope, former United States Senator from Idaho, who had a reputation as a consistent New Dealer and was definitely on the public side of the power question.[4] Harcourt A. Morgan was made chairman after Arthur E. Morgan's removal, and held the post for three years. When he requested release from this responsibility in 1941, the President designated Mr. Lilienthal as chairman, Mr. H. A. Morgan continuing as a member of the board.

THE DIRECTORS AS ADMINISTRATORS

The board of directors was largely free from statutory restrictions in setting up the administrative organization of the corporation. The act merely provided: "The board shall . . . appoint such managers, assistant managers, officers, employees, attorneys, and agents as are necessary for the transaction of its business, fix their compensation, define their duties, require bonds of such of them as the board may designate, and provide a system of organization to fix responsibility and promote efficiency." Some of the earlier Muscle Shoals bills had gone much further than this in dealing with the problem of administrative control in the corporation. In the meas-

3. Mr. Lilienthal was reappointed to a full nine-year term in 1936, and Mr. H. A. Morgan in 1939.
4. Mr. Pope was reappointed to a full term in 1942.

ures vetoed by Presidents Coolidge and Hoover, provision was made for a general manager of the corporation who would be its chief executive officer, responsible to the board of directors for the efficient conduct of its business. The general manager was to be appointed for a ten-year term but could be removed for cause. He was to appoint, with the advice and consent of the board, two assistant managers, one for the fixed nitrogen program, the other for the power operations. The board members under this plan were not to be full-time officials; in fact, they were prohibited from serving more than 100 days a year at their posts. Thus it was made clear that the administrative control of the corporation was to be in the hands of the general manager and his assistants, with the board functioning purely in a policy-forming role.

The T.V.A. Act as finally adopted substituted for this arrangement the provision for a full-time board of directors, with no general manager, which had characterized all of the Norris bills. The administrative implications of this type of board were brought to the attention of Senator Norris as early as 1922 by O. C. Merrill, executive director of the Federal Power Commission, when he said to the senator:

> I don't know whether your measure proposes that the three directors shall have equal authority in management of the business. If so, I would doubt its advisability. I think there should be a group of men, whether three as proposed here or more, whose business it shall be to determine the general policies, the general lines under which the operation shall proceed, etc., but that when you get down to actual administration you should concentrate the authority in an individual and make that individual responsible to the group that establishes the policy.[5]

Senator Norris assured Mr. Merrill that such was his idea, but he did not revise his bills to clarify the board's relation to the administration of the corporation.

Consequently, when the T.V.A. was established, the board members were free to decide for themselves the extent to which

5. Hearings before Senate Committee on Agriculture and Forestry, 67th Cong., 2d sess., p. 770 (June 3, 1922).

they should participate in the actual administration of the corporation's activities. There were three feasible alternatives. They could stay out of administration altogether, leaving that field to the responsibility of a general manager appointed by them. They could give administrative responsibility to one of their own number. Or all three directors could undertake administrative duties. At the organization meeting of the board on June 16, 1933, the board chose the second alternative. Chairman Arthur Morgan was designated as general manager of the corporation, whose functions and duties "were to be those customary to the General Manager of a private corporation, and to include the coordination and general administration of the various activities of the Corporation, subject to the continuing authority of the Board of Directors acting as a Board." In taking this action the directors were more or less ratifying an existing situation. For as the chairman, and as the first member appointed to the board, Arthur Morgan had naturally assumed the leadership in the organization period of the T.V.A. The grant of managerial powers doubtless seemed a natural and logical step under the circumstances.

Giving administrative authority to one member of a board in this fashion, however, is likely to work poorly under the most favorable circumstances. It may succeed if the administrative member is a very strong personality and the other directors are weak or have only part-time positions.[6] If the statute definitely prescribes the powers and duties of the administrator there is also a possibility of success. In the case of the T.V.A. none of these conditions was met. All three board members were strong and competent, with full-time positions. The statute gave the chairman no special powers, and did not require the other two board members to accept a subordinate position in the execution of the corporation's program.

Under the circumstances, then, it was not surprising that the

6. The experience of certain of the British public corporations is of interest here. The chairman of the Central Electricity Board is the administrative head of the corporation, but he is the only full-time member of the board. The chairman and vice-chairman of the London Passenger Transport Board are the administrative heads of that organization, but again they are the only full-time members on the board. See Lincoln Gordon, *The Public Corporation in Great Britain* (New York, 1938).

original administrative plan was abandoned within two months. During this period the other two directors had become increasingly dissatisfied with what they felt to be the lack of an adequate plan of administration or an effective over-all method of control and review of the T.V.A. program. They believed that in the absence of such a plan the T.V.A. was being committed to unconsidered projects by the statements and speeches of some of its employees. It was known, for example, that the other two directors had some anxiety as to the scope and nature of the project which Chairman Morgan was undertaking in the construction of the town of Norris.

The views of the other directors were presented to Chairman Morgan at a board meeting on August 5, 1933.[7] A plan of organization was outlined which they felt should be immediately adopted to end the confusion then prevailing. In substance, it called for the dividing up of primary responsibility for each phase of the T.V.A. program among the three directors. Each director was to be allotted a sphere of activity within which he was to operate as the responsible administrative chief. This responsibility included the tentative formulation of recommendations on policy, personnel, and budget in each area, the submission of these recommendations to the board of directors as a whole, and the execution of the program as authorized.

The essence of this plan was that each director should act in two capacities—as one of the three members of a policy-forming board, and as the administrative head of one segment of the total T.V.A. program. The director as administrator was to be responsible to the board as a whole, was to receive his instructions from it, and was to make his reports to it. If under the allocation plan an activity assigned to one director overlapped or conflicted with that of another director, the two were to confer together as administrative heads, not as a board, to work out the problem. To the extent that other methods of coordination were required, this should be a special responsibility of the chairman of the board. The function of dovetailing separate activities into an integrated program was prop-

7. The memorandum prepared by the two directors is printed in *Hearings,* pp. 105–7.

erly one attaching to the chairmanship, the other two directors felt, adding that this role was quite different from any concept of general manager.

The adoption of this plan of organization was of course a foregone conclusion, since its authors were a majority of the board. Chairman Morgan, while going along with his co-directors in the proposal, did take occasion to justify his administrative leadership.[8] His goals, he said, had been to insure the proper taking over of activities already under way (such as the drafting of plans for Norris Dam by the Army Engineers), the setting up of the necessary administrative machinery for such functions as accounting and personnel, which would have to be performed no matter what the details of the program, and the securing of key personnel on whom the board could rely for advice in planning its activities. He pointed to the difficult physical conditions under which the new organization had worked, involving the transfer from Washington to Knoxville and the setting up of a new establishment, the pressure of job applications, the absence of the other two board members during most of the period, and so on. Chairman Morgan felt that some degree of confusion was inevitable under these conditions, and indeed that it was better than a quick semblance of order and plan which failed to keep pace with necessary tasks and proceeded without full appreciation of the complex problems involved. Chairman Morgan's credo was well-stated in the preface which he wrote for the T.V.A. organization manual issued in March, 1935, in which he said: "I personally detest regimentation, red tape, and bureaucracy, and am willing to endure a limited amount of confusion in order to give freer play to loyalty, initiative, and enthusiasm."

The plan of allocation adopted by the board at its meeting on August 5, 1933, gave Chairman Morgan responsibility for the general engineering program, including all matters concerned with Norris Dam; the educational and training program, other than agricultural; land and regional planning, and subsistence homesteads, including a "few experiments" with homesteads at Norris; matters

8. His memorandum on the subject is printed in *Hearings*, pp. 107–9.

relating to social and economic organization and planning; forestry, soil erosion, and Civilian Conservation Corps relationships; and matters concerning raw material for fertilizer. The chairman was to share with Harcourt Morgan responsibility for matters relating to industry and encouragement of cooperatives. He was also given the special task, as chairman, of "integration of the parts of the program into a unified whole, including the administration of the general functions such as accounting." [9]

Harcourt Morgan was assigned to supervise all matters relating to agriculture, including rural life planning and rural agricultural industries; the entire chemical engineering program, involving not only fertilizer research and production, but also research and development in the manufacture of "cement and dry ice"; and public relations in East Tennessee and adjoining areas. To Mr. Lilienthal went all matters pertaining to the power program, supervision of the legal department and the land acquisition program, and "the economics of transportation."

The T.V.A. was thus launched on an experiment with an unorthodox plan of administrative organization, the principal characteristics of which were that it merged policy-formulation and administration in the same hands, and set up three administrators with coordinate authority. Under the circumstances prevailing at the time, however, it may well be that this plan was the best temporary solution of the organizational problem. The situation facing the T.V.A. was that an extremely diversified group of activities had to be undertaken with the utmost speed. The administrative task involved would have made physically impossible demands upon any single administrator or general manager. It was clear that each of the broad fields of T.V.A. activity would need its own responsible head. The directors themselves were each expert in one of the Authority's branches of operation, and capable of undertaking administrative duties in connection with them. Policies for the various programs had to be developed which could not be arrived at *a priori*, but which had to emerge out of the realities of the existing situ-

9. *Hearings*, p. 110.

ation. The administration of the enterprise, moreover, had to be infused with the spirit which had brought this unusual regional agency into existence, and kept up to the standards which the board members had set for it.

All things considered, it is quite possible that the assumption by the directors of responsibility both for formulating and administering the program made possible much of the spectacular achievement of the T.V.A. during its first year or two of operation. In the complicated situation which existed, this simplicity lessened the difficulty of getting projects under way. As makers of policy the directors were kept close to reality by the knowledge that they themselves had to translate their plans into going enterprises. As administrators the decisions of the directors were guided by their full knowledge of the goals and larger purposes of the program. It is probable that if administrative control had been centralized in some fashion when the corporation was just getting under way, the complicated nature of the program and the necessity for working out administrative relationships would have acted as a real brake on progress.

Nevertheless, the fact remains that this organizational plan was essentially an expedient which could be made to operate only with the conscious effort and good will of the participants. It created unusual problems of coordination of the efforts of the different administrative divisions. It put the directors in a position where they were almost certain on occasions to confuse their dual roles, or to borrow support from their legal status as directors for their administrative acts. Certainly it was true that this trisecting of administrative responsibility tended to diminish the policy-forming responsibility of the board as a whole. For example, the extremely important power policy announced by the T.V.A. in August, 1933, was not an official product of board consideration. According to Mr. Lilienthal,[10] it was drafted by Mr. Arthur Morgan and himself after a visit to the White House, and was immediately released to the press. It was never officially adopted by board action. While this may seem unimportant,

10. *Hearings,* p. 785.

in view of the fact that two of the three members of the board approved the statement, the incident does serve to indicate how easy it was for the directors to forget in what capacity they were acting at a particular time. An even better example is furnished by Mr. Lilienthal's announcement of tentative wholesale power rates in New York without their prior submission to the board as a whole. The authority delegated by the board to Mr. Lilienthal to conduct T.V.A. power operations and negotiations was probably broad enough to justify his action in this case, but as he himself subsequently recognized it was a matter of such importance as to have merited submission to the board for formal approval.[11]

The organization of the board itself during this early period was sketchy and inadequate. Meetings were held irregularly, when necessary or possible, but rather frequently, numbering 80 during the first year of operations. There was at first nothing in the way of a formal agenda for the meetings. Even in the matter of the corporation's minutes of board meetings, there was for some time a failure to adopt a regularized procedure, and often minutes of preceding meetings were not finally approved until some months later. The principal problems were not, however, those relating to the organization of the board as a board, but involved rather the organization for administrative control and coordination of the total T.V.A. program. Here the most interesting and important development was that of the office of coordinator.

THE FUNCTION OF THE COORDINATION DIVISION

Steps were taken early in the development of the T.V.A. toward supplying the need for a central administrative office. As noted above, Chairman Morgan was made responsible for the administration of "the general functions such as accounting," presumably including such additional auxiliary services as personnel, purchasing, central office services, and so on. During the first few months the chairman's responsibilities in these fields were largely assumed by one of his assistants, Carl Bock, who was a personal friend and long-

11. *Hearings*, p. 776.

time associate of Mr. Morgan in his engineering firm. Mr. Bock undertook the task of securing office space and equipment, managing office services, and procuring transportation equipment and facilities. He acted as secretary to the board, and assisted in planning budgets and coordinating programs. Within a short time this function and these duties were institutionalized and elaborated in the creation of a coordination division, headed by a coordinator.

The concept of the coordinator's office called for it to exercise liaison, service, advisory, and even control functions. The coordinator was charged with direct responsibility for coordination of the Authority's policies and plans as approved and authorized by the board, and the distribution of information and instructions in regard to them. He was to maintain liaison with the individual departments and divisions of the T.V.A. and the projects on which they were engaged, to analyze and appraise reports on proposed projects, and to prepare operation progress reports. As a central service agency, the coordination division was to maintain a technical engineering library and to supervise general office services. In addition, the coordinator was to advise with the major operating executives on management problems, and to assist them in the organization of their contemplated plans and the preparation of reports and supporting data for presentation to the board. Finally, the coordinator was to control expenditures within the limitation of allotments, with the cooperation of the budget supervisor, and to issue orders for all authorized expenditures for materials, pay rolls, and services.

Although these latter control powers never developed, the coordination division did have an important job to do in transmitting, disseminating, and coordinating within the organization the policies and plans approved by the board. Its objective was to effect cooperation and integration between all activities in order to insure economical and efficient operation. From the beginning, the development of the coordinator's office was through an evolutionary and largely unplanned process. The value of the position lay in its potentialities for centralization and unification. The coordinator had a roving commission to bolster up the weak administrative spots and supply a measure of integration in the operation of a new and rapidly expanding organization.

Once established, the coordination division increased gradually in size, functions, and importance. Mr. Bock, the first coordinator, was soon replaced by John Blandford, who came to the T.V.A. from the post of director of public safety in Cincinnati, and who had no personal connections with any of the three directors. Thus the coordination division was cleared for a larger role in the organization than it might have assumed had it continued in the charge of Chairman Morgan's close associate. The division accepted responsibility for services which seemed logically to belong to none of the existing divisions, such as that of facilitating and supervising the removal of families from T.V.A. reservoir lands. The coordinator maintained contact with the various T.V.A. field offices. Regional coordinators were established in the geographical areas where T.V.A. activities were under way. Assistant coordinators were set up to maintain relationships with the management and the planning divisions, and later assistant coordinators for the electricity and engineering departments were added.[12]

Despite this considerable development of the coordination division, the coordinator did not acquire the functions or status of a general manager. He and his assistants were at all times agents and intermediaries. They were quite literally coordinators, who investigated, persuaded, reported, brought opposing viewpoints or policies together, and prepared alternate courses of action for presentation to the higher authorities. They were not administrative officials speaking with authority and setting the pace of the program, but merely way-stations on the administrative lines which converged upon the three directors. A contemporary designation of the coordination division as representing "the control stage of the organization" was far from accurate.

The unsatisfactory nature of this administrative arrangement

12. An organization chart of the coordination division as of 1935 is given in the report of the National Resources Committee, *Regional Factors in National Planning,* p. 95.

may be indicated more clearly by considering how it operated in the important function of budget preparation. Budget-making in the T.V.A. served two purposes, and was divided into two stages. First came the preparation of what was known as the "external budget," to determine the amount of money to be requested from Congress for the next fiscal year. After Congress had acted on the appropriation, there came the second stage, preparation of the "internal budget" designed for internal control of the Authority's operations. The budget was thus the principal planning instrument of the board, and as such its proper preparation and consideration were matters of prime importance.

As the first step in budget preparation, the various project organizations in the T.V.A. made estimates of the financial needs of the activities in their respective fields for the ensuing fiscal year, known as allotment requests. They were assembled in the finance division, and transmitted to the coordinator for review and submission to the board. The coordinator had no real authority in the process of budget preparation, and in no field did the board's failure to delegate any substantial powers to this official place more difficulties in the path of effective administration. The coordinator could and did discuss tentative budgets with department and division heads, make suggestions, and attempt to coordinate programs. Unquestionably he made a contribution in this way; moreover, his function of budget review was perhaps his most valuable method for keeping in touch with the activities of the various divisions. But always he had to stop short of making any real decisions.

The result of this system was that the board itself had to bear the entire brunt of budget revision and approval. Extensive budget hearings were held by the board each year. Many of the projects presented the board would be examining for the first time. Important planning decisions had to be made hurriedly under pressure of producing a budget. And while the directors were considering the budget they were at the same time acting as administrators of the corporation's affairs, so that they could devote only part of their attention to budget matters.

Under these conditions it is not surprising that budget hearings extended over a period of several months each year, and that the budget was never ready at the beginning of the fiscal year to which it related. In 1935 portions of the budget were not finally approved until November, five months after the beginning of the fiscal year. This is only one example of a situation that called for more than mere coordination. It called for the exercise of powers of control and decision, but these were powers with which the coordinator was not equipped.

As time passed, the inadvisability of attempting to combine policy-formulation and administrative responsibility in the hands of the board members became more and more evident. In an agency as large as the T.V.A., and with problems as difficult and demanding, it meant that the directors were going to slight one or both of their major responsibilities. Their primary task was to determine what the policies of the Authority were to be, and where it was going. It became increasingly obvious that their administrative responsibilities were preventing the most effective fulfillment of this function.

Apart from all other factors, however, continued operation under the original administrative plan was made impossible by the serious breach which had developed between Chairman Morgan and the other two directors. Antagonism appears to have existed between the chairman and Mr. Lilienthal from an early stage in the Authority's history, although the state of the relations between the two men did not become a matter of general knowledge until the expiration of Mr. Lilienthal's term in 1936, when Chairman Morgan protested to President Roosevelt against his reappointment.[13] Regardless of the original causes of this rupture, the difficulties were unquestionably accentuated by the fact that each of the directors

13. The newspapers had reported as early as October, 1933, serious differences existing between Chairman Morgan and Mr. Lilienthal, and there were reports that the latter was to become chairman and that Mr. Morgan was to be limited strictly to the construction projects. See *The Nashville Banner*, October 5, 1933. The best account of the differences between the two directors at this early stage is contained in the article, "Sweetness and Light vs. Power and Light," 7 *Today* 14–15 (1937). See also J. C. Poe, "The Morgan-Lilienthal Feud," 143 *Nation* 385–86 (1936).

was administering a portion of the T.V.A. program, and the serious effect of the split was increased because each board member was in administrative control of subordinates who loyally subscribed to the views of their respective chiefs. Thus the board's differences were not confined to that body, but seeped down through the entire organization. With the principal administrative officials of the organization involved in the controversy and taking sides over the issues raised, an impasse was reached which came dangerously close to wrecking the morale of the Authority. Disagreement among policy-makers is expected and may be quite salutary; disagreement among co-administrators may easily be disastrous.

THE ESTABLISHMENT OF A GENERAL MANAGER

The remedy for the Authority's administrative ills was fortunately a rather obvious one. It was well stated by Marshall E. Dimock, who wrote after a survey of the T.V.A. in 1935:

> . . . the board of directors should be the policy formulating unit, and although exercising complete surveillance and ultimate control over the management, should not interfere with administrative details. Under such an arrangement, the crying need is for a general manager of the corporation, who is given complete administrative control over every phase of the organization's activity. Such an officer is nowhere to be found in the T.V.A., since the directors have been reluctant to relinquish the administrative powers which they have assumed.[14]

There was almost universal agreement with this point of view, and immediately after Mr. Lilienthal's reappointment in May, 1936, the board took action to create the office of general manager. Mr. Blandford, who had been serving as coordinator, was appointed acting general manager, with the responsibility of formulating plans designed to perfect the administrative organization and to adapt it to the new plan of operation. Chairman Morgan apparently acquiesced in the action of the board, though he later refused to sign the minutes of the meeting on the ground that they did not ac-

14. National Resources Committee, *Regional Planning in National Development*, p. 114.

curately record his understanding of the action taken. It should be mentioned that Mr. Blandford had not supported the chairman in his controversy with Mr. Lilienthal, and that he was regarded by Mr. Morgan as a member of the opposing camp. On later occasions Mr. Morgan complained bitterly that the effect of the changed administrative plan was to restrict his access to and control over the engineering staff, and he undoubtedly regarded this as a principal goal of the reorganization plan, which he held to be part of a plot against his authority. There can be no doubt, however, that the establishment of a general manager was an imperative step if the T.V.A. was to hang together as an effective operating organization, and in the highest degree essential so long as the composition of the board remained unchanged.

The transition from coordinator to general manager control was effected gradually.[15] It was undoubtedly facilitated by reason of the fact that the same man held both positions. In his new capacity Mr. Blandford directed the attention of the entire personnel to a rethinking of the agency's organizational and administrative problems. He asked for and received from most of the principal supervisory officials, oral and written statements of administrative needs and suggestions for reorganization. In some fields the general manager began to exercise increased responsibility almost immediately, as in the preparation of the budget for the fiscal year 1937. Extensive budget hearings were held by the general manager, which were intended to replace to a large extent the hearings held by the board in former years. He reviewed the proposed projects and expenditures, and attempted to prepare a satisfactory budget document for presentation to the board, which held its own hearings as in previous years. But because of this preliminary work, the hearings were more effective and were concluded more rapidly.

It was not until a year after the original establishment of the

15. It was so gradual, indeed, that the *Engineering News-Record*, in an article of December 31, 1936, expressed the opinion that the appointment had been largely a gesture, "since current indications are that each of the three board members remains more or less supreme in the formulation of policies in the sphere assigned to him."

office of general manager that the plan was consummated by granting to this official true managerial powers. On June 16, 1937, the board adopted, over the protest of Chairman Arthur Morgan, the first of a series of resolutions completely reorganizing the administrative structure of the Authority. Under the new organization the general manager, to which post Mr. Blandford was now definitely appointed, was constituted the chief administrative officer of the corporation, to whom all departments and their administrative officers were to report.[16] Subject to such controls as the board might from time to time establish, he was made responsible for the execution of policies and decisions of the board. It was his function to assist the board in the process of policy-formulation by preparing the agenda for board meetings, presenting subjects for board action, keeping the board informed as to the corporation's activities, preparing special reports requested by the board, and making recommendations as to the affairs of the Authority. When decisions had been made and policies formulated by the board, it was the general manager's function to notify the administrative organization of such action.

Further, the general manager was charged with the preparation and submission to the board of the annual budget estimates and with the administration of the budget as approved. The importance of the budgetary function and its potentialities for coordination and control of activities were recognized by attaching the chief budget officer of the T.V.A. to the general manager's staff. A second assistant was the director of information, who was to advise the general manager in matters pertaining to public relations and to coordinate official reports. The general manager was also, of course, to be aided by the chief administrative officers of the corporation in the general formulation of plans and policies. The new plan of organization undertook to facilitate the administrative control of the

16. The only exceptions were that the general counsel was to be directly responsible to the board as to legal opinions, and the comptroller was likewise directly responsible to the board as to the disbursement of T.V.A. funds. This latter arrangement was revised in 1941, when the comptroller was made responsible to the general manager in all matters pertaining to finance.

general manager by a general reorganization of the operating departments, which will be discussed in the next section.

The theory and practice of general management as it has developed in the T.V.A. under Mr. Blandford and his successor, Gordon Clapp, are extremely interesting. The popular concept of the general manager as a high-pressure executive, with five telephones on his desk, making split-second decisions on complicated technical questions, issuing instructions to his subordinates, keeping a battery of secretaries busy—all this is completely foreign to T.V.A. experience. From the beginning the policy of the general manager's office was decentralization and delegation of authority. Considering the wide range of activities in which the T.V.A. was engaged, such a policy was practically inevitable. For no one man could have been found with the capacity to direct the dam construction program, fertilizer research, agricultural development, power production and marketing, and so on. These are all fields for specialists, and the true role of the general manager in such a situation is to act as a coordinator of the specialists.

It may seem paradoxical, having contended that the earlier position of T.V.A. coordinator failed because that official did not have sufficient powers of control, to urge that the most important task of a general manager with controlling authority is to delegate most of that control responsibility to subordinates so that he may himself be left free for the task of coordination. Yet it is only through such a formula that control can be effectively exercised in a large and diverse organization. The most important responsibility of a general manager under such conditions is not to issue orders, but to organize the work of his agency in such a way as to bring the details of one part of the enterprise into relationship with other details of the program at points in the organization where they ought logically to come together. Mr. Clapp, who was appointed to the post of general manager of the T.V.A. in 1939, has stated the problem succinctly and admirably:

> The role of general management . . . is certainly not to attempt to keep a close check on everything that is going on in

the T.V.A. That sort of concept would so hamstring the T.V.A. as to deprive it of the drive, imagination, and experience of its staff. . . . No man in an agency with as broad a program as this, involving so many different subject matters, can possibly presume to sit in a focal position and pass authoritative judgments on everything that comes within the ken of the T.V.A. . . . General management in the T.V.A. . . . attempts to achieve the benefits of decentralization, to free the staff for effective achievement and general direction within a broad framework prescribed by policy . . . [and] to see that the right minds, the right subject matters, come to bear in the right sequence to lead up to the best decisions.[17]

There is another aspect of general management in an agency which is headed by a politically-appointed and publicly-responsible board, and that is the responsibility of acting as intermediary between the board and the technical staff. Here again we may call upon Mr. Clapp's own statement:

The real function of general management in the T.V.A., I would say, it to attempt to bridge the gap between a staff that is organized largely upon the basis of technical groupings and who think along terms of expertness and special subject matter in their fields, and the Board of Directors who bear the ultimate responsibility for the success of the Authority's work and who must, of necessity, think in terms of broad public effect, of broad consequences, of the expertness and rightness of direction in which the whole program is moving. There is a gap between these two levels of work. The role of general management is to help interpret each of those levels one to the other and help create the kind of atmosphere that will make the compromises which spell good administration understandable, wise, and workable.

Standing in this strategic position between the two levels, the general manager must face in two directions. With respect to the board of directors, his primary responsibility is the formulation of issues for decision. These issues may arise out of problems encountered by administrative officials in their respective programs,

17. Extemporaneous remarks before a seminar of T.V.A. employees, May 22, 1941.

or they may be raised by the directors themselves, or they may grow out of congressional action or public controversy. No matter how the issue arises, the board needs to have gathered for it all the pertinent information on the question, it needs to have the views and recommendations of the specialists in this particular field within the T.V.A., and it wants to be sure that all of such specialists have been consulted or will feel that their views were given consideration. These responsibilities fall upon the general manager.

In the formulation and documentation of major issues, the T.V.A. general manager is likely to use the following procedure. A staff-management conference technique has been worked out, which brings together the appropriate technical staff and management officials for discussion with the object of coordinating their respective judgments, uncovering and reconciling conflicts between subject matter fields, isolating important questions, and stating possible alternative solutions. The results of the conference and the consensus reached are summarized by the general manager, and the issue is then ready for board consideration.[18]

It has been found, however, that a formal board meeting does not furnish an ideal forum for reviewing the data and recommendations thus submitted by the general manager or exploring the ramifications of an important question of policy. And so the matter may go first to a board-management conference, where a few of the staff officials directly concerned (but by no means all of the participants in the original staff-management conference) will meet with the board for the purpose of making the results of the previous conference available and of elaborating on specific points in which the board members might express an interest. By reason of the work already done, the board is able to begin at the point where the staff-management conference stopped, and has the advantage of prior sharpening and formulation of issues. At the conclusion of the conference the board members may have reached a decision which will simply require formal ratification at the next regular board meeting.

18. This discussion is based in part on the remarks of Mr. Robert E. Sessions, former assistant to the general manager, before a seminar of T.V.A. employees.

It may be that the result arrived at will require the undertaking of a new activity or the making of a comprehensive study by a T.V.A. department, in which case the staff official involved will be directed to prepare a formal project authorization, which can be approved without further discussion at the next board meeting. By organizing these lines of communication and by managing their use, the general manager's office fills an indispensable role in the decision-making process. Its job is, as Mr. Clapp put it, "to see that the right minds, the right subject matters, come to bear in the right sequence to lead up to the best decisions."

Many of the most important decisions are made in the course of budget preparation. Most T.V.A. activities are covered by project authorizations which are presented to the board in support of new work to be undertaken, and which when approved by the board furnish a continuing authority for the conduct of the particular project until it is completed, or at least for a definite stated period. Where such project authorizations have been adopted, the annual budget-making process does not require decisions as to whether these projects shall be undertaken, but simply as to what amount shall be allotted for the coming fiscal year. It is the general manager's responsibility to hold budget hearings at which the heads of the various operating departments appear with their requests for funds. In 1941 the press of other duties led the general manager to delegate the bulk of this function to the chief budget officer. In any case, the budget is given definite form, and the initial decisions are made, in the general manager's office, and here again the task of ultimate decision by the board of directors is enormously simplified.

In his other major role, the general manager faces toward the staff, with the responsibility of translating the board's policies for administrative assignment. This task is to a large extent self-accomplished through the organizational hierarchy and the budget, and by the system for notification of board action. In part it is a task which will already have been accomplished by reason of the participation of the staff in the original formulation of policies. The goal of general management in fulfilling this responsibility is not to direct the program in a centralized way, but to make clear the broad framework of policy within which T.V.A. activities are to proceed, leaving to specialists the making of decisions within that framework. The end-result is thus a rather loose and flexible scheme of administration, in which conscious application of the principles of decentralization keeps the general manager's office from becoming a bottleneck no matter how big the job of the organization becomes or how fast the problems pile up.

With this conception of its function, it is easy to see why the T.V.A. general manager's office has never developed into a large organizational unit. It is in fact surprisingly small. Aside from the budget office and the office of the director of information, the general manager's staff has in the past been made up of two assistants. One of them reviewed, prepared, and appraised recommendations on matters of program and policy content which required action either by the general manager or the board. The other assistant was responsible for administrative coordination, reviewing, preparing, and appraising recommendations on matters relating closely to the executive functions of the general manager's office, and dispatching, routing, and coordinating matters handled by the office. When both of these assistants were recently called to other posts by the war, Arthur Jandrey, director of personnel, was appointed assistant general manager, a new position created in May, 1942.

Because responsibility has been judiciously distributed among the staff, and because of the confidence of the board in the general manager and the staff, the general manager's office has been equal to the difficult task given it, and has proved the validity of the theory of general management adopted.

THE DEPARTMENTAL ORGANIZATION

Each department of the T.V.A. is organized on the basis of a written charter, in the form of an "administrative bulletin," explicitly stating the duties and responsibilities of the department, the powers of its officials, and the divisional organization within the department. The purpose of these bulletins is to define clearly the

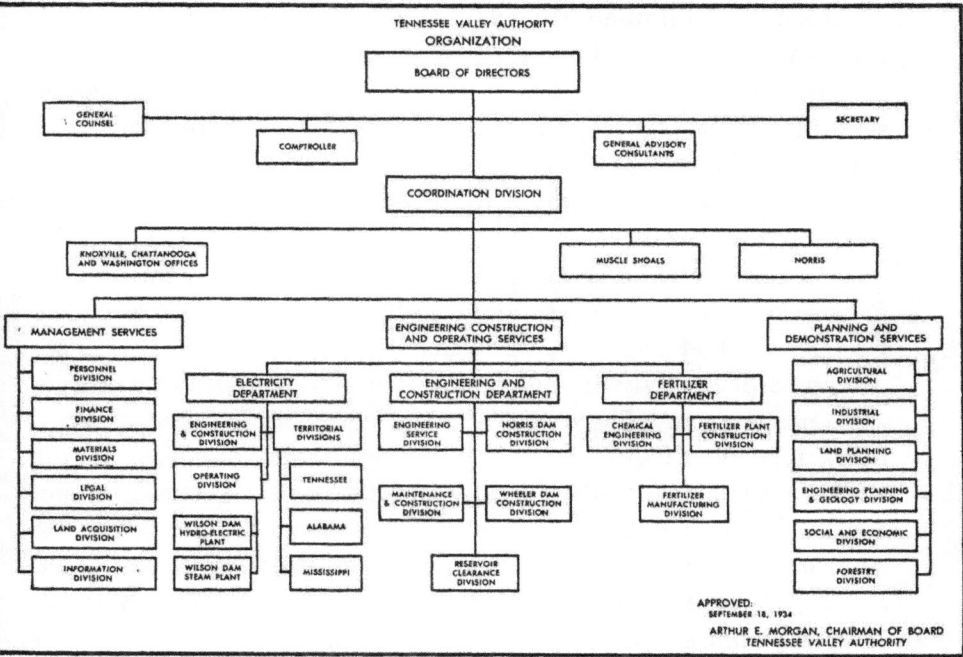

TENNESSEE VALLEY AUTHORITY ORGANIZATION

BOARD OF DIRECTORS

GENERAL COUNSEL

SECRETARY

COMPTROLLER

GENERAL ADVISORY CONSULTANTS

COORDINATION DIVISION

KNOXVILLE, CHATTANOOGA AND WASHINGTON OFFICES

MUSCLE SHOALS

NORRIS

MANAGEMENT SERVICES

ENGINEERING CONSTRUCTION AND OPERATING SERVICES

PLANNING AND DEMONSTRATION SERVICES

PERSONNEL DIVISION

FINANCE DIVISION

MATERIALS DIVISION

LEGAL DIVISION

LAND ACQUISITION DIVISION

INFORMATION DIVISION

ELECTRICITY DEPARTMENT

ENGINEERING & CONSTRUCTION DIVISION

OPERATING DIVISION

WILSON DAM HYDRO-ELECTRIC PLANT

WILSON DAM STEAM PLANT

TERRITORIAL DIVISIONS

TENNESSEE

ALABAMA

MISSISSIPPI

ENGINEERING AND CONSTRUCTION DEPARTMENT

ENGINEERING SERVICE DIVISION

MAINTENANCE & CONSTRUCTION DIVISION

NORRIS DAM CONSTRUCTION DIVISION

WHEELER DAM CONSTRUCTION DIVISION

RESERVOIR CLEARANCE DIVISION

FERTILIZER DEPARTMENT

CHEMICAL ENGINEERING DIVISION

FERTILIZER MANUFACTURING DIVISION

FERTILIZER PLANT CONSTRUCTION DIVISION

AGRICULTURAL DIVISION

INDUSTRIAL DIVISION

LAND PLANNING DIVISION

ENGINEERING PLANNING & GEOLOGY DIVISION

SOCIAL AND ECONOMIC DIVISION

FORESTRY DIVISION

APPROVED:
SEPTEMBER 18, 1934

ARTHUR E. MORGAN, CHAIRMAN OF BOARD
TENNESSEE VALLEY AUTHORITY

program responsibilities of the departments and to delegate to them commensurate administrative authority. While it is not possible to describe here the departmental organization of the T.V.A. in detail, or to trace through the different plans of departmentalization that have been used, it is desirable to indicate the major organization units and to comment on some of the problems encountered and procedures employed in this field.

Under the original organization plan, Chairman Arthur Morgan headed the engineering and construction work of the T.V.A., with the title of chief engineer. Carl Bock was assistant chief engineer. Under their direction the organization for the dam construction program was built up, consisting at first of two construction divisions for the Norris and Wheeler dams, plus a reservoir clearance division, an engineering service division, and a general maintenance and construction division. The Norris and Wheeler dams were both designed by the Bureau of Reclamation, so that no design organization was required at first. Each of these two major construction projects was in charge of a construction engineer and a construction superintendent, who reported directly to the Knoxville central office. Centralized control of this sort was possible since there were only two projects under way, and since both were within reasonable distance of Knoxville.

As the construction program expanded, the departmental organization had to be enlarged and reorganized to keep pace with it. Under the chief engineer, three major departments evolved, concerned respectively with engineering planning, engineering design, and construction.[19] There was also the post of general office engineer, responsible for supplying central office services to the engineering departments, handling matters of budget and budget control, engineering procedure, organization, reports, and so on. The main outlines of the organization thus established were confirmed and regularized in the general reorganization of 1937. Chairman Morgan's tenure as chief engineer was of course terminated at that time, and Colonel Theodore B. Parker, previously head of the T.V.A. construction department, was named to that post. He was made responsible for the direction and general supervision of the three major engineering departments, and for advising the general manager on engineering matters. The general office engineer was to assist him in coordinating and administering the work of these departments.[20]

The first of the three major engineering units was called the *water control planning department*, with the function of general planning for the entire river control enterprise. Necessary basic data were secured in this department through the work of its hydraulic data, maps and surveys, and geologic divisions, which were then turned over to a project planning division for utilization in the de-

19. An engineering and construction department organization chart as of 1936 is given in the *Engineering News-Record* for December 31, 1936.
20. *Hearings,* p. 4698.

velopment of definite plans for the dams and related engineering works.

The second department was the *design department*, under a chief design engineer, which was to prepare the complete technical designs and specifications for dams, reservoirs, locks, powerhouses, and other structures and equipment, all within the general pattern and according to the hydraulic requirements of the water control planning department. The original organization of the design department called for the establishment of separate project design divisions for each major construction job. Consequently, the design of each unit proceeded to a certain extent on a self-contained basis, although each division had available the services of certain staff engineers who were specialists in particular fields, such as architecture or electrical engineering, and who contributed their specialized knowledge to the design of each project. A considerable measure of standardization was thus secured.

However, an improved plan of organization was worked out and put into effect in 1940. The new plan abolished the separate divisions and threw the preparation of all preliminary and final designs and specifications into a single project design division. Such centralization obviously would permit economies and uniformities in design not attainable under the former plan. In order that this desirable centralization might not have undesirable effects upon the degree of attention given to individual projects, a project design engineer was assigned from a newly-created project design staff to take responsibility for engineering coordination and expediting of design work and procurement *for each project*. Thus, while the design work on all projects was being carried on by a single organization, there was one official responsible for the progress of design on each major project. It was his job to obtain approval of the fundamental engineering assumptions and layouts; to review all designs and obtain the necessary approvals from superiors; to coordinate the design work on his project with all other affected departments of the T.V.A.; and to act as a center of information on the status of

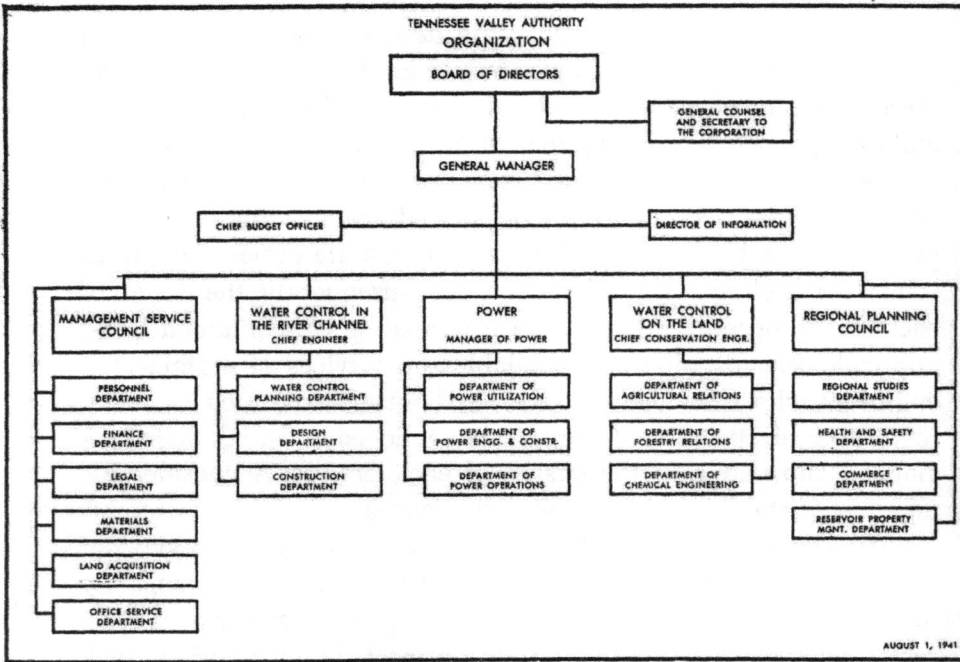

TENNESSEE VALLEY AUTHORITY
ORGANIZATION

BOARD OF DIRECTORS

GENERAL COUNSEL AND SECRETARY TO THE CORPORATION

GENERAL MANAGER

CHIEF BUDGET OFFICER — DIRECTOR OF INFORMATION

MANAGEMENT SERVICE COUNCIL — WATER CONTROL IN THE RIVER CHANNEL (CHIEF ENGINEER) — POWER (MANAGER OF POWER) — WATER CONTROL ON THE LAND (CHIEF CONSERVATION ENGR.) — REGIONAL PLANNING COUNCIL

PERSONNEL DEPARTMENT — WATER CONTROL PLANNING DEPARTMENT — DEPARTMENT OF POWER UTILIZATION — DEPARTMENT OF AGRICULTURAL RELATIONS — REGIONAL STUDIES DEPARTMENT

FINANCE DEPARTMENT — DESIGN DEPARTMENT — DEPARTMENT OF POWER ENGG. & CONSTR. — DEPARTMENT OF FORESTRY RELATIONS — HEALTH AND SAFETY DEPARTMENT

LEGAL DEPARTMENT — CONSTRUCTION DEPARTMENT — DEPARTMENT OF POWER OPERATIONS — DEPARTMENT OF CHEMICAL ENGINEERING — COMMERCE DEPARTMENT

MATERIALS DEPARTMENT — RESERVOIR PROPERTY MGNT. DEPARTMENT

LAND ACQUISITION DEPARTMENT

OFFICE SERVICE DEPARTMENT

AUGUST 1, 1941

design, specifications, placing of contracts, and approval of manufacturers' drawings. It is an interesting organizational arrangement for rendering centralized service to a number of individual projects without sacrificing the advantages of autonomous treatment and individualized attention for those projects.

In addition, the design department included an inspection and testing section, responsible for the inspection, testing, and expediting of all construction materials and equipment, and a highway and railroad division, engaged in planning and designing access roads and railroads and relocating highways and railroads as required by the flooding of T.V.A. reservoirs.

The third major engineering department was the *construction department*, operating under a chief construction engineer. In order to localize responsibility for construction work, separate divisions were set up for the construction of each of the active projects. The project engineer heading each division was responsible for the engineering and construction work of the entire project, based on designs furnished by the design department. Work on each project was divided into two branches, engineering and construction, headed respectively by a construction engineer and a construction superintendent. There was also a project accountant for each project. Besides the project divisions, there were in the construction department three general service divisions—construction plant, construction and maintenance, and reservoir clearance. The first of these was responsible for the development of a construction plant at each project, and the maintenance of records of performance, valuation, accountability, and availability. The second did the small jobs such as building camps and necessary roads, and had an administrative setup that was always in existence so that it could be used to start a large job or finish one, thus avoiding the use of a large dam organization where that was not necessary. The third division removed vegetation and everything else from the reservoirs before the dams were closed.

The organization of the power activities of the T.V.A. and its operating personnel, numbering in 1941 about 3,000 employees, has presented a number of problems. In the early days, Mr. Lilienthal was himself in charge of power developments. Llewellyn Evans, who had been manager of the municipal power plant at Tacoma, was appointed chief electrical engineer in charge of the power division under Mr. Lilienthal. In 1934 the department of electricity was organized, with Mr. Evans in charge of system and market planning, and A. H. Sullivan in charge of administration. The department included an engineering and construction division and an operating division, as well as territorial divisions covering the three states in which T.V.A. power was being sold. The original department of electricity did not undertake sales promotion activities, as this work was carried on by the Electric Home and Farm Authority, a separate organization set up by the T.V.A. directors. However, when the E.H.F.A. was made nation-wide in scope in 1935, a division of sales and promotion to operate in the T.V.A. area was organized in the department. Negotiation of contracts for disposal of power was in charge of a new-contracts committee, composed of two representatives of the electricity department and one from the legal department, acting under the direct supervision of Mr. Lilienthal.

The 1937 reorganization removed Mr. Lilienthal from direct administrative responsibility, and provided for the establishment of the position of chief power economist, making this official responsible for the two power departments—the *department of power planning* and the *department of operations.* The first of these departments was to be under the direction of a chief power planning engineer, aided by a technical staff and working through four operating divisions—system studies, rates, contracts, and surveys and investigations. The department of operations was to work under the supervision of a manager and was divided into four functional divisions (engineering and construction, power operations, telephone and communications, and electrical development) and four territorial divisions. The divisional managers in each of these geographical areas were made responsible for the operation and maintenance of all transmission and distribution lines and facilities within their area, subject to the functional supervision of the division of power operations. The division managers were also to render assistance in the negotiation of power contracts, subject to the functional supervision of the division of electrical development, and were generally responsible for the public relations of the T.V.A. with respect to power operations in their territories.

The organization plan provided in the 1937 reorganization was not put into effect completely.[21] The top post of chief power economist was not filled, and coordination between the two power departments had to be supplied by their own action or by the general manager. The post of manager of the department of operations was likewise not filled, and several of the divisions mentioned above were never actually established. By 1941 the increase in power per-

21. See testimony of J. A. Krug, *Hearings*, pp. 5191–97.

sonnel, the change in emphasis from construction and development to operation, and dissatisfaction with existing procedures led to another reorganization. The new setup was headed by a manager of power, who was to be aided by a general office engineer, and to have three major power departments under his control—*power engineering and construction, power operations,* and *power utilization.* J. A. Krug, who had been chief power planning engineer, was appointed to the post of manager of power, which is the counterpart to the position of chief engineer in the engineering departments. However, Mr. Krug's office has not developed to the same extent as that of Colonel Parker's in size or techniques of administrative control.[22]

The third major grouping of T.V.A. activities is that of the three departments whose common goal is water control on the land. These departments carry on the T.V.A. fertilizer, agricultural, and forestry program, and were brought together under the supervision of a single official, with the title of chief conservation engineer, by the 1937 reorganization. Prior to that time, the fertilizer department had been organized on a separate basis, under the general supervision of Harcourt Morgan and under the immediate direction of Dr. Harry Curtis, chief chemical engineer. Prior to 1937 Harcourt Morgan was also responsible for the separately-organized agricultural division, which handled the fertilizer utilization activities and the general T.V.A. agricultural program described in an earlier chapter. Finally, the forestry activities were in the hands of a forestry division responsible to Chairman Arthur Morgan.

The effect of the 1937 reorganization was to bring these three major lines of activity into a closer relationship with each other by making them responsible to a single head. The post of chief conservation engineer, which was comparable to that of chief engineer and chief power economist (later manager of power) heading the other two major departmental groupings, was filled by Neil Bass, who had served from 1933 on as assistant to Director Harcourt

22. Mr. Krug has been on loan to O.P.M. and its successor, the War Production Board, since June, 1941.

Morgan. The names of the agricultural and forestry divisions were changed to the departments of agricultural relations and forestry relations, in order to emphasize that the T.V.A. was not so much undertaking to carry on active operating programs of its own in those fields, as to encourage, facilitate and expedite the work of existing state and local agencies. The chief conservation engineer has functioned principally as a coordinator for the three departments under his supervision, and has undertaken little in the way of supplying them with central administrative direction or services.

Aside from the three principal groups of operating departments just described, there were after the reorganization of 1937 four regional survey and demonstration departments and six management service departments. The former group included departments for regional studies, health and safety, commerce, and reservoir property management; the latter departments covered the fields of personnel, finance, law, materials, land acquisition, and office services. A description of the organization and functions of these ten departments would carry this discussion to an undesirable length, and consequently only a few of the major points of interest will be touched upon.

The establishment of the reservoir property management department represented an interesting solution of a difficult problem. Prior to 1937, the various operating and maintenance jobs that had to be performed in and around the T.V.A. reservoirs were divided among the T.V.A. divisions on a functional basis. For example, the T.V.A. had purchased considerable acreage around its reservoirs above the high water line for the purpose of reservoir protection. Some of this land was in forests, and they were handed over to the forestry division for administration. Some were agricultural lands, which were administered by the agricultural division. Camp and village management was under the coordination division. Operation of the recreational areas maintained in connection with the various dams and reservoirs was split up among several divisions. Responsibility for malaria control attached to the health and safety division. Schools provided for the children of employees living in T.V.A. villages and camps were managed by the T.V.A. personnel division.

Under this kind of arrangement, it was difficult to relate one operation to another taking place in the same reservoir, and no plans were drawn for the management of reservoir lands and properties from an over-all T.V.A. point of view. The reorganization of 1937 sought to solve the problem by turning over these various responsibilities to a single management and operating agency, the reservoir property management department.[23] The department was organized on the basis of a central policy-determining and reviewing office at T.V.A. headquarters, plus field or area organizations under area managers administratively responsible for all activities of the department in their respective areas. The area managers were given titles and responsibilities varying with the state of development of the area program and its local importance.

In order that integrated administration might operate successfully with such diversified responsibilities, the reservoir property management department was directed to call upon other T.V.A. departments for technical advice and planning assistance. Thus the department of forestry relations was to furnish a management plan for forest lands owned by the T.V.A., and the agricultural relations department was to supply plans and advice as to the best use of its agricultural lands. The reservoir property management officials would look to the regional studies department for guidance as to the most promising areas and methods for recreational development. If the plan was to operate successfully, these interdepartmental contacts would have to be maintained on a systematic and understanding basis. After some experimentation, it became evident that the best way to clarify and define such relationships was through the adoption of a series of written agreements between the departments involved, stating specifically their respective roles in the administration of what was essentially a joint program. Thus the operation of schools in T.V.A. towns and villages was covered by an agreement between the reservoir property management department and the personnel department. The former was, according

23. See testimony of L. N. Allen, *Hearings*, pp. 3682–3701.

to the terms of the agreement, to prepare the general program plans and budgets, and to conduct the program; the latter was to review and approve such plans and to assess the progress of the program. Only in the negotiation of contracts with local governments on educational matters did the personnel department have the primary responsibility.

Of the six management service departments, those concerned with personnel and finance are probably of most general interest. The organization for personnel administration will be discussed in a later chapter. The finance department is under the supervision of a comptroller, who is responsible for the general administration of the financial and accounting policies of the T.V.A. There are separate divisions for chemical accounting, power accounting, and construction accounting. The work of the latter division is done at offices located at the dam sites and other construction centers, by personnel administratively responsible to the construction department. The central accounting division in Knoxville keeps the general records, including cash accounts, accounts receivable, general property-control accounts, field-office control accounts, liability accounts, records of commitments, and the expenditure accounts for the administrative and service departments. This division assists in the administration of the T.V.A. budget by keeping a record of the obligations charged to each allotment release, and by currently examining purchase and personnel requisitions for budgetary authority.[24]

The treasurer of the T.V.A. is a subordinate of the comptroller, heading the treasury division. This division handles the receipt, deposit, and custody of all funds, the preparation of all checks, and the maintenance of necessary fund and cash records. Finally, there

24. As already noted, the budget officer is attached to the general manager's office, and is not in the finance department. Although budgetary allotments and commitments are not formally recorded on the books, the procedures of traditional government accounting are adhered to by detailing these items on monthly financial statements for the purpose of determining unencumbered balances of each activity. See *Financial Statements of Certain Government Agencies*, Senate Doc. No. 172, Part 1, 76th Cong., 3d sess., p. 327 (1940), for a description of general accounting practices.

is an auditing division which is responsible for the assembling, audit, and approval of all vouchers for payment, the supervision and audit of pay rolls, the audit of revenues and receipts, the administration of travel in accordance with approved travel regulations, and the handling of all correspondence with the Comptroller General on auditing questions.

The four regional survey and demonstration departments and the six management service departments have a common status in that they all report directly to the general manager. This is in contrast to the practice in the three groups of operating departments, which as noted have all been brought under single responsible heads. Instead of adopting this same device for the planning and management departments, an attempt has been made to introduce a measure of coordination for these departments below the level of the general manager's office by providing for the planning departments a *regional planning council* and for the management agencies a *management service council*. Councils of this sort, composed of the heads of the appropriate departments, have existed from the early days of the Authority. They were continued by the reorganization of 1937, the general manager serving as chairman of both councils, and the director of personnel and the director of regional studies acting as secretaries of the respective councils. The general purpose of the management service council was to assist the general manager by coordinating and developing recommendations on matters involving management policies or practices of interdepartmental significance, and to serve as a center of discussion and review on general problems of public administration of common interest to the management staff. The regional planning council was to perform a similar function in the field of survey, demonstration, and planning policies and practices.

In actual practice, the contribution of the councils to coordination and improved administration was never very great. In the early years the regional planning council was fairly active, 18 meetings having been held during the year 1935. The chairmanship during this period was filled by the assistant coordinator for the planning services, and the meetings were typically attended by a dozen or more officials, including nearly always representatives of outside departments such as legal or information. Much of the work of the council was carried on by committees, which were appointed on an *ad hoc* basis as needs arose, and which were used principally in coordinating the surveys and studies made by the planning departments in the various reservoirs. The council attempted to eliminate duplication in programs, made numerous recommendations to the board, and was the forum for much general discussion. The management service council met on fewer occasions; the members concerned themselves with such problems as procedure for handling claims against the T.V.A., policy governing employees' speeches and articles, and the regulation of mimeographing and printing.

Both of the councils had lapsed into inactivity by 1937, and were reorganized at that time, with the general manager serving as chairman of both. In their new incarnation the councils again failed to win a permanent place in the administrative organization. There was of course general agreement that they could not and should not assume administrative responsibilities or functions. As agencies of coordination their principal usefulness lay in the development of a common fund of information among the major staff officers. The councils were in a sense forums to which the general manager could from time to time refer matters for advisory opinions, but because of the variety of problems that occurred and the need for speed in handling them, the cream of the subject matter was generally skimmed off in other methods of staff and management coordination, leaving scanty material for council consideration. In 1940 the general manager finally announced that neither of the councils would be assembled again unless suitable subject matter was found for their action.

The experience of the T.V.A. with these councils indicates the limitations of large committees of this sort in achieving current coordination. In a going organization most matters cannot await the infrequent meetings of a large, fixed-membership group. Where department heads are properly executing their functions, the day by day problems are coordinated currently through normal channels and by conferences with the officials directly concerned. Those problems that remain unsolved above the departmental level are proper subjects for the attention of the general manager or his assistants. Advisory assistance to the general manager on long range problems can probably be better handled by *ad hoc* committees limited to those persons directly concerned with the subject matter, rather than by the use of general councils.[25]

A more effective device for securing coordination and collaboration among the various departments is the series of "administrative codes" prepared by the general manager's office. One such code, issued in June, 1942, dealing with coordination of plans for T.V.A. reservoir land purchase and use, furnishes an unusually good example of this technique and shows in addition how the principle of delegation is applied. One of the most difficult problems encountered at every T.V.A. dam project has been to determine what and how much land should be purchased for the reservoir. The engineers, the land planners, the foresters, the agricultural staff, and the social and economic experts would all have views on the subject, and would make recommendations. The board would then adopt whatever taking-line policy it considered desirable for the immediate project.[26]

By 1942 the board had come to the conclusion that it was a mistake to thresh this question out anew every time a dam got under way, and so adopted by resolution a general policy to control all future reservoirs. Application of the policy was turned over to the general manager, who was thereafter to approve the purchase of land and land rights. The general manager in turn issued an administrative code delegating his responsibility for application of the

25. These were the conclusions reached by Donald Fowler and Wesley McClure, of the T.V.A. personnel department, in a report prepared for a T.V.A. seminar on March 20, 1941, which the writer has used in the above discussion.

26. The T.V.A. at first followed a very liberal policy of land acquisition, purchasing a protective strip around the reservoirs extending from one-eighth to one-quarter of a mile above the high-water line. The present policy is not to purchase land above the zone of reservoir fluctuation, and to make a greater use of easements and the purchase of flowage rights.

policy to the T.V.A. chief engineer. This official was directed to prepare recommendations on land acquisition, and to secure the views of other departments through the department of regional studies. The chief engineer's recommendations, with notation of any variations from departmental viewpoints, were then to go back to the general manager, who would make the final decision. By such use of administrative codes the T.V.A. has been able, as Mr. Clapp says, "to develop reasonably precise arrangements for securing the desired sequences for collaboration between and among the several departments."

This chapter has of necessity presented only a rapid glimpse into T.V.A. internal administration. How T.V.A. operations are conditioned by the Authority's regional status has already been noted, but the effect of its corporate nature remains to be analyzed. It has not been possible to go into the work of the operating departments. The story of T.V.A. organization for purchasing, for land acquisition, for the performance of other vital administrative tasks, remains untold. Most important of all, it has been impossible to describe the spirit of T.V.A. administration, a spirit engendered out of the enthusiasm of a staff whose best efforts were challenged by a task which they found continually absorbing—a spirit which expressed itself in constant re-appraisal of administrative effectiveness and a search for administrative methods that would have the most meaning in terms of the total T.V.A. program.

7: T.V.A. and the President

> "Internal jealousies and dissensions . . . will
> ever arise among men equal in power, without a
> principal to decide and control their differences."
> —*Thomas Jefferson*

T HE RELATIONSHIP of the Tennessee Valley Authority to President Roosevelt has been a very close one. His role in the adoption of the T.V.A. Act has already been indicated. The directors were appointed by him, and as a government corporation outside the regular departmental system the board reported directly to him. The general responsibility which all executive agencies owe to the President was buttressed by various specific provisions in the T.V.A. Act giving him powers and duties in connection with the T.V.A. All ordinary tasks of policy formation and decision were of course performed by the board of directors. But when major decisions had to be made, or where particularly difficult problems or disagreements among the directors were involved, it was to the President that the board looked for direction and assistance.

The occasions when such presidential intervention occurred, or was requested, were fairly numerous. At the beginning Chairman Morgan consulted frequently with the President, outlining proposed plans and receiving approval and suggestions. An early disagreement over power policy was settled by a visit to the White House, following which the first statement of T.V.A. policy in this field was drafted and issued. In November, 1933, the President requested the T.V.A. to undertake the immediate construction of Wheeler Dam. In 1934 he allocated $25,000,000 from an emergency appropriation for T.V.A. use. In 1936 the President took an active part in attempting to solve the difficulties between the T.V.A. and the private utility companies, and held the power pooling conference already discussed. He had several contacts with Mr. Wendell Willkie on T.V.A. matters. In 1937 the President appointed a committee to represent him personally in looking into the administrative difficulties of the T.V.A., and to prepare a report for his use.[1] He visited the T.V.A. area on several occasions, and in other ways manifested his very real interest in the continuing operations of the agency, which was obviously very close to his heart.

THE STRANGE CASE OF ARTHUR E. MORGAN

The most dramatic example of presidential intervention in T.V.A. affairs was, of course, his removal of its first chairman, Arthur E. Morgan, in 1938. This action was the climax of a bitter personal feud on the board of directors which had long handicapped the work of the T.V.A. and which almost destroyed it. It is unfortunate that a disproportionate amount of attention must be devoted to a discussion of these difficulties, but it is necessary because they bulk so large in the administrative development of the T.V.A. and in the public attitude toward it.

The character of Arthur E. Morgan, the central figure in this drama, has been sketched in the preceding chapter. President Roosevelt, after bitter experience with Mr. Morgan, referred to him as a man "temperamentally unfitted to exercise a divided authority." [2] Mr. Morgan's contention was, on the other hand, that he was the victim of a plot or conspiracy engineered by his two fellow-directors and participated in by many of the principal officials of the organization. According to Mr. Morgan, his difficulties began "within a few weeks after the organization of the T.V.A." [3] The first untoward incident among the directors was the criticism of the

1. The members were Mr. Ernest G. Draper, then Assistant Secretary of Commerce, Rear Adm. Archibald L. Parsons, U.S.N., and Mr. Herbert Emmerich, then deputy governor of the Farm Credit Administration.
2. Senate Doc. No. 155, 75th Cong., 3d sess., p. ix.
3. Ibid., p. 68.

chairman's administration of T.V.A. affairs submitted by the other two directors at the board meeting of August 5, 1933, which resulted in the allocation of administrative responsibilities among the board members and the deposing of Chairman Morgan as general manager. H. A. Morgan described to the congressional investigating committee his reaction and that of Mr. Lilienthal to the chairman's administrative conduct during these first few weeks.[4] With respect to the first board meeting, H. A. Morgan testified:

> Instead of following an orderly course Dr. Arthur Morgan plunged the meeting into detailed administrative matters without joint consideration of the meaning of the act—without consideration of the major objectives of the project that Congress had authorized, the necessary procedures for budget control and employment, and the structure of a working organization. We were called upon to review great stacks of correspondence, most of which dealt with matters which properly should have been delegated to others after an organization had been set up. In the same first meeting we were then asked by Dr. Morgan to approve semi-commitments he had already made as to a number of key personnel. The men in question were already at work. Following meetings were of the same pattern.[5]

According to H. A. Morgan, he and Mr. Lilienthal were finally led into open objection by the elaborate program of activities which the chairman presented at the board meeting of July 30, 1933.[6] This list included some of the immediate and proper objectives of the Authority, but it also contained items which H. A. Morgan considered "impracticable and highly visionary or clearly outside the scope of our responsibility under the law."[7] He was particularly disturbed to learn that the chairman had apparently made a number of

4. *Hearings*, pp. 97–112.
5. *Ibid.*, pp. 98–99.
6. *Ibid.*, pp. 100–2.
7. *Ibid.*, p. 102. For example, there were proposals that the T.V.A. might begin the production of Portland cement and dry ice; that a commission should be organized "to study the proper functions of the real estate man in an organized society;" and that a study should be made "of the succession of authority as a guide in our relations to organizing cooperatives." These and similar proposals grew out of Mr. Morgan's belief that the T.V.A. was to be used for the encouragement of a "designed social and economic order."

commitments prior to submission of these proposals to the board. H. A. Morgan concluded that he could not continue on the board unless some method was adopted "whereby each member of the Board would be limited in individual action to those fields with which each was intimately familiar and whereby there would be preserved to the Board as a board the prerogatives of review and decision with respect to the broader policy questions." [8] Since Mr. Lilienthal felt the same way, the two directors agreed on the plan of dividing administrative responsibility already described. Chairman Morgan apparently accepted this check in good spirit at the time,[9] but he later contended that this was the beginning of a conspiracy against him by the other two directors.[10]

Other differences developed between the chairman and his associates. Mr. Lilienthal opposed the plan for an area restriction on T.V.A. power sales, which was included in the 1934 contract with the Commonwealth & Southern Corporation. He had grave doubts about the scale of the Norris town project, the construction of which under Chairman Morgan's supervision was marked by many administrative muddles and by costs far above the original estimates. Both directors found the chairman to have a strong visionary streak, expressed in such forms as a speech in which he appeared to be arguing for a separate coinage system for the Tennessee valley.

On the other hand, Chairman Morgan was, according to his subsequent statements, dissatisfied almost from the beginning with the conduct of the power and agricultural programs. He objected to Mr. Lilienthal's announcement of wholesale rates without submitting them for final board approval, to the handling of the allocation problem, to the conduct of the negotiations with Mr. Willkie, to the financial reporting of power operations, to the claims of "yardstick" significance for the power program, and so on. He objected to the administration of the T.V.A. fertilizer program in large part through the land grant colleges, which he considered to constitute "a power-

8. *Ibid.*, p. 103.
9. See text of his reply, *Hearings*, pp. 107–9.
10. See his letter to Rep. Maverick, reprinted in *Hearings*, p. 230.

ful political bureaucracy." [11] The net result was that at the end of the first three years there was bitter antagonism between the chairman and the other two board members. The feeling had been fairly well confined, however, to the directors and their immediate associates, and strangely enough not a single dissenting vote had been recorded on formal board actions.

One reason for this unanimity, it later appeared, was that Chairman Morgan had been biding his time, awaiting the expiration of Mr. Lilienthal's three-year term of office. Prior to the expiration, Chairman Morgan announced to several people, including H. A. Morgan and Senator Norris, that he would himself resign if Mr. Lilienthal was reappointed.[12] When Mr. Lilienthal was reappointed, the chairman did not resign. Instead, he left on an extended vacation, and did not return to Knoxville for almost two months. When he did return, he began to express opposition to the board actions taken by the majority members and to record in the minutes of the board his objections to the way numerous projects had been handled. For example, he refused to sign the minutes of the meeting of May 22, 1936, at which the general manager plan had been adopted, because the minutes did not record his understanding of the action taken.[13] One year later, when the new organization plan was definitely put into effect, he voted against the plan and against the appointment of Mr. Blandford as general manager.

Controversy also developed over the proposed Fontana dam, the site for which was owned by the Aluminum Company of America. The dam was important to the T.V.A. plan for unified river control, and Chairman Morgan was interested in working out a plan with the company whereby the T.V.A. would receive the site and build the dam, the company to be compensated by T.V.A. power. However, Congress turned down the Fontana project in acting on the T.V.A. appropriation in 1936. Under these circumstances, the

11. See *Hearings*, p. 233.
12. He later denied this, but the record seems to be against him. According to Mr. H. A. Morgan, he told at least two T.V.A. officials that he was considering recommending them to President Roosevelt for appointment to the Lilienthal vacancy. See *Hearings*, pp. 112–13.
13. *Hearings*, pp. 119–20.

board decided to drop the negotiations on the question of securing the dam site, and on May 19, 1936, took formal board action limiting further discussions with the company to the matter of selling it T.V.A. power. Chairman Morgan disagreed with this action, and he and one of his subordinates continued discussions with the company.[14] Mr. Lilienthal and his staff meanwhile had concentrated upon securing a contract for the sale of T.V.A. power to the Aluminum Company, and such a contract was signed later in 1936. The chairman attacked this contract as one which "failed to protect the public interest." In fact he seemed to develop a general suspicion that Mr. Lilienthal was trying to give T.V.A. power away to industrial customers at unjustifiably low rates, for he also protested that there was a "joker" in the 1937 contract with the Arkansas Power & Light Company which he had discovered and caused to be eliminated.[15]

Another series of incidents arose out of the negotiations carried on in 1936 with the Commonwealth & Southern Corporation, in connection with the expiration of the 1934 contract. These negotiations were in Mr. Lilienthal's charge, and the chairman was not satisfied that he was reporting Mr. Willkie's attitude correctly. As noted in a previous chapter, Mr. Willkie wished the T.V.A. to accept an area restriction, and to agree to sell power outside that area only through his companies. Mr. Lilienthal characterized this stand as a demand for a "monopoly" of T.V.A. power, and Chairman Morgan objected to this term.[16] When the board decided in August, 1936, to adopt a policy of no territorial restrictions on sale of T.V.A. power, the chairman voted against it. Chairman Morgan also believed that Mr. Lilienthal wanted the power pool proposed at that time to fail, and so he endeavored to work out on his own responsibility a power pool plan to present to the conference called by the President. In this work he secured the assistance of a private utility executive, an ac-

14. Senate Doc. No. 155, 75th Cong., 3d sess., pp. 48–49.
15. *Hearings*, pp. 231–32. For T.V.A. defense and analysis of these contracts, see *ibid.*, pp. 5296–5304.
16. For Mr. Morgan's position, see *Hearings*, pp. 25–35; for Mr. Lilienthal's views, see *Hearings*, pp. 150–52, and Senate Doc. 155, pp. 59–61.

tion which the other two directors hotly condemned.[17] It was during this same period that the board members unanimously decided at a meeting to send the President a telegram asking that he arrange a meeting with them for the purpose of discussing power problems. The actual sending of the telegram was left to the chairman, who for one of the two or three reasons which he subsequently gave, decided not to send it, a fact which the other directors did not learn for several days. They later stressed this incident as an example of the chairman's obstructive attitude.[18]

One of the most serious steps which Chairman Morgan's antagonism toward Mr. Lilienthal (and the T.V.A. power program as developed by him) led him to take was in connection with the trial of the *Tennessee Electric Power Company* case against the T.V.A. in Chattanooga during the winter of 1937–1938. In a conference with the counsel for the T.V.A. a few days preceding the trial, Chairman Morgan criticized some of the power transactions and suggested the possibility that the court might enjoin a part of the power operations and leave the rest of the program intact. "Repeatedly," according to James L. Fly, general counsel of the T.V.A., "he came back to the same problem of finding some theory of the case or possible judicial decision whereby certain of the power activities might be enjoined." [19] If there had been any thought of putting the chairman on the witness stand for the T.V.A., it was abandoned by counsel after this incident.

In the preparation of this case for trial, T.V.A. lawyers had many contacts with T.V.A. engineers concerning the preparation and presentation of technical material and testimony. While the case was in progress, on December 14, 1937, the chairman wrote a letter to Mr. Fly, charging that the T.V.A. legal staff had called upon the engineers "to give testimony of a misleading character." [20] Mr. Fly immediately wrote to Mr. Morgan, asking him to substantiate his

17. *Hearings,* pp. 14–24 (Morgan's position); Senate Doc. 155, pp. 54–62 (Lilienthal's position).
18. Senate Doc. 155, pp. 64–67.
19. *Ibid.,* p. 45.
20. *Hearings,* pp. 222–29; Senate Doc. 155, pp. 44–48.

charges or withdraw them. So did John Lord O'Brian, who was assisting the T.V.A. legal staff as special counsel in this litigation,[21] and who said in a letter of December 22: "In all of my close contact with this case, I have never observed any conduct, or heard any suggestion, from either lawyers or engineers not in accordance with the higher standards of their respective proprieties."[22] He requested Chairman Morgan to give him any specific information which he had to the contrary, so that the court might be protected from misleading testimony. A vague response came from Mr. Morgan on December 30. After reading it, and again going over the preparation of engineering testimony, Mr. O'Brian wrote on January 9, 1938: ". . . I am more than ever confirmed in the opinion which I previously expressed to you that the case has been handled with unusual ability and in accordance with the highest standards of integrity. . . . Your charges, coming while the case was actively on trial, have had a disrupting and demoralizing effect upon all the attorneys and upon the conduct of the Authority's case."[23] A special meeting of the T.V.A. board was held on this matter, which the chairman at first refused to attend. When he did appear, he refused to substantiate the charges he had made. The board then adopted two resolutions, one condemning Arthur Morgan's conduct as an unwarranted interference with the management of T.V.A. business, and the second a vote of confidence in its legal counsel and engineers.

No organization could continue to operate effectively under such conditions. An explosion of some sort was imminent. For the most part the difficult state of relations among the board members had been kept from general public knowledge. On various occasions during the year 1937, however, the chairman gave some public expression to his views on T.V.A. power policies.[24] The most forthright statement of his attitude was contained in an article he wrote for the

21. Mr. O'Brian was a Republican, had served as an assistant attorney general in the Hoover administration, and was a recognized leader of the American bar.
22. *Hearings*, p. 226.
23. *Ibid.*, p. 228.
24. See *New York Times*, January 17, 1937; *Saturday Evening Post*, August 7, 1937.

September, 1937, issue of the *Atlantic Monthly*, in which he said: "The writer is a minority member of the Board of Directors of the Tennessee Valley Authority, of which he is the Chairman. In important respects he differs from what he judges to be the actual power policy of his associates. This statement therefore reflects his personal views, and not the working policy of the TVA on the power issue. Neither does it undertake to criticize in detail what the writer believes to be the improprieties of that policy." [25] In another passage which could have been aimed only at his colleagues on the board, he referred to "public men" who use "arbitrary coercion" and "false or misleading propaganda," and added: "I have no confidence in the supposed liberalism of people who use such methods. Whoever will use unfair methods for the public probably will use unfair methods against the public for his own advantage." Another critical reference to T.V.A. power operations went as follows: "In the operation of public 'yardstick' systems there should be no hidden subsidies, no undisclosed government assistance to local public power systems. . . . If there is government subsidy, it should be in the open."

These remarks were eagerly seized upon by spokesmen for the private utilities. In the same issue of the *Atlantic Monthly*, Mr. Willkie commented on Mr. Morgan's article in these words: "Dr. Morgan is the only government official of standing who has had the courage to state that 'in the operation of public "yardstick" systems there should be no hidden subsidies.' He of course would not say this if he were not conscious that such exist. Unfortunately, he has not carried the decision in the councils of those who control government power policy or the TVA."

The other two directors considered the chairman's article as impugning "the integrity of the Tennessee Valley Authority and the honesty and motives of its Board of Directors." Their sense of responsibility for the T.V.A. program prevented them, they said, from "answering attacks of this character in the forum which Dr. Morgan has chosen," but the board did adopt a resolution condemning the

25. "Public Ownership of Power," 160 *Atlantic Monthly* 339, 346 (1937).

chairman's action "as injurious to the project and to the public interest." [26] A copy of this resolution was sent to the President, and he was also informed by letter of the damage which Mr. Morgan's public statements were likely to cause in the forthcoming litigation with the utility companies. President Roosevelt immediately wrote to the chairman, suggesting "that there is a very definite obligation on you either to withdraw what your colleagues believe to be an impugning of their integrity or that you present whatever specific facts you may have, if any, to justify your statements." [27] According to the President, Mr. Morgan came to see him a few weeks later and said that no attack on the integrity of his fellow directors had been intended. The final showdown was thus momentarily postponed.

FLOODED MARBLE: THE BERRY CLAIMS

When the ultimate break in relations did come, the immediate cause was not power policy, but certain claims made against the T.V.A. by Major George Berry (later U.S. Senator from Tennessee) on account of damage to his allegedly valuable marble properties by the flooding of the Norris reservoir. These claims had been pending since the early days of the Authority, but their settlement did not become urgent until 1936. The position of T.V.A. officials on this matter was clear from the beginning. They felt that the marble involved was commercially worthless, a conclusion based on the reports of their own geologists and outside consultants. Major Berry and his associates, on the other hand, contended that the properties were immensely valuable, sums up to $5,000,000 being mentioned.

Under these circumstances, the T.V.A. could have proceeded under its statute to condemn the mineral rights involved, the value of the property being determined by three commissioners appointed by a federal district court. This was not done. Instead, in the summer of 1936 the T.V.A. and Major Berry entered into a "conciliation agreement" in which the parties agreed to the appointment of a con-

26. Resolution of August 31, 1937; see Senate Doc. 155, p. 43.
27. Senate Doc. 155, p. 4.

ciliator who was to make an independent examination of the claims, to receive confidentially materials and documents from each side, and to serve as a medium between the parties in assisting them to arrive at an agreement. He was not to make any award or recommendation, and either party could terminate the arrangement by written notice. It was understood by the parties that Dr. John W. Finch, director of the U.S. Bureau of Mines, would be secured as conciliator. The agreement was approved by the T.V.A. board on July 13, 1936, at a meeting from which Chairman Morgan was absent.[28]

The T.V.A. had never before made use of such an agreement, but in this case it was felt to be the best method of handling the controversy. For there were certain risks involved in filing immediate condemnation proceedings. While the T.V.A. was confident the marble was valueless, Major Berry would present experts who might very well convince the lay commissioners otherwise, or at least induce them to make a compromise award of a sizeable character. The fact was not overlooked that Major Berry was a local resident, and that this factor might react in his favor in a lawsuit with the government. Accordingly, T.V.A. officials grasped at the conciliation idea, hoping that the advice of an outside expert might convince Major Berry that his ideas of value were illusory. They had no doubt that Dr. Finch would come to this conclusion.[29] In any case, the activities of the conciliator were not to be binding on either party, and if the plan failed the T.V.A. could then proceed to condemn.

Chairman Morgan disagreed entirely with this method of handling the claim. He was convinced from the various geological reports that the marble had no commercial value, and he doubted whether Major Berry was presenting the claim in good faith. In June, 1936, before the conciliation agreement was adopted, he wrote to the other two board members expressing this position, and sug-

28. The text of the agreement is given in Senate Doc. 155, pp. 13–14.
29. Indeed, Dr. Oliver Bowles, a subordinate of Dr. Finch in the Bureau of Mines, had examined the Berry properties in 1935 and reported them valueless from a commercial standpoint. See *Hearings*, p. 63.

gesting that the President should be informed of the facts, since Berry was at that time rather close to the Roosevelt administration.[30] He objected to the conciliation agreement because it treated the claimant as though he were proceeding in good faith; Mr. Morgan contended that it would be difficult later on to charge bad faith after having entered such a "friendly agreement." He believed, moreover, that the agreement was in effect a concession on the part of the T.V.A. that some payment was due Major Berry.[31]

In August, after the agreement had been adopted, Chairman Morgan undertook to secure from Major Berry evidence to confirm his belief that the claims represented a deliberate attempt to hold up the government. He requested Mr. Berry to supply the T.V.A. with a list of his options and leases with their dates; [32] to explain how he came to be financially interested in these claims; to reveal how much had been invested in working these marble properties, and how much of that investment had been made before the building of Norris Dam was assured; to state the total amount of his claim for damages, and so on. Major Berry refused substantially all the information requested, indicating that the request was not in accordance with the conciliation procedure.[33]

There was delay in getting the conciliation machinery into operation. The full T.V.A. board met again with Major Berry and his associates on February 24, 1937, and the following day the board revalidated, over Chairman Morgan's protest, the conciliation agreement.[34] In doing this the two directors favoring the agreement were careful to state in the resolution that "the Board hereby reemphasizes that such an arrangement is in nowise to be construed as a validation of any claims, nor is either party to be bound in any way

30. President Roosevelt appointed him to the post of coordinator of industrial cooperation in the N.R.A. in September, 1935.

31. This contention derives some support from the language of the agreement, which begins: "In an effort to arrive at an agreement as to the amount to be paid by the Authority to Major Berry. . . ." See Hearings, p. 195.

32. For the most part the claims rested upon leases to mineral rights. It was suspected that the leases had been secured, not with any thought of commercial operation, but solely to establish a basis for claims against the government.

33. For text of both letters, see Hearings, pp. 82-85.

34. Senate Doc. 155, p. 14.

by reason of the fact that Dr. Finch has been called in as intermediary, or by any proposals, recommendations, or informal findings which he might make." Chairman Morgan entered a written protest against the board action, stating in part:

> Some or all these options or leases, it appears, were perfected or revived after the construction of the Norris Dam was a practical certainty. . . . My letter to Mr. Berry of August 9, 1936, asked for information which would largely remove any unfounded concern on this matter. Mr. Berry has not furnished that information. Unless and until such information is furnished I feel that I cannot approve the contract for the services of conciliation to consider physical values which might by implication give good standing to possible improprieties or lack of good citizenship. If the Tennessee Valley Authority Board considers it advisable to secure the opinions of additional outside consultants, the same quality of consultation can be secured directly, without the involvements or implications of a contract for conciliation.[35]

Chairman Morgan was then directed by the board to write to Secretary Harold L. Ickes, the department head to whom Dr. Finch was responsible, asking that Dr. Finch's services be made available. The chairman complied, but sent along his own written protest to the board and the other documents he had accumulated on the case. The matter was thus presented in such a dubious light that Secretary Ickes refused the request. With Dr. Finch unavailable, the conciliation agreement died, and condemnation proceedings were then begun by the T.V.A.

Mr. Morgan was thus correct in claiming, as he later did, that he prevented the carrying out of the conciliation plan. On the other hand, his suspicions of the agreement seem on the basis of all the evidence to have been unwarranted. The agreement was admittedly a device peculiar in nature and subject to misrepresentation. If there had been a desire to treat Major Berry kindly, as a loyal Democrat, labor leader, and valuable Roosevelt supporter, an agreement of this sort might have been manipulated for such a purpose. But a long

35. *Hearings*, pp. 69–70.

and careful congressional investigation failed to find evidence of any such purpose. The agreement was favored by the T.V.A. legal staff and by its geologists. The only conciliator ever considered was Dr. Finch, in whose hands the public interest would have been well protected. Major Berry's lawyers did argue before the condemnation commission subsequently that the agreement was proof that the T.V.A. recognized the properties to have some value, but the point had no weight in their final decision.

This disagreement over the wisdom of the conciliation agreement constituted only the preliminary skirmish in the battle over flooded marble. As preparations for trial of the condemnation case proceeded in the T.V.A. legal department, Chairman Morgan became convinced that the lawyers were making no effort to discover evidence bearing on the question of Major Berry's good faith in pressing these claims. He felt that the T.V.A. was deliberately seeking to limit its argument to the contention that the marble was commercially valueless. If this had been true, it would not have been particularly surprising. For after all the purpose of condemnation proceedings is to establish value, and evidence as to the good faith of the claimant in making claims of value would presumably be admissible only as it threw light on the question of value.

In any case, it does not appear that the chairman was correct in his assumptions. Everyone connected with the case felt as Chairman Morgan did that there was a strong possibility of bad faith on the part of the claimants, but there simply was no tangible evidence in support of this conclusion such as would be required in court proceedings. There was, according to Evans Dunn, T.V.A. attorney who handled the condemnation case, a continuous search for material and evidence which would support a contention of fraud, but there was no success until in November, 1937, shortly before the trial was to begin. At that time one of the men who had been associated with Major Berry in securing the leases on which the claims were based, decided to tell what he knew about the entire affair. With his assistance certain damaging powers of attorney were discovered and evidence was obtained showing that the leases in question were secured with the definite knowledge that the properties would be flooded by the Norris reservoir.[36] Fortified by this evidence, the T.V.A. was able to present an overwhelming case to the condemnation commission.[37]

All of the evidence which the T.V.A. was able to secure on the question of bad faith was presented to the commission. Major Berry's own opinion was that he was treated very badly indeed by the T.V.A. attorneys.[38] However, Chairman Morgan was not satisfied. As the hearings in the case drew to a close, he came to the conclusion that not all of the relevant facts had been submitted. Consequently he wrote a letter to the chairman of the condemnation commission, stating that he had some evidence to give. Against the advice and over the protest of the T.V.A. counsel, he took the witness stand on December 20, 1937, to relate the story of his long-standing suspicions as to the claims and of his objections to the conciliation procedure. Under cross-examination by the T.V.A. counsel, Chairman Morgan admitted that in February, 1937, when the conciliation agreement had been revalidated, he had none of the specific evidence of bad faith on which the T.V.A. relied in the trial. His conclusions were based simply on the suspicious circumstances surrounding the claim, such as Major Berry's refusal to furnish information requested, and the fact that everyone knew the Cove Creek dam was scheduled for construction at the time the leases were secured. But these suspicions were not evidence admissible in legal proceedings, as Mr. Morgan himself admitted on the stand.[39]

Chairman Morgan subsequently contended that his appearance before the commission and explanation of the conciliation agreement were "necessary to protect the public." [40] The commission, however, in its report to the federal district judge paid no attention to the chairman's testimony, and indeed made no reference what-

---

36. *Hearings*, p. 206.
37. For a detailed statement of the preparations for the case, see *Hearings*, pp. 203–8.
38. Senate Doc. 155, pp. 20–21.
39. *Hearings*, p. 209. He later denied making this admission (see his letter of March 2, 1938), but again the record is against him.
40. *Hearings*, p. 73. For his complete statement, see *ibid.*, pp. 59–94.

ever to the whole question of good faith of the claims. Their findings were limited simply to the question of value, on which they held that "the properties cannot be profitably operated commercially and that the various defendants are entitled to no award." [41]

The chairman's statement on the witness stand was not without effect, however. It was universally construed as an attack upon his colleagues and as an expression of distrust in the T.V.A. counsel. On January 18, 1938, the other two directors addressed a memorandum to President Roosevelt, recounting the serious situation that had developed, charging the chairman with "rule or ruin" methods, and listing the types of opposition to majority board action of which Mr. Morgan had been guilty. In the following words they indicated their belief that the chairman should resign:

> There have been many instances in American public life in which a public officer, having been unable to persuade his colleagues or his superiors to his own views, has retired to private life and, standing up as a private citizen, has continued to contest and seek to upset a policy with which he disagreed as a public officer. To this there can be no possible objection.
>
> If, however, he remains as an executive officer of an agency with the decisions of which he is out of sympathy, an obligation rests upon him not to use his vantage point as an executive to obstruct the carrying out of determined policies.[42]

The President, however, took no action as a result of this communication.

The decision of the condemnation commission was announced on March 1, 1938. Chairman Morgan, according to the *New York Times*, "took the commission's decision as a complete vindication of the stand he took at the outset, and in which he was not supported by his associates, that the Berry claims were nothing short of an attempt to exploit the government." [43] He immediately seized the opportunity to issue a public statement charging that the Berry case

41. For complete text, see Senate Doc. 155, pp. 11–13.
42. *New York Times*, March 5, 1938, p. 2.
43. *Ibid.*, March 3, 1938, p. 1. During this period Mr. Morgan used the *New York Times* and its political writer, Mr. Arthur Krock, as his journalistic mouthpiece.

typified the lack of "honesty, openness, decency and fairness in government" with which he had had to contend on the board, and calling for a congressional investigation. The significant portions of his statement, released on March 2, 1938, are as follows:

> The Berry marble case represents the kind of difficulty with which, as chairman of the TVA board, I have been faced in the effort to maintain good standards of public service. To a steadily increasing degree I have contended with an attitude of conspiracy, secretiveness, and bureaucratic manipulation, which has made the proper and effective conduct of TVA business increasingly difficult.
>
> During this period the public has been steadily and, I believe purposely, led to believe that the difficulties within the TVA have been due primarily to differences as to power policy or to just another "family quarrel." The real difficulty has been in the efforts to secure honesty, openness, decency, and fairness in government. . . .
>
> The TVA deserves a fair and open hearing, which is full and impartial with nothing hidden, and without predilection for or against any person or against the TVA itself. The investigating body should be provided with sufficient funds to make possible a first-hand examination of the obscure financial records of the power program, and of all other important phases of the TVA which come into question.
>
> The fertilizer policy for example, was adopted without being disclosed to the TVA Board, and no impartial technical appraisal and report of the fertilizer program ever has been made to the board or to the public.
>
> It would seem that such an investigation could best be conducted by a joint House and Senate committee on which all important attitudes toward the TVA would have adequate representation.[44]

Chairman Morgan could hardly have attacked the personal integrity of his colleagues in any more direct or serious fashion. The press immediately began referring to the "T.V.A. scandal." The *Chicago Journal of Commerce* put the following interpretation on the statement:

44. *New York Times*, March 3, 1938, p. 2.

Bluntly, Dr. Morgan charged that only his intervention had prevented the consummation of an agreement whereby his two colleagues would have permitted Senator George L. Berry, Democrat, of Tennessee, to "exploit," "hold up," and "defraud" the Government. . . . Dr. Morgan accused Mr. Lilienthal of having threatened Tennessee Valley Authority staff members who criticized the Berry claims. . . . The possibility of a wide-open scandal over the fertilizer program . . . was hinted. . . . Chairman Morgan declared that his fellow director, H. A. Morgan, directed the determination of prices for . . . purchases of phosphate lands. In this case and in the Berry case the board majority took the handling of land acquisition out of the usual Tennessee Valley Authority channels, the Chairman charged.[45]

Similar stories appeared in other newspapers.

As a reply to the charges, President Roosevelt released for publication on March 4 the January 18 memorandum of the other two directors, with its suggestion that the chairman should resign. To counter this blow, and to convey an intimation that he would refuse to resign, the chairman released on March 6 a letter which he had written the preceding month (February 14) to Representative Maury Maverick of Texas. In this letter he had poured out his charges against the power policy generally and certain industrial power contracts specifically, his objections to the fertilizer program, his contention that the other two directors had conspired against him and overridden his suggestions, his belief that the general manager plan was a device for denying him contact with his own staff, and so on. He revealed his bitterness toward Mr. Lilienthal in the following passage: "There is a practice of evasion, intrigue, and sharp strategy, with remarkable skill in alibi and the habit of avoiding direct responsibility, which makes Machiavelli seem open and candid. It took me a year or more of close association to be convinced that the attitude of boyish open candor and man-to-man directness was a mask for hard-boiled, selfish intrigue. . . ."[46] Concerning the Berry marble case, he had written: "The Berry marble

45. March 3, 1938; reprinted in *Hearings*, p. 246.
46. *New York Times*, March 7, 1938; reprinted in *Hearings*, pp. 229–34.

claims, in my opinion, were an effort at a deliberate, bare-faced steal. The other two directors had the same evidence of this that I did. For a year and a half I tried to work it out in confidence in the Board, and without publicity, and only spoke out at the last minute. The public and the Congress do not yet know the extent to which that was improperly handled." His letter closed with a martyr-complex statement that it would be "pleasanter to resign," but that "to surrender the chance to make some contribution to decency and effectiveness in government does not seem to be the right course."

THE PRESIDENT ACTS

Under these circumstances President Roosevelt, always slow to act in difficulties of this kind, could no longer hope that the situation would work itself out. He therefore, on March 8, requested the three directors to appear at the White House for a conference on March 11. From Chairman Morgan he received the astoundingly impertinent reply: "On considering the matter, in view of my experience with the other two members of the Board, I am convinced that the type of conference proposed with them and the President cannot now serve any useful purpose. Therefore, the President should not plan on my presence." [47] To a second presidential request, the chairman sent another negative reply, as follows:

During a long period I have repeatedly and unsuccessfully endeavored to secure your adequate consideration of very grave difficulties in the T.V.A. and as a final resort as a protection of the public interest was forced to make the situation public. In the present situation I believe those difficulties should be considered by a congressional committee rather than by an effort to compose the issues in your office. [48]

It was only after a third telegram had been dispatched, in which the President stated that a "clear duty rests on me to get the facts," that Chairman Morgan agreed to appear.

Thus President Roosevelt had before him on March 11 the three members of the T.V.A. board for a hearing of an unprecedented

47. Senate Doc. 155, p. 17.
48. *Ibid.*

sort. The proceedings were recorded and immediately released to the press. After outlining the development of the unfortunate situation, the President asked Mr. Morgan what evidence he had of dishonesty or malfeasance on the part of his colleagues in the Berry case to support the public charges he had made. In reply, Chairman Morgan announced his refusal to answer the question, saying:

> I am of the opinion that this meeting is not, and in the nature of the case cannot be, an effective or useful fact-finding occasion. To properly substantiate the charges is not the work of a morning. . . . Such information and appraisal can best be obtained and made available to the people, to Congress, and to the President by a congressional committee which will make an impartial, comprehensive, and complete investigation of the Authority's affairs.[49]

This determination to get a congressional investigation led Mr. Morgan to refuse all participation in the hearing, except for certain minor explanations. The field was thus left to the other two directors, who replied to those charges of the chairman which were sufficiently specific to permit it, and presented the evidence for their own charges against the chairman. At the close of the session President Roosevelt indicated his disappointment at Chairman Morgan's attitude, and in order that the chairman might have a chance to change his mind adjourned the hearing for one week.

At the resumed hearing the chairman was still adamant. He had prepared a statement which he insisted on reading, refusing to allow the President to interrupt with questions. His contention still was that only a congressional investigation would be adequate for the purpose, since the facts could "be shown only by witnesses who may have to be subpoenaed and where there must be facilities for examination, cross-examination, and argument, which are not available here." [50] The President immediately called attention to section 17 of the T.V.A. Act, which gives the President powers to select assistants for an investigation into the management of T.V.A. prop-

49. Senate Doc. 155, p. 7.
50. *Ibid.*, p. 77.

erties.[51] He indicated that either under this section, or on the basis of his general powers under the Constitution, he could set up an investigatory procedure with the compulsory powers which Chairman Morgan had said would be necessary. He then asked Mr. Morgan whether he would participate in such an investigation. The chairman indicated that he could not come to a sound decision "under the stress of the moment." The President then closed this second session by giving Mr. Morgan three days in which to decide "whether you are going to be guilty of contumacy by refusing to appear in a continuation of this inquiry or whether you are going to appear and answer the questions which are going to be put to you." [52]

On March 21, the final scene of this extraordinary drama was enacted. Mr. Morgan gave his reply, which was a refusal to participate further in the proceedings. Mr. Roosevelt then indicated that he had prepared two memoranda for the occasion. The first was based on the assumption that Mr. Morgan would decide to submit to the President's investigation procedure, and in it he outlined the arrangements that would be set up to give Mr. Morgan "full advice of counsel, full time to prepare any documentary evidence that you might want to bring in. . . ." [53] Chairman Morgan's answer prevented the use of this memorandum. Instead, the President was forced to turn to his second memorandum, in which he reviewed the controversy and noted the chairman's refusal to offer explanations for his "reckless and astounding conduct." The President summed up the situation as he saw it in these words:

> Arthur E. Morgan's whole attitude toward this inquiry in itself gives credence to the charge that he has been unwilling to cooperate with his fellow directors in the administration of the act and that he is temperamentally unfitted to exercise a divided authority. His fellow directors have responded as a matter of course and have given specifications to support their

51. This section was drafted in rather limited terms; it had been included in the act to permit the President to investigate reports that there had been preferential treatment of private power companies at Muscle Shoals under War Department control.

52. Senate Doc. 155, p. 96.

53. *Ibid.*, p. 98.

grievances. With the exception of a few fragmentary questions and answers on the Berry marble claims, Arthur E. Morgan has stood aloof and refused to cooperate in this proceeding or even to supply the simplest facts asked of him by his own administrative superior. . . .

I have tried to be mindful of the debt the public owes to Arthur E. Morgan for past services, of his sense of the righteousness of his own convictions, and of the patience with which the public interest demands that a situation of this kind be worked out if possible. I have therefore struggled with this problem for over a year, and, in its present acute form, for 6 months. I have been patient.

But, as I have said before, there is a limit to patience. I must greatly consider the position in which Dr. Harcourt Morgan and David Lilienthal find themselves. Some decision on this record is due to them, in all fairness. If there should be no decision after Arthur E. Morgan has refused to substantiate his grave and libelous charges against them, they would be definitely, seriously, and permanently injured in their rights and standing as citizens and as public officials.

Furthermore, I must greatly consider the continuing operations of an important Government agency. It would violate my constitutional duty to take care that the laws are faithfully executed if I should leave unsupported charges hanging indefinitely over the heads of two officials who have cooperated in the difficult task of divided authority and thereby permit a recalcitrant, noncooperative official further freedom to sabotage Government operations at a crucial time.

Finally, I must also consider the consequence of permitting the establishment of a precedent whereby any subordinate in the executive branch of the Government can refuse to give to his superior or to the Chief Executive himself facts sought in order to straighten out difficulties which he charges exist in his own departmental work; can refuse accountability to the Chief Executive for his actions as a member of the executive branch, even though he be charged with misconduct in office; and can insist that orderly executive functioning and discipline be maintained only through the processes of legislative committees. It is worth while to consider what would happen to the efficiency of Government if this suggestion were made the general rule. Obviously the Congress has full power of investigation; but, obviously also, the Constitution of the United States declares that "the executive power shall be vested in a President of the United States." Under such circumstances indulgence of my personal wish to continue my patience with Arthur E. Morgan would be unfair to his colleagues, to his Government and to the public. I therefore feel obliged to act upon the evidence now before me.[54]

The President's action took the form of requesting Mr. Morgan publicly to withdraw his charges impugning the honesty, good faith, integrity, and motives of his fellow directors, or else to resign. If Mr. Morgan refused to take either course, the President added that he would suspend or remove him from his post. Mr. Morgan replied in typical fashion: "It is my judgment that my resignation at this time would not be in the public interest. Therefore, I do not tender my resignation. I wish also to say that I challenge the suggestion and deny the right and the power to remove or to suspend me." [55] On the following day President Roosevelt, having received no further statement from Mr. Morgan, removed him "as member and chairman of the board" of the T.V.A., the removal to be effective March 23, 1938.

Thus the President's role ended. Mr. Morgan was successful, however, in securing the congressional investigation toward which all his efforts had been directed. It is fortunate that such an investigation was held. Without the forum thus provided, it would have been impossible for the public to know whether Arthur E. Morgan was a martyred idealist surrounded by crooks to whom it was unsafe to extend ordinary courtesies, or a man driven by delusions of persecution and the prodding of an injured ego into obstructionism and a battle against imagined evils.

The joint congressional committee set up to investigate the T.V.A. met on May 25, 1938, to hear the eagerly-awaited testimony which the ousted chairman had refused to give to the President. The intervening period had served to build up public expectation of the irregularities to be disclosed. The *Saturday Evening Post* speculated as to whether there was a "little black bag" in the T.V.A. Sen-

54. *Ibid.*, p. 103.
55. *Ibid.*, p. 104.

ator Henry Styles Bridges declared there was in the T.V.A. a public scandal compared with which Teapot Dome would look like a sewing circle intrigue.[56] The *Washington Evening Star* on the day of the opening of the investigation said: "The long-awaited story of corruption in the Tennessee Valley Authority—if any exists—was to be told by Dr. Arthur E. Morgan today." [57]

After this build-up, Mr. Morgan was a great disappointment to the scandal-mongers. For it immediately appeared that in making his grave charges of dishonesty against his fellow directors he had been using words not in their ordinary senses but in accordance with a private vocabulary of his own. He said: "I have not charged that any director of the T.V.A. has taken bribes or stolen money; nor have I charged that any director has profited financially through any transaction of the Authority." [58] He had not been talking about such material things as money, or little black bags. What he had meant was that his co-directors in the execution of their public duty and responsibility had "not been open, candid, fair, and straightforward," and hence there had not been "honest administration of a great public trust." In other words, he had been using the term "dishonest," to which the public attaches only one meaning in connection with public office, as a synonym for a lack of openness and fairness! Mr. Morgan never once apologized for his reckless use of words to the colleagues whom he had charged with dishonesty because they did not agree with him, and never publicly recognized that he had done any injustice to them by allowing his vague and unsupported charges to hang over them for months.

Having thus deflated the investigation, which his tactics had been obviously calculated to secure, he went on to indicate the nature of his charges. He itemized them as follows:

1. Inaccurate and misrepresentative reports to the President, the Congress, and the public.
2. Mismanagement of the power program.

56. *Chicago Tribune,* March 20, 1938; quoted in *Hearings,* p. 239.
57. Quoted in *Hearings,* p. 148.
58. *Ibid.,* p. 6.

3. Lack of candor in statements to the Congress and the public concerning the power program.
4. Improper and misleading accounting, reporting and publicity in reference to the "yardstick" program.
5. Collusion, conspiracy, and mismanagement in administration.
6. Subservience to political and other special interests.[59]

It is impossible to go into the examples and evidence which Mr. Morgan presented to support these charges, which even on their face are for the most part not extremely serious. Congressional committees are not set up to investigate "lack of candor" or "misrepresentative reports." Many of the items which Mr. Morgan brought out in his testimony, even if true, were minor matters or questions on which there could be legitimate difference of opinion. Before a committee that had been expecting evidence of "corruption" or "little black bags," Mr. Morgan offered charges that Mr. Lilienthal was dishonest and untruthful because in a report to the President he had said that the T.V.A. power program started "from scratch" (failing to inform the President that the War Department had sold power there previous to 1933, a fact which the President well knew), and because Mr. Lilienthal had spoken of Mr. Morgan's collaboration with a vice-president of the Insull company, without mentioning that the company had ten other vice-presidents! Some of Mr. Morgan's charges had an admittedly personal basis—witness his complaints that the majority of the board had been guilty of "petty dictation, of treating the chairman with that dictation and coercion that has been a characteristic of the T.V.A. Board. . . ."[60]

On the other hand, some issues of real consequence were presented. The most important concerned the handling of the Berry claims. As has already been made clear, his principal objection was to the conciliation agreement, concerning which he stated to the committee:

I held that the procedure adopted was wholly improper for a Board entrusted with the expenditure of Government

59. *Ibid.*, p. 6.
60. *Ibid.*, p. 24.

funds; that with the evidence of bad faith and of a clear attempt to secure a large sum of Government money for worthless claims before it, the procedure of conciliation was not only bad administration but a breach of public trust. . . . This action did not show frank, disinterested, and honest public service. . . . The whole conduct of the *Berry Marble case* shows not only an insensibility to proper standards of conduct of public business but also a deliberate effort to give special consideration to a public official on claims which had been established to be worthless by abundant information already in the hands of the Board, and which later an independent tribunal found to be valueless, in spite of efforts to "soft pedal" facts in the hearings before that tribunal.[61]

Mr. Morgan thus reiterated his suspicions, the scanty basis for which has already been discussed. The charge about "soft pedalling" facts can be definitely disproved. Mr. Morgan's charges against the T.V.A. counsel who handled the case, Evans Dunn, were particularly unfounded and unjust to an extraordinarily capable, honest, and hardworking lawyer. As for the agreement itself, it clearly protected the public interest and the justification offered by the two board members and the major T.V.A. staff officials was never successfully challenged. The general conclusion of the majority of the congressional investigating committee concerning Mr. Morgan's charges was: "Dr. A. E. Morgan's charges of dishonesty, resulting in the investigation of the Authority are without foundation, not supported by the evidence, and made without due consideration of the available facts." [62]

From the viewpoint of the present writer, there cannot be the slightest doubt that this conclusion was correct.[63] Indeed, the facts justify a much more affirmative conclusion—that the T.V.A. has on the whole been administered with a degree of honesty, competence, imagination, and purposefulness seldom equalled in the history of American public administration. This of course does not mean that

61. *Ibid.*, pp. 60, 62.
62. *Report of the Joint Committee*, p. 237.
63. The complete evidence on which this conclusion was based may be found in the published hearings of the joint congressional committee. In addition, the author has had many opportunities for judging the integrity of T.V.A. administration.

there have not been mistakes in judgment, errors in the selection of personnel, human weaknesses of all sorts in the direction of this huge program. The best evidence that these errors do not bulk large in comparison with the Authority's tremendous accomplishments is found in the fact that the T.V.A. emerged from the congressional investigation unscathed and with reputation unimpaired. It is rare indeed for so searching an inquiry to produce so few skeletons from administrative closets.

For this record of creative achievement great credit must go to all three of the Authority's original directors. It is unfortunate that a peculiar combination of naivete, obstinacy, and egotism led Arthur Morgan to use his great talents and his high reputation for the unworthy purpose of attacking colleagues as honest, as sincere, and as devoted to the T.V.A. as he.[64] It is pertinent, in closing this episode in T.V.A. administration, to quote the charitable comment of the congressional investigating committee, which concluded: "Mr. Lilienthal and Dr. H. A. Morgan acted with forbearance and dignity during the severe strain to which they were subjected, and with due consideration for proper administrative discretion. This cannot be said of Dr. A. E. Morgan."[65]

THE QUESTION OF PRESIDENTIAL AUTHORITY

One of the factors underlying Mr. Morgan's resistance to the President, or at least used to rationalize this resistance, was a contention that the directors of the T.V.A. were ultimately responsible to Congress rather than to the President. This position was implied in several statements made by Mr. Morgan during the hearings, and when President Roosevelt notified Mr. Morgan of the intent to remove him, Mr. Morgan stated explicitly: "I challenge the

64. For an indication as to how fully the public was misled by Mr. Arthur Morgan's conduct, Miss Dorothy Thompson's article on "L'Affaire Morgan" is typical. She saw here a similarity to the Dreyfuss case, and believed that "a distinguished public servant, a man of unselfish service, unchallenged personal integrity, and complete incorruptibility" was being railroaded, purged, and subjected to "smear" tactics! The article is reprinted in *Hearings*, pp. 266–67.

65. *Report of the Joint Committee*, p. 239. Willson Whitman gives an excellent characterization of A. E. Morgan, *op. cit.*, pp. 136–47. He concludes: "Like Moses, he was a good head man until he got mad."

suggestion and deny the right and the power to remove or to suspend me." [66]

After the removal Mr. Morgan initiated legal action to make good his claim. His attorneys brought suit against the T.V.A. in the local chancery court for Knox County, Tennessee, asking for an award of salary and for a declaratory judgment that the removal was unlawful. The T.V.A. had the case transferred to a federal district court, which ruled against Mr. Morgan in August, 1939.[67] Since the suit raised an important question in constitutional law, an analysis of the decision is in order.[68]

The T.V.A. Act contained two passages, and only two, bearing upon the removal of T.V.A. directors. Section 4 (f) provided that "any member of said board may be removed from office at any time by a concurrent resolution of the Senate and the House of Representatives." Section 6 was as follows:

> In the appointment of officials and the selection of employees for said Corporation, and in the promotion of any such employees or officials, no political test or qualification shall be permitted or given consideration, but all such appointments and promotions shall be given and made on the basis of merit and efficiency. Any member of said board who is found by the President of the United States to be guilty of a violation of this section shall be removed from office by the President of the United States. . . .

It was Mr. Morgan's contention that this specific grant of power to the President to remove a director under stated circumstances showed a congressional intent to limit the power to this single cause. In dealing with this contention the district court had first to consider whether such a limitation on the President's removal power, if

---

66. *Hearings,* p. 104.
67. *Morgan v. T.V.A.,* 28 F. Supp. 732 (1939).
68. For legal discussions of this controversy, see "Morgan v. United States—the President's Power of Removal," 51 *Harvard Law Review* 1246–51 (1938); Arthur Larson, "The President's Power of Removal," 16 *Tennessee Law Review* 259–90 (1940); R. A. Swain, "The President's Power of Removal and the TVA," 9 *George Washington Law Review* 703–13 (1941); also 39 *Michigan Law Review* 1410–12 (1941).

adopted by Congress, would be constitutional. For in the well-known case of *Myers* v. *United States* [69] the Supreme Court had held that the President's power to remove executive officers could not be limited by congressional action. However, in the subsequent case of *Humphrey's Executor* v. *United States* [70] the doctrine of the Myers case had been limited to "purely executive officers"; where officers exercising quasi-judicial and quasi-legislative powers were concerned (such as members of the Federal Trade Commission), Congress could constitutionally limit the President's power by specifying certain grounds or causes which alone would justify removal. The district court in the instant case assumed, without deciding, that a director of the T.V.A. would fall within the principle of the Humphrey case, and consequently that Congress would have the power to prescribe valid limitations with respect to removal.

But whether Congress had exercised this power in enacting the T.V.A. statute was another question. There was no specific limitation on the President's removal power. If any existed, it had to be implied from the fact that Congress had reserved to itself the power to remove by concurrent resolution, and had stated one specific cause for which the President was directed to remove. The district court could find in these provisions "no legislative intent to limit the power of the executive with respect to removal, and in the absence of such intent the power exists."

Mr. Morgan appealed this unfavorable decision to the circuit court of appeals. Here his counsel contended that the two methods of removal specified in the statute were exclusive, and that the general power of removal attributed to the President by the *Myers* decision was not applicable in the case of the T.V.A., because it was "an independent agency of the government exercising quasi-legislative functions with the members of its Board of Directors responsible to Congress and not to the President." [71] In more detail, the contention was that the provision for congressional removal by

69. 272 U.S. 52 (1926).
70. 295 U.S. 602 (1936).
71. *Morgan* v. *T.V.A.*, 115 Fed. (2d) 990, at 991 (1940).

concurrent resolution [72] indicated "a deliberate intention by the Congress to set up a mode of removal which expressly excludes the President," and that this method was intended to provide the only means of removal, except as section 6 imposed on the President a mandatory duty to remove for stated causes. Counsel for Morgan further argued

> . . . that the plain intent of the Congress, gathered from the Act as a whole, is completely to exclude any discretionary power of the President to remove, so that the Congress may implement its own policies thereby as distinct from any executive policy, and that in addition to relying upon a technical rule of statutory construction, the appellant may properly rely upon the higher rule that a statute is to be interpreted by the meaning it has as a whole.[73]

One of the factors relied upon as showing congressional intent to limit the President's control was the creation of the agency as a corporation, "thus negativing any idea of an organization within an executive department, and subject to executive control."

The circuit court of appeals, in an opinion delivered in December, 1940, rejected this view. The court could not accept the contention that the concurrent resolution device was intended as the exclusive method of removal. The opinion pointed out that the T.V.A. Act was passed in 1933, when the broad rule of the *Myers* case was the law on this subject, and that if Congress had intended any such limitation on the President's powers, it would have recognized the necessity of stating the limitation as explicitly as it had done in connection with the position of the Comptroller General, established in 1921.[74] Moreover, the nomination of Mr. Morgan's

72. A concurrent resolution does not require approval by the President to become effective, whereas a joint resolution does. Senator Norris was responsible for this unusual provision for removal by concurrent resolution. He included it in his Muscle Shoals bills during the 1920's because he feared that Republican presidents would appoint as directors men who did not believe in a public power program, and who might sabotage the work of the agency. He wanted to have available to Congress a method of removing such appointees. It is ironical that Mr. Morgan sought to use the provision to secure a result opposite to that Senator Norris had intended.

73. 115 Fed. (2d) 990, at 992.

74. The statute provided that the Comptroller General could be removed "in no other manner except by impeachment" (42 Stat. 24).

successor had been confirmed by the Senate after discussion as to whether or not a vacancy existed.[75] Looking at the act as a whole, the court found some provisions indicating "the intent of Congress to keep in close touch with the development of the activity entrusted to the Authority," but it also found "many provisions in the Act which impose supervisory duties upon the President." [76] The court added that if section 4 (f) were to be given the construction suggested, it would probably be unconstitutional.[77]

A final contention remained to be considered. Counsel maintained that the T.V.A. exercised "quasi-legislative powers," and that therefore the President was without power to remove directors during the terms for which they were appointed, by reason of the *Humphrey* decision. The court's answer was:

> It requires little to demonstrate that the Tennessee Valley Authority exercises predominantly an executive or administrative function. . . . True, it is, that in executing these administrative functions, the Board of Directors is obliged to enact by-laws, which is a legislative function, and to make decisions, which is an exercise of functions judicial in character. In this respect its duties are, in no wise, different, except perhaps in degree, from the duties of any other administrative officers or agencies. . . . The Board does not sit in judgment upon private controversies, or controversies between private citizens and the government, and there is no judicial review of its decisions, except as it may sue or be sued as may other corporations. It is not to be aligned with the Federal Trade Commission, the Interstate Commerce Commission, or other administrative bodies mainly exercising clearly quasi-legislative or quasi-judicial functions—it is predominantly an administrative arm of the executive department. The rule of the Humphrey case does not apply.[78]

Mr. Morgan, battling to the last for a contention without basis in law, sought a review of the decision by the Supreme Court, but

75. 84 *Cong. Rec.* 140–42, 236–38.
76. 115 Fed. (2d) 990, at 993.
77. Citing *Springer* v. *Philippine Islands,* 277 U.S. 189 (1928).
78. 115 Fed. (2d) 990, at 993–94.

certiorari was denied in March, 1941. The legal position of the
T.V.A. as a regular executive and administrative agency, responsible
to the President as well as to the Congress, was thus definitely established.

ADMINISTRATIVE AUTONOMY

The court decision just noted was not only sound law; it was
also sound administration. Denial of the President's removal power
would have rendered him unable to end administrative chaos in the
T.V.A., and would have thrown on Congress a supervisory responsibility which it is not and cannot be organized to accept.[79] But, accepting the fact that the President must be ultimately responsible
for the T.V.A., and that the Authority must recognize a responsibility to the President, there still remains a substantial area of choice
as to the most effective and desirable method of implementing that
responsibility.

From the beginning the T.V.A. has been outside the regular departmental system, with no intermediary between the directors and
the President. Most of the other New Deal corporations were also
set up on a basis of independence from any existing departments,
and they came to form a considerable portion of the confusion of
independent agencies which aroused the interest of Congress and
the President in reorganization of the governmental structure.[80] The
solution envisaged by the President's Committee on Administrative
Management, reporting in 1937, was to place the various corporations under supervisory agencies in appropriate departments, thus
bringing them within the regular departmental system of responsibility and limiting the President's span of control. A degree of independence for these supervisory agencies (of which the Farm
Credit Administration was the prototype) was to be insured, if

79. The history of the General Accounting Office furnishes a horrible example
of the failure of congressional supervision. See President's Committee on Administrative Management, *Report*, pp. 21–25.

80. "The Executive Branch of the Government of the United States, has thus
grown up without plan or design like the barns, silos, shacks, tool sheds, and garages
of an old farm." President's Committee on Administrative Management, *Report*, p. 32.

necessary, by giving them a semi-autonomous status within their department.[81]

The general goal of bringing the independent corporations within the departmental organization was largely achieved in 1939 by the reorganization plans issued by President Roosevelt under authority of the Reorganization Act of that year. The Farm Credit Administration with its subsidiary corporations was transferred into the Department of Agriculture. The nonagricultural lending corporations were brought together in a new Federal Loan Agency, which was a department in everything but name. Several other corporations were "departmentalized," and some corporations which had already been located in a department were transferred to more appropriate departments. The net result of the program of reorganization was that the President was relieved of direct responsibility for every corporation except the T.V.A. and the Federal Deposit Insurance Corporation.

Why did the T.V.A. escape the effects of this general trend toward integration? The case for extending departmental control would seem to be as strong in the case of the T.V.A. as for the other corporations. The need for lightening the President's burden of responsibility as much as possible is unquestioned. His attention to the affairs of the T.V.A. cannot be other than intermittent, and his control spasmodic in character. If a cabinet member were given responsibility for oversight of the T.V.A., he would be more able to keep in continuous touch with the operations of the corporation, to interpret governmental policy to it, and to accept responsibility for its operations before Congress. The question as to what department or agency the T.V.A. might logically fit into is not an easy one. Probably the Department of the Interior would be the most acceptable departmental home for the T.V.A., since it already contains the Bonneville Administration and the power projects of the Bureau of Reclamation.

While the case for departmental control of the T.V.A. may thus

81. See the monograph by Herbert Emmerich, "Government Corporations and Independent Supervisory Agencies," in President's Committee on Administrative Management, *Report*, pp. 295–308.

seem to be a strong one, it cannot be accepted without considering the merits of the case for administrative autonomy. There can be no doubt that Congress did intend, in creating the T.V.A., to depart widely from the ordinary bureau pattern and to establish an agency with a considerable measure of independence from presidential control. The terms of nine years given the T.V.A. directors are, so far as the writer is aware, longer than those of any other appointive officers in the executive branch of the federal government.[82] Responsibility for this status is largely attributable to Senator Norris, whose idea was originally to limit the harm that the Republican presidents of the 1920's could do to this public power agency. But even with a friendly President in the White House, Senator Norris has not changed his mind on the desirability of regional autonomy for enterprises of this type. The issue has been squarely raised by pending legislation establishing a permanent organization for disposing of power from the Bonneville and Grand Coulee dams. As opposed to the present arrangement which makes the Bonneville Power Administration simply a bureau in the Department of the Interior, Senator Norris has fought for an independent regional authority headed by a T.V.A.-type board.[83]

The T.V.A. has sought by many different means to emphasize its autonomy, and to stress what it conceives to be the advantages of this status. To insure that its center of balance will be located in the Tennessee Valley, it maintains only a small office force of about ten employees in Washington. To make clear its divorce from purely partisan politics, its directors systematically refrained from any participation in the presidential campaigns of 1936 and 1940. Mr. Lilienthal has on many occasions called attention to the importance of the T.V.A. experiment in "decentralized administration of centralized authority." He has argued that, while centralization of power in the hands of the national government is increasingly necessary, such concentration is subject to the same dangers,

82. The next longest term is that of seven years for members of the Interstate Commerce Commission. The Comptroller General, who has a fifteen year term, is considered to be a legislative officer.
83. See *Time*, Nov. 17, 1941, pp. 15–16.

temptations, and abuses that have characterized the management of centralized business. Administration from Washington is bound to suffer from lack of knowledge of local conditions and regional customs; it tends to exclude and ignore local and state institutions and agencies; and there are bound to be vexing delays in arriving at decisions and putting them into effect in the field. One way of solving these problems, Mr. Lilienthal maintains, is the T.V.A. method of expressing centralized authority through a decentralized regional administration. From this point of view, perhaps the most important administrative contribution of the T.V.A. has been its self-conscious effort "to discover just how far and how effectively in its administration a Federal program can be brought closer to the people and their problems, how far a Federal agency can take local and State instrumentalities into active partnership." [84]

It may well be that Mr. Lilienthal, in his enthusiasm for the T.V.A. pattern, has sought to prove too much from its example. Over-centralization is admittedly a chronic weakness of federal administration, but there are methods of remedying it without setting up autonomous regional authorities. Nonetheless, the fact remains that these remedies are too often not adopted. The experience of the Bonneville Power Administration, which has had a job quite similar to that involved in the T.V.A. power program, shows how difficult it is to secure any release from Washington departmental controls. As a unit of the Interior Department, all of the important decisions of the Bonneville Administration have had to be made or approved in Washington, and its principal officials have been required practically to commute from coast to coast. This the T.V.A. has avoided by its decentralized and autonomous status.

No consensus seems to have been achieved, however, on the value of the T.V.A. type of autonomy. In spite of Senator Norris, it appears that the Bonneville Administration, which is now on a provisional basis, will be given permanent status in the Interior De-

84. Address before the University of California, Nov. 29, 1940. See also his articles, "TVA and Decentralization," 29 *Survey Graphic* 335–37 (1940), and "Administrative Decentralization of Federal Functions," 5 *Advanced Management* 3–8 (1940).

partment.[85] Another regional proposal which shows signs of life is that for establishing an Arkansas Valley Authority, but the various bills introduced in Congress for that purpose have varied widely on this issue of organization.[86] One measure proposed an authority headed by a three-man independent board exactly on the T.V.A. model, while a second would have made the authority a regional agency in the Department of the Interior, to be headed by a single administrator.

Another question which remains unsettled is whether the T.V.A. board of directors is the best type for an autonomous regional agency.[87] In view of the important policy-forming responsibilities involved, it might well be argued that a full-time three-man board is less desirable than a larger board of part-time directors, who could more completely represent various interested viewpoints. It might even be possible for some of the members of such a board to be appointed by or through certain regional institutions, thus binding the agency and the region closer together. On the other hand, the present T.V.A. system is not without its advantages, principally in the concentrated attention which full-time directors can give to the agency's problems.

The ultimate test of autonomy for regional development, conservation, and power agencies would come if five or six authorities of this kind were set up throughout the country. In that event interregional conflicts over policy and program might develop which would prove autonomy unworkable, and make central coordination a necessity, whether provided on a regulatory basis by such an agency as the Federal Power Commission, or on a management basis by a central department.

85. See S. 2430, 77th Cong., introduced April 1, 1942, by Senators Homer T. Bone and Monrad C. Wallgren with administration support.

86. S. 280, 77th Cong., 1st sess. (original and amendment); S. 2226, 77th Cong., 2d sess. See H. W. Blalock, "The Arkansas Valley Authority," 28 *Public Utilities Fortnightly* 195–98, 279–86, 341–49 (1941).

87. The most recent Arkansas Valley Authority bill sets up a five-man board, with four of the members to be part-time directors, and three to be residents of the Arkansas Valley area. The fifth board member is the administrator of the Authority.

This chapter has been concerned with the external controls over the T.V.A. exercised by, and the relationship of the T.V.A. to, the executive office. The pattern which emerges is that of a definite presidential responsibility for and ultimate authority over the administration and policies of the T.V.A. While it may be objected that this is a role to which the President cannot possibly give proper attention, the record shows that he has maintained reasonably close contact with the Authority's development and problems. Doubt as to whether this has been the best arrangement for external control of the Authority may be resolved by considering the two principal alternatives. Locating the T.V.A. in one of the regular departments would have profoundly modified some of its most characteristic features. Complete autonomy and absence of responsibility to the President would have been objectionable under any circumstances, and would certainly have required the substitution of systematized democratic controls emanating from the region itself. It is midway between these extremes of central control and regional autonomy that the T.V.A. has steered its course.

8: Corporate Freedom

> "Congress has held the Departments, and the
> Departments have seemingly resigned themselves,
> to principles thoroughly sound, yet geared to the
> tempo of a vanished age. . . . We cannot be condi-
> tioned today, especially in our dire emergency, by
> the pace of the old gray mare. We must command
> the speed and efficiency of a multiple-cylindered en-
> gine. These can be attained, and have been at-
> tained, by the device of the American government-
> controlled business corporation, an achievement in
> swift statecraft and creative force seldom excelled
> in the history of American political institutions."—
> *L. B. Wehle*

THE T.V.A. was organized as a corporation with the definite expectation that this form would give it a status different from
that of ordinary government departments, a freedom in administration which was believed justified and desirable in carrying on the
program with which it was entrusted. President Roosevelt in his
initial message to Congress on this subject suggested the creation of
"a corporation clothed with the power of government but possessed
of the flexibility and initiative of a private enterprise." [1] The congressional conference report on the T.V.A. bill contained these
words: "We intend that the corporation shall have much of the essential freedom and elasticity of a private business corporation." [2]
It is the purpose of the present chapter to determine the extent to
which these goals have been achieved, and to note whether the
T.V.A. has, by reason of its corporate form of organization, been

1. House Doc. 15, 73d Cong., 1st sess.
2. House Report 130, 73d Cong., 1st sess., p. 19.

able to secure the elasticity of management, the autonomy of finance, and the freedom from governmental intervention, which have been cited as the results made possible by this form of organization. In other words, it is a study in what may be called "the corporate freedom" of the Tennessee Valley Authority.

THE THEORY AND PRACTICE OF CORPORATE FREEDOM

When the T.V.A. was created in 1933, a considerable fund of experience had accumulated in this country with respect to the government owned corporation, a form of government organization generally agreed to represent an interesting and useful addition to the older departments, bureaus, commissions, and boards. "The functions of government," it has been well said, "are much more susceptible of modification than is its anatomy." [3] The government corporation was all the more important because it appeared to constitute a real modification in the anatomy of government administration.

The modern American experience with government owned corporations goes back to only 1904, when as an incident to the building of the Panama Canal, the United States purchased the Panama Railroad Company,[4] a corporation chartered under the laws of the state of New York in 1849. The existing corporate organization was retained under government ownership because it was believed that corporate methods and powers would prove more successful than would ordinary government procedures in the operation of the railroad, shipping line, and supply services that were to be carried on. The government's control over the corporation was exercised through the Secretary of War, who was a member of its

3. C. H. Wooddy, *Recent Social Trends in the United States* (1933), p. 1274.
4. The first and second Banks of the United States were, of course, government-owned in part. Other early federal agencies organized as corporations were the National Academy of Sciences, incorporated in 1863, and the National Soldiers Home (1866). This latter institution John A. McIntire considers "probably the first government corporation properly so-called." See his "Government Corporations as Administrative Agencies: An Approach," 4 *George Washington Law Review* 161–210 (1936). Also see, more generally, H. A. Van Dorn, *Government Owned Corporations* (New York, 1926), and John Thurston, *Government Proprietary Corporations* (Cambridge, 1937).

board of directors and appointed the other 12 members. Under government ownership the corporation continued to conduct its business much like a private agency, and to exercise the powers given by the charter of incorporation.[5] The Attorney General early held that employees of the corporation were not "employed by the United States."[6] In a subsequent decision involving the power of the directors of the corporation, the Attorney General observed that the rule adopted by the government had been to treat the railroad as a "wholly independent corporation," and that the directors' powers would therefore have to be determined "by reference to the ordinary principles of corporation law."[7] The corporation was financially self-supporting and did not, after the first few years, receive appropriations from Congress. On the contrary, it paid annually from 1924 to 1938 dividends of 5 to 10 per cent on the corporation's stock into the federal treasury, as well as a special 40 per cent dividend assessed by Congress in 1932 to supply funds for building the Madden Dam in the Canal Zone. The corporation was not subjected to the provisions of the civil service laws, and its accounts were not submitted to the regular government audit. In short, its administration was in many respects more characteristic of a private company than of a government department.

The first large-scale use of the corporate device for governmental purposes occurred during the first World War, when such important agencies as the Shipping Board Emergency Fleet Corporation, the U.S. Grain Corporation, the War Finance Corporation, the U.S. Housing Corporation, and others were set up in this form. Some of these agencies were incorporated directly by act of Congress, while others were brought into existence under the incorporation laws of various states and the District of Columbia. All of them operated with the freedom of commercial organizations, performing their emergency duties with a flexibility and vigor that

5. For an account of the administration of this corporation under government ownership see M. E. Dimock, *Government-Operated Enterprises in the Panama Canal Zone* (1934).
6. 25 Op. Atty. Gen. 466.
7. 30 Op. Atty. Gen. 508.

had hardly time to be questioned before the war was over and liquidation was begun. The Fleet Corporation, however, continued in existence long after the war was over, and its experience contributed a great deal to an understanding of the potentialities and limitations of the corporate form when used for governmental purposes.

The corporation was created by officials of the Shipping Board with an initial capitalization of $50,000,000.[8] The corporation took the position that this capital constituted a revolving fund to be used without further congressional authorization, and that its status was that of a private corporation not subject to government regulatory statutes and restrictions. The policy of the Fleet Corporation, however, was to comply with all such statutes insofar as "they are not in conflict with and do not, when applied, act as obstacles to the efficient operation and maintenance of Government owned vessels which are engaged in a commercial enterprise of a highly competitive nature."[9] Congress gave support to the claims of the corporation for special status by providing that the Comptroller General should audit the financial transactions of the Fleet Corporation "in accordance with the usual methods of steamship or corporate accounting."[10] This exemption from the regular government audit was approved by the Supreme Court, which stated in a case involving this corporation: "Indeed, an important if not the chief reason for employing these incorporated agencies was to enable them to employ commercial methods and to conduct their operations with a freedom supposed to be inconsistent with accountability to the Treasury under its established procedure of audit and control over the financial transactions of the United States."[11]

8. Congress authorized sale of the corporation's stock to private investors, with the limitation that such holdings could not be a majority interest. No such sales were ever made, for obvious reasons. In addition to its capital, the corporation subsequently received over $3,000,000,000 in appropriations to finance the ship construction program and later to meet the corporation's deficit in its merchant fleet operations. The corporation was given the same freedom in spending appropriated funds as it enjoyed in connection with its original capital (40 Stat. 183).

9. House Doc. 321, 72nd Cong., 1st sess., p. 3.

10. 42 Stat. 444 (1922).

11. *Skinner & Eddy Corp.* v. *McCarl*, 275 U.S. 1 (1927).

Several other decisions of the Supreme Court were also to the effect that the Fleet Corporation was not to be treated as an ordinary government department.[12] On the other hand, the court did on occasions hold the corporation to be representative of the government itself.[13] Relying upon these decisions, the Comptroller General came to the conclusion that the Fleet Corporation acted at times as a private corporation, and at other times in a governmental capacity. In its operations as a shipping concern and in the administration of its transactions with outsiders, it could proceed as a private corporation, but its internal relationships would be subject to the limitations and regulations applicable to government agencies.[14] Thus, although the Fleet Corporation was given a curious dualism of character, its special administrative status and semiprivate nature were officially recognized.

During the decade of the 1920's the most interesting government corporation established was the Inland Waterways Corporation. From 1920 to 1924 the War Department carried on a barge line service, inherited from the war period, on the Mississippi River through the agency of the Inland and Coastwise Waterways Service. The difficulties encountered in attempting to operate within the regular governmental framework were so great that Congress was asked to create a corporation to take over the enterprise. Under the corporate form of organization, it was stated, the corporation's capital would free the business from the hazards of annual appropriations by Congress and from the itemized allocations in appropriation acts. Likewise the capital would provide funds for unforeseen emergencies, while additional funds could if necessary be secured by borrowing. The corporation would be free from the supervision of the Comptroller General and would enjoy more flexibility in con-

12. *Sloan Shipyards Corp.* v. *Emergency Fleet Corp.*, 258 U.S. 549 (1922); *United States* v. *Strang*, 254 U.S. 491 (1921).

13. *Emergency Fleet Corp.* v. *Western Union*, 275 U.S. 415 (1928); *United States* v. *Walter*, 263 U.S. 15 (1923). For a discussion of this question see John Thurston, *Government Proprietary Corporations*, Chap. 2.

14. House Doc. 111, 71st Cong., 1st sess., p. 44.

tractual relations, both of these features being considered desirable in a business enterprise.[15]

Congress acted favorably on this request and created the Inland Waterways Corporation, to be under the direct control of the Secretary of War.[16] The corporation was given capital amounting to $12,000,000, plus existing properties and equipment valued at over $10,000,000, and it proceeded to build up a substantial transportation business operating with practically the freedom of a private corporation. Employees of the corporation were not placed under civil service.[17] The act made no provision for audit of the corporation's accounts, and as a result the Comptroller General did not attempt to exercise his auditing control over the corporation, or to enforce upon it federal regulatory statutes.[18]

The Reconstruction Finance Corporation was the last government corporation created before the New Deal era. It was established along the lines of the War Finance Corporation, with a seven-man board of directors, one of whom was to be the Secretary of the Treasury. The corporation was given an original capitalization of $500,000,000, and was authorized to borrow additional sums to be used as a revolving fund for the making of loans. The corporation's freedom from the accounting control of the Comptroller General was guaranteed by the following provision in the act: "The board of directors of the corporation shall determine and prescribe the manner in which its obligations shall be incurred and its expenses allowed and paid." [19] The corporation did not regard it-

15. Hearings before House Committee on Interstate and Foreign Commerce on H. R. 6647, 68th Cong., 1st sess.

16. 43 Stat. 360 (1924). Control was transferred to the Secretary of Commerce in 1939 by Reorganization Plan No. 2.

17. Executive Order No. 7916 of June 24, 1938, extending the civil service, was held by the Attorney General to apply to this corporation (39 Op. Atty. Gen. 61). The Reed Committee, reporting in 1941, recommended that the clerical, administrative, and fiscal employees be brought into the civil service. See Report of President's Committee on Civil Service Improvement, House Doc. 118, 77th Cong., 1st sess. (1941), Chap. 11.

18. For a study of this corporation, see M. E. Dimock, *Developing America's Waterways* (1935).

19. 47 Stat. 6 (1932).

self as bound by regulatory statutes, though in practice they were conformed to, if possible.

Through the operation of these four corporations and others of less importance, the United States had accumulated by 1933 a considerable experience with the corporate device as employed for governmental purposes. The use of the corporate form of organization had been shown to be generally effective in securing a substantial freedom from ordinary government financing, auditing, and personnel practices, and had allowed the adoption of methods suited to a commercial undertaking. This experience had been fairly well assimilated and recorded by students of government. As early as 1917 W. F. Willoughby had clearly outlined the nature and uses of the corporation in government administration. In an article published at that time he proposed that government services having an industrial and revenue-producing character, services concerned with the administration or exploitation of the public domain, and the general supply services and manufacturing plants of the government should be given by Congress a status as "distinct subsidiary corporations," to which Congress would stand in the position of a holding corporation. Willoughby explained:

> Essentially this means that each such service will be given a legal, administrative and financial autonomy. Each will have its organic act, or charter, providing for its creation and defining its jurisdiction, powers and duties; its board of directors; its directing staff and subordinate personnel; its own plant, equipment and other property which it will possess in its own name; its own revenue and expenditure system; its distinct accounting and reporting system separate from that of the general government; and its own well-defined sphere of activities. Each, in a word, will have all the characteristics of a public corporation.[20]

By 1926 the experience with corporations enjoying such "legal, administrative and financial autonomy" had been so extensive that Harold A. Van Dorn was able to prepare a systematic appraisal of

20. "The National Government as a Holding Corporation: The Question of Subsidiary Budgets," 32 *Political Science Quarterly* 507 (1917).

this organizational form. His analysis stressed the various kinds of freedom which had been characteristic of these corporations— freedom in financing, in purchasing, in personnel matters, and from congressional interference. He also noted the pattern of overhead organization resulting from the presence of a board of directors, and the principle of liability to suit in the courts. At the time the T.V.A. was created, then, the theory of corporate freedom was well understood and was solidly based on the prevailing practice. Because of the corporate form of their organization T.V.A. officials assumed that they would have a considerable measure of administrative autonomy and that certain of the external governmental controls over their organization would be somewhat looser than in the case of ordinary government departments. In actual practice the quest for corporate freedom turned out to be only partially successful, as the following discussion will make clear.

CONTROL BY CONGRESS

No concept of "corporate freedom" ever contemplated complete lack of control by, or accountability to, the Congress, a status as impossible as it would be undesirable. Willoughby's case was simply against a detailed congressional control which he felt Congress had not the time or wisdom to supply. Van Dorn spoke of the desirability of eliminating congressional "interference," but recognized that corporate agencies should be "by no means independent of ultimate Congressional control." [21] Such ultimate control is inevitably present in the congressional power to create, abolish, or modify the powers of government corporations.

In the case of the T.V.A., Congress has used its legislative power sparingly. The basic act adopted in 1933 has been amended on only five occasions, [22] and generally for the purpose of facilitating, rather than restricting or "interfering" with T.V.A. operations. The amendments adopted in 1935 were for the most part sponsored by the T.V.A. itself in order to repair deficiencies which two years

21. *Op. cit.*, p. 277.
22. 49 Stat. 1075 (1935); 53 Stat. 1083 (1939); 54 Stat. 626 (1940); 55 Stat. 599, 775 (1941). See Ransmeier, *op. cit.*, Chap. 3.

of operation had shown to exist in the T.V.A. Act, and to make the corporation's powers more clear and definite. The most controversial of the issues considered by Congress at that time was the relationship of the T.V.A to the General Accounting Office, and here, as will be noted later in this chapter, Congress acted to uphold the T.V.A. In 1939 the Authority found it necessary, in order to carry through the purchase of Commonwealth & Southern properties, to come to Congress for an amendment modifying its power to issue bonds. On this occasion Congress proved rather obdurate, and the necessary legislation was secured in a much more restrictive form than the T.V.A. had requested. The following year the T.V.A. presented to Congress its recommendations with respect to payments in lieu of taxes on its properties to local governments, and Congress adopted them substantially as offered. Finally, in 1941 the longstanding quarrel of the T.V.A. and the General Accounting Office was brought to a conclusion by an amendment satisfactory to both parties. On the whole, the T.V.A. has been fortunate in its legislative relationships. Definitely unfriendly proposals in the form of legislation have been uniformly defeated.[23]

From the point of view of continuing control, the most important congressional power has been that over T.V.A. appropriations. It is in this field that the position of the T.V.A. contrasts most markedly with the traditional   concept of corporate freedom. The cornerstone of the administrative autonomy of the earlier corporations was their financial independence. Because they had been endowed with capital and were able to use their revenues, it was un-

23. The most recent legislative vendetta against the T.V.A. was organized by its erstwhile friend, Senator McKellar, after circumstances had forced him to yield on the building of Douglas Dam, which he had bitterly opposed. In the spring of 1942 he introduced crippling T.V.A. legislation (S. 2361, 77th Cong.), made personal attacks on Mr. Lilienthal, and told the Senate amazing yarns to the effect that T.V.A. had wanted to stop building dams after the first two, and that he had compelled them to continue the program. See his speeches of May 1, 4, 5, and 6, 1942. Senator Stewart, who supported McKellar in this fight, came up for re-nomination shortly afterwards, and was saved from defeat on the issue of "tampering" with the T.V.A. only by the Crump machine in Memphis. Further information on McKellar's attitude is found in Herbert Corey, "The Federals Are Coming," 29 *Public Utilities Fortnightly* 729–36 (1942), and Senate Committee on Agriculture and Forestry, Hearings on S. 2361, 77th Cong., 2d sess. (March, 1942).

necessary for them to seek appropriations from Congress. As Van Dorn put it, if a government corporation has to depend upon appropriations, it has lost "one of the chief characteristics which commended it as an efficient agency for carrying on a business function of government. As long as it must look to Congress for annual detailed appropriations it is in the same dependent position as a bureau or a board. The camouflage of a corporate name will in no wise protect it from political pressure." [24]

The reliance of the T.V.A. on appropriated funds has been in large part the inevitable result of the size and kind of program it was called upon to administer. The corporation was established without any capital, except for the properties turned over to it. It was given authority to issue bonds in the amount of $50,000,000, but limited to use for construction purposes.[25] For other purposes there was no alternative except appropriations, and consequently a sum of $50,000,000 was requested from Congress when the T.V.A. was first set up. This amount was included in the $3,300,000,000 appropriation for national industrial recovery voted in 1933. In connection with the T.V.A. appropriation, Chairman Morgan appeared before the House subcommittee in charge of deficiency appropriations and attempted to give some idea of how the sum would be spent, but his estimates were of necessity extremely rough. The greater part was to go for Norris Dam, in the construction of which the T.V.A. did not propose to use its bonding power. The appropriation was to be available until expended, and not bound by the usual fiscal year limitation. Several members of the subcommittee objected to this procedure, but Chairman Morgan said he was unable to estimate the sum required for the fiscal year, and maintained that the T.V.A. should not have to run the risk of having a subsequent appropriation refused with its dam half completed.[26]

24. *Op. cit.*, pp. 167–68.
25. The insertion of this provision was suggested by President Roosevelt, on the basis of the experience of the Port Authority of New York. Senator Norris was not enthusiastic about the plan. The bond section as finally adopted was a compromise between the Senate and House bills, and was not satisfactory.
26. Hearings, "Fourth Deficiency Appropriation Bill for 1933," 73d Cong., 1st sess., June 9, 1933, pp. 33–34.

This first T.V.A. appropriation received little attention on the floor of Congress. As to form, the appropriation was made in a single lump sum. The Cove Creek dam and powerhouse was the only project specifically mentioned in the appropriation act. The complete absence of any itemization may have been the result of congressional recognition of the Authority's corporate status, but it was more probably due to the emergency conditions prevailing at the time.

It is also interesting to note that this first appropriation was secured without any contact with the Bureau of the Budget. The T.V.A. officials tended to assume that their organization was immune from such control, along with other emergency agencies. In the fall of 1933, however, the T.V.A. reconsidered this position and acceded to the Bureau's request that a budget for the following fiscal year be prepared and submitted. The fact that the T.V.A. program was in a formative stage, and that its officials were without previous experience with the regular budget procedure, made preparation of a satisfactory budget somewhat difficult, but approval was finally secured from the Bureau of the Budget.

Absence of a complete understanding between the two agencies, however, was shown in the budget document presented to Congress, in which the Bureau made no request for an appropriation to cover contemplated T.V.A. obligations. Instead, the document noted that the amount required was "to be supplied by sale of securities." [27] This suggestion was a complete surprise to T.V.A. officials, and proposed a type of financing against which they had definitely decided. Actually, appropriated funds were secured for the 1935 fiscal year, but not by means of a direct appropriation to the Authority. Instead, a lump sum of $899,675,000 was appropriated for four emergency agencies "to be allocated by the President." The T.V.A. received $25,000,000 from this appropriation for the fiscal year 1935.

The process of budget preparation and appropriation for the following fiscal year was marked by several changes. First, the

27. *The Budget of the U.S. Government, 1935*, p. 56.

T.V.A. was divested of its emergency status, becoming a regular agency whose appropriation needs were to be met out of the regular budget. Second, an annexed budget was used in presenting the financial requirements of the Authority. The use of annexed or subsidiary budgets for financially independent or semi-independent governmental agencies has long been advocated by fiscal experts. Foreign governments have made wide use of this type of budget for public enterprises. It was employed by the United States for the first time in the 1936 budget, and the purpose was explained in President Roosevelt's transmittal message as follows:

> Annexed budgets are set up for the major self-supporting or self-contained units of the Government, namely, the Post Office Department, the Reconstruction Finance Corporation, the Tennessee Valley Authority, and the District of Columbia. The use of such budgets permits the receipts and expenditures of each of these units to be clearly and completely presented in gross figures and in balanced form, as has not hitherto been done. By following this method, the net figures for each unit, which may be either appropriation needs or surplus receipts, are calculated and then carried to the General Budget Summary.[28]

The theory behind this use of an annexed budget for the T.V.A. was excellent, although it was scarcely accurate to refer to the T.V.A. at that time as a "self-supporting or self-contained" unit. For in the 1936 budget total T.V.A. obligations were estimated at over $63,000,000, while revenues expected totalled only $6,210,000. Under these circumstances the practical advantages of the annexed budget were not too great, but it became more appropriate in later years as revenues increased.

When the legislative stage arrived on the 1936 appropriation, the T.V.A. presented for the first time detailed supporting statements covering its projects.[29] However, the appropriation retained its lump sum character, the language of the act simply specifying

28. *Ibid.*, *1936*, p. xiv.
29. At these hearings the T.V.A. was represented by all three board members. At the hearings of the two previous years, Chairman Morgan had appeared alone.

the dams and sites upon which expenditures were authorized. While there was thus no attempt to bind the T.V.A. to the specific estimates presented to Congress, the chairman of the House appropriations committee did state his understanding that these estimates "ought to be your budget that would not only guide you but bind you, unless some great emergency happened." [30] Mr. Lilienthal indicated his agreement with this point of view, although Chairmain Morgan said that he "assumed there was a reasonable amount of leeway."

The pattern of appropriation control thus established has continued largely unchanged during subsequent years. The process of review of estimates by the Bureau of the Budget and authorization of expenditures by Congress is essentially the same as that for any ordinary government agency. Over the course of the years the annual T.V.A. appropriation became stabilized at around $40,000,000, until the national defense emergency made it necessary to speed up T.V.A. construction activities and to add new dams to the program. The supplementary appropriations voted the T.V.A. in 1940 and 1941 were put through Congress on the recommendation of the Advisory Commission to the Council on National Defense and the Office of Production Management. Appropriations for the ten fiscal years 1934 to 1943 total two-thirds of a billion dollars.

In addition to appropriations, the T.V.A. has secured funds from two other sources. First, it has been permitted to retain its revenues, earned primarily of course from the sale of power. Normal practice requires government agencies which receive fees or payments for services to turn them immediately into the general treasury, from which they can be paid out only pursuant to regular appropriations. In government business enterprises, however, the nature of the activity is generally felt to justify a different rule, and retention of revenues has been a normal practice. The original T.V.A. Act accepted this idea by providing that net proceeds from operations were to be paid into the Treasury only at the end of

30. Hearings, "Second Deficiency Appropriation Bill for 1935," 74th Cong., 1st sess., p. 543.

Table IV

CONGRESSIONAL APPROPRIATIONS TO THE T.V.A., FISCAL YEARS 1934–1943

Fiscal Year	Amount Appropriated
1934	$50,000,000
1935	25,000,000 *
1936	36,000,000
1937	39,900,000
1938	40,166,270
1939	40,000,000
1940	39,003,000
1941	66,500,000
1942	196,800,000
1943	136,100,000
Total	$669,469,270

* Allocated by the President.

each calendar year. In determining "net proceeds," the T.V.A. was permitted to deduct from its gross revenues "the cost of operation, maintenance, depreciation, amortization, and an amount deemed by the board as necessary to withhold as operating capital, or devoted by the board to new construction." This language was so broad as to ensure that, during the construction period at least, there would be no net revenues.

When the T.V.A. Act was being amended in 1935, the House became much disturbed over this practice, and proposed that the T.V.A. should be forbidden to spend its revenues "except in consequence of annual appropriations thereof by Congress." [31] The Senate did not concur, however, and the amendment finally adopted made little change in the existing procedure. The T.V.A. was authorized to retain such part of its proceeds "as in the opinion of the Board shall be necessary for the Corporation in the operation of dams and reservoirs, in conducting its business in generating, transmitting, and distributing electric energy and in manufacturing, selling, and distributing fertilizer and fertilizer ingredients."

31. See 79 *Cong. Rec.* 10971 (1935).

Under this authorization the T.V.A. has been able to retain all its revenues, applying them against the programs and projects to which they are related and thus decreasing to that extent the appropriations required. No net proceeds have been paid into the Treasury. It should be made clear, however, that revenues which are spent are budgeted for, accounted for, and audited in the same fashion as appropriated funds. Moreover, the revenues are not deposited in banks or invested, as is the practice in some government corporations, but are placed to the credit of the T.V.A. in the U. S. Treasury.

The availability of its revenues has given a flexibility to T.V.A. financing which its officials have considered extremely important and necessary. For example, in 1940 national defense needs made it suddenly necessary to open up and operate the Muscle Shoals steam plant. This eventuality had not been foreseen when the budget for the fiscal year had been prepared, and so no funds had been requested for this purpose. Without the authority to use its own revenues, the T.V.A. would have had to wait until an appropriation could be put through Congress in order to begin the production of badly needed power.

The T.V.A. exercised this right to spend its revenues largely without question from 1935 to 1942. When the Senate undertook consideration of the T.V.A. appropriation for the fiscal year 1943, however, Senator Kenneth D. McKellar made an attack on this practice part of his general campaign against the Authority. He won a partial victory in the Senate, but because of the strength of the T.V.A. case, as well as the general feeling that this was simply a political attack, his amendment was excluded from the appropriation bill as finally passed. The T.V.A. thus properly retains the right to use its revenues.

A third source of T.V.A. funds has been the sale of bonds, which have been issued to the amount of some $65,000,000. As already noted, the provision in the original act authorizing issuance of bonds to finance construction was so drawn as to make it of little use. When the act was being amended in 1935, the T.V.A. proposed that this unused bond section be eliminated in favor of a new one which would authorize bonds for the acquisition of existing electric distribution systems and transmission lines. It was believed that the progress of municipal ownership was being hampered because integrated utility companies were refusing to break up their systems by selling them piece-meal to the various cities which wanted to buy them. The best way of facilitating these purchases without causing dismemberment of existing systems, T.V.A. officials felt, would be for the T.V.A. to purchase the entire system of any company threatened with a loss of part of its properties, and then to re-sell the individual distribution systems to the cities and counties concerned. The proposed amendment provided that the T.V.A. was not to purchase any properties unless it appeared practicable to dispose of them. This procedure, it will be noted, was essentially that which the T.V.A. had followed with the properties it had first purchased, those of the Mississippi Power Company. To finance purchases of this character, the T.V.A. asked Congress for authorization to issue $100,000,000 in 50 year, 3½ per cent bonds, fully guaranteed by the United States both as to principal and interest.

Congress refused to accept the T.V.A. point of view. The amendments finally adopted did not permit the T.V.A. to purchase existing power systems, but merely authorized it to assist public agencies and non-profit organizations in acquiring their own systems by extending credit to them. For this purpose the T.V.A. was permitted to issue bonds up to $50,000,000. The original bond provision authorizing a $50,000,000 issue for construction purposes was also retained in the Act.

For some time neither of these authorizations appeared likely to be of much use to the Authority. However, in September, 1938, bonds to the amount of $3,000,000 were issued under the original section 15 for the acquisition of certain assets from the Tennessee Public Service Company, and subsequently $5,300,000 additional was secured under the same section. The bonds, bearing 2½ per cent interest, were sold at par to the Reconstruction Finance Corporation. In December, 1938, the new bond section (15a) was utilized in issuing bonds amounting to $272,500, bearing 2⅛ per cent interest and maturing in ten years, which were sold to the Treasury at par. The purpose of this issue was to extend credit to two cooperative organizations which were buying distribution systems.

The most important issuance of T.V.A. bonds came in connection with the purchase of Commonwealth & Southern properties. In order to secure the funds needed for this purpose, the T.V.A. requested Congress in 1939 to rewrite the two bond sections into a new and somewhat broadened authorization to issue $100,000,000 in bonds. The proposal met an unfavorable reception in the House, which cut the amount and wrote in a limitation on the territory to be served by the T.V.A. There was for a time serious danger that the T.V.A. agreement with the Commonwealth & Southern would fall through because of congressional failure to make funds available. However, a compromise was finally reached on a provision much more restrictive in character than the T.V.A. had proposed. The bond authorization was limited to $61,500,000 and, while no territorial restriction was included, Congress specified in detail the purposes for which the funds were to be used. This authority was to expire on January 1, 1941, and the two earlier bond sections were nullified. Under authority of this 1939 amendment, the T.V.A. secured the funds to consummate its contract with the Commonwealth & Southern, issuing to the United States Treasury interim certificates amounting to a total of $56,500,000 and bearing ½ per cent interest. The understanding was that the Treasury was entitled to receive at a later date definitive bonds bearing interest not to exceed 3½ per cent.

The T.V.A. program has thus been financed in only a relatively minor degree by borrowing. It would clearly have been preferable for more of its funds to have been secured in this fashion, instead of having them supplied by congressional appropriations on which there is normally no obligation to pay interest or expectation of repayment. Obviously the T.V.A. should not have been required to secure all its funds by the sale of securities, for its multiple-purpose program, as we have seen, includes many non-commercial and non-income producing elements. But it would have been logical to require that all direct power costs and common costs properly allocable to power be met out of borrowed funds, the interest upon which would be a proper charge upon the power program.

This approach was not taken for various reasons. For one thing, no one knew what charges were to be made against power until 1938. Moreover, at the beginning the prospects for revenue from power sales were so discouraging that the T.V.A. hesitated to load itself with fixed debt charges. As Mr. Lilienthal said in 1935, "it seemed unwise to issue bonds which carry fixed charges until a definite basis of revenues has been established." [32] Chairman Arthur Morgan had earlier expressed the view that the T.V.A. should husband its bond-issuing authority against the chance that Congress might some day refuse further appropriations; it would then be needed to finish up projects already begun.

The fact that borrowing was inadequately used in financing T.V.A. power projects need create no difficulty, however, for there is no reason why the funds appropriated to cover power costs should not be treated as advances on which the Treasury is entitled to receive interest. As a matter of fact, such has been the intention of the Authority from the beginning,[33] and the various amortization plans and long-term forecasts of financial prospects which the T.V.A. has issued, have all contemplated that the government would receive interest on its power investment as well as ultimate repayment of the principal. No actual payments into the Treasury by way of interest have as yet been made, however.

The T.V.A. statute leaves the Authority entirely without direction in the matter of interest payments and amortization. These are matters that might well have been given congressional attention, and in fact they were the subject of some legislative proposals that did not find their way into the final act. For example, the House draft of the T.V.A. bill in 1933 would have required the T.V.A. to create

32. Hearings before House Committee on Military Affairs, "Tennessee Valley Authority," 74th Cong., 1st sess., p. 68.
33. As noted in chap. 4, interest on the power investment was taken into account in fixing wholesale power rates.

a sinking fund for Wilson Dam for the purpose of amortizing the investment in the dam and returning to the Treasury its entire cost within 60 years. Further, interest of 2 per cent was to be paid into the Treasury on that portion of the dam's cost chargeable to power. The same provisions were to be effective for all other dams the T.V.A. might build. These proposals were eliminated from the bill before final passage, Senator Norris contending that the sinking fund plan would be unworkable because power would be only an incident in the program and the great bulk of expenditure would be for other purposes.

In spite of the absence of any statutory provision on the subject, Congress has shown on several occasions that it expects a substantial return on the moneys advanced to the T.V.A. One year after the T.V.A. was set up, in May, 1934, Chairman Morgan was questioned by the House appropriations subcommittee concerning the organization's plans for amortization. He replied that, while no definite policy had been adopted, he believed that after the preliminary organization period, the program should be amortized in 25 years. In 1936 Mr. Lilienthal presented to the same subcommittee a fairly complete amortization plan, providing for liquidation of the entire investment (not merely the power costs) in 50 years without use of a sinking fund. Interest was to be paid on the direct power investment only, at a rate of 3½ per cent. The plan was of necessity based on estimates of future revenues, costs, and power capacity, and is of importance now only as it shows the development of the approach to this problem.

The congressional investigating committee touched on this same problem in 1938. In the analysis of T.V.A. power rates made by the committee's engineer, it was concluded that an interest charge of 3¼ per cent and an amortization charge of 0.825 per cent on the power investment (both direct and allocated) should be figured in the power costs. The conclusion of the committee itself, in its majority report, was that

> power revenues, insofar as the marketing problems permit, should return to the Federal Treasury all direct and allocated

indirect costs of construction paid for out of Federal funds, chargeable to the power program. The return of capital advances of this character, with adequate interest accumulations, will discharge the obligations which the rate payer on the Authity's system may in fairness be called upon to liquidate.[34]

While the principle of interest payment and amortization is thus accepted, it has yet to be put into effect. There has been no binding legislative determination as to what is expected from the T.V.A. along this line, and no final statement from the T.V.A. as to what amortization plan it proposes to adopt or at what rate and on what investment it will pay interest. As noted, no actual payments have been made into the Treasury; the sums that might have been paid for these purposes have simply been retained by the T.V.A., reducing to that extent the appropriations necessary. In the interests of a straightforward commercial approach, such payments should actually be made into the Treasury, although it would mean at the present time that the T.V.A. annual appropriation would have to be increased by an equivalent amount. Even if the payment is to be simply a bookkeeping transaction, the basis of the calculations should be definitely determined without further delay.

REPORTING TO CONGRESS

Appropriations control is the most important continuing control which Congress exercises over the T.V.A., and the appearance of T.V.A. officials before the appropriations subcommittees constitutes the principal congressional avenue of communication with the organization. Another important source of information is the annual report of the Authority. This document has developed from the meager 60-page pictureless pamphlet of 1934 to the present volume of several hundred pages. A large part of the report consists of material which Congress has required to be published. Included in this category are all contracts for the sale of power (the printing of which took 220 pages in the 1940 annual report), and a list of the salaries of all employees receiving in excess of $1500 per year.

34. Senate Doc. No. 56, 76th Cong., 1st sess., p. 153.

Perhaps the most important feature of the document is the annual financial report and comptroller's statement. The preparation of its financial statements has caused the T.V.A. no little trouble, for several reasons. One was that the statements had to cover the operations of a program that was in part commercial and in part noncommercial. Another was that the statements had to serve the dual purpose of showing the financial position of the Authority and of reporting to Congress on the use of appropriated funds. The possible conflict resulting from these requirements may be illustrated by noting the problems presented in preparation of the T.V.A. balance sheet.

Insofar as appropriated funds were spent for the construction of dams, power lines, and other properties, there was no difficulty. These expenditures appeared in the balance sheet under the heading of fixed assets. But a part of T.V.A. expenditures was for such purposes as forestry projects, soil erosion control, social and economic research, land planning, and so on—expenditures which created no corporate assets in any ordinary sense of the term, no physical structures or income-producing properties. Consequently the T.V.A. did not attempt to give effect to these so-called "developmental" expenditures in its first financial report (fiscal year 1934).[35] They did not appear at all on the asset side of the balance sheet, and on the liabilities side they were deducted from the appropriation advances to secure the "appropriated capital" figure.

While this procedure seemed quite proper, it did mean that the balance sheet did not reflect the Authority's complete financial position nor account for all funds received from Congress. Because of this fact, the 1935 financial statement adopted a different policy, presenting a balance sheet in which the principal asset classification was not fixed assets but "net investment in programs," under which heading were included net expenditures of all T.V.A. programs.[36] The principal purpose of the 1935 statement was conceived to be an accounting to Congress for expenditures made, and so the theory

35. *Annual Report, 1934*, pp. 56–57.
36. *Ibid.*, 1935, p. 63.

that every expenditure increased an asset had to be adopted. The liabilities side of the balance sheet was headed "appropriations and liabilities," and listed the total appropriations without any deduction. The resulting statement was not a very satisfactory one, and it was hardly a "balance sheet" by ordinary standards.[37] In recognition of that fact, a similar statement in the 1936 and 1937 annual reports was called simply a "statement of application of funds," one side of which was headed "appropriations and liabilities" and the other "application of funds."

The 1938 financial statements reflected the influence of a new comptroller, Mr. E. L. Kohler. The principal statement was once more designated as a balance sheet, with standard headings and classifications.[38] In a return to the theory of the 1934 statement, the fixed asset classification was restored, and expenditures resulting in tangible assets having a substantial service life were capitalized and accounted for as fixed assets. All other expenditures were treated as "program expense," and revenues from the sale of power and other sources were credited against the total gross expense of such programs. On the liabilities side of the balance sheet the resulting net expenses of all programs were deducted from total appropriations received. The recorded net worth of the T.V.A. was thus considered to be contributed capital (appropriations plus property turned over to the T.V.A.) less "the net operating expenses chargeable thereagainst." [39]

Of the six "programs" into which the T.V.A. activities were divided for accounting purposes (navigation, flood control, power, fertilizer, related property operations, and development activities), only two brought in any substantial revenue (power and fertilizer),

37. After looking at this statement, a critic of the T.V.A. wrote: "There need be no hesitation in saying that if any private corporation subject to the regulatory authority of any Washington bureau attempted to offer in the name of a financial statement the travesty that receives this designation in the Authority's annual report, it would subject itself to heavy penalties." James G. Mitchell, "The TVA Decision and the TVA," 47 *The Annalist* 333 (February 28, 1936).

38. *Annual Report, 1938*, pp. 137–38. See *Hearings*, pp. 5995–6185 for Mr. Kohler's detailed explanation of the new statements.

39. *Annual Report, 1938*, p. 123. A simplified version of the T.V.A. balance sheet is given in Table V.

Table V

ASSETS

Cash and cash funds

Cash in U.S. Treasury checking accounts:

General purposes......................	$4,874,919
Emergency continuing fund (Sec. 26)......	1,000,000
Unexpended bond proceeds..............	3,557,654
Balance of appropriations.................	20,098,436

$29,531,009

Current receivables

Wholesale power customers.................	3,307,854
AAA, FWA, and other federal agencies......	427,345
Other..................................	454,899

4,190,098

Long-term receivables (municipalities and cooperatives).........................	3,986,761
Inventories..............................	3,521,007

Fixed assets (at cost, less accrued depreciation)

Multiple-use dams.......................	198,016,217
Other electric plant.....................	83,983,231
Fertilizer plant.........................	3,650,003
General plant...........................	7,280,568
Construction in progress..................	92,364,974
Investigations for future projects...........	351,410

385,646,403

Total.............................. 426,875,278

and only the power program was intended to be run on a commercial basis. Up through 1938 power revenues were not covering power operating costs. From 1939 on, however, there has been substantial annual net income from power, which means that net worth is now contributed capital plus net power income less net expenses of the other programs.

Table V

T.V.A. BALANCE SHEET, JUNE 30, 1941

LIABILITIES

Current liabilities

Accounts payable	$9,844,208	
Employees' accrued leave	2,984,636	
Unpaid pay roll	1,271,957	
Retirement system	142,767	
Accrued bond interest	136,700	
Federal agencies	13,615	
		$14,393,883
Funded debt		65,072,500

Funds appropriated and property transferred,
    less net expense of programs:

Appropriations	336,569,270	
Transfer of assets (Wilson Dam, etc.)	33,898,307	
	370,467,577	

Net expense (or income *) of programs,
    1933–41

Power	*12,184,643	
Navigation	3,840,086	
Flood control	2,619,615	
Fertilizer	13,292,822	
Related property	4,949,902	
Development activities	10,540,900	
	23,058,682	
		347,408,895
Total		426,875,278

As was noted in an earlier chapter, the congressional investigating committee took the view that a single balance sheet covering all T.V.A. programs was undesirable, in that it failed to distinguish between commercial and non-commercial activities. The committee considered it proper, in the case of a non-revenue-producing program such as flood control, to consider "net expense" as a deduction from capital, since expenditures for flood control are not "losses," but simply expenses. The same consideration would apply to all other T.V.A. activities except power. In that field the committee felt that financial results should be reflected in terms of profit and loss.

It is the view of the author that there is no objection to the single balance sheet now issued by the Authority, with its attached statements of net income or expense for the various programs, including power. But, as pointed out already, the writer does feel that in addition to these statements, a separate balance sheet and income and expense statement should be prepared covering power only, much as the British Post Office presents such statements for its telephone and telegraph services. At present the reader of T.V.A. financial statements has to dig out these power data for himself. Separate power reports could be issued without jeopardizing the constitutional position of the T.V.A. power program, or losing sight of the fact that power is simply one partner in a multiple-purpose program of regional development.

INVESTIGATION BY CONGRESS

Congressional authority over administrative agencies rests on a great trilogy—the power to legislate, the power to appropriate, and the power to investigate. This third power is one which hangs over the head of every administrator like a brooding omnipresence. Usually it manifests itself in some routine fashion such as a congressional request for information; only occasionally does it materialize in a full-fledged congressional investigation. But when an investigation does come, it is likely to be an event long remembered in the history of the agency investigated.

The circumstances under which the T.V.A. was subjected to the scrutiny of a joint congressional committee in 1938 have already been indicated in part. The insistence of Chairman Arthur Morgan upon such an investigation and his calculated campaign to secure it were welcomed by the enemies of the T.V.A. Its friends were at first inclined to resist this pressure. Senator Norris came forward with a substitute proposal for an investigation by the Federal Trade Commission. However, he subsequently withdrew the suggestion when it became apparent that nothing less than a full congressional inquiry would be capable of quieting the uproar which Chairman Morgan's charges had caused.

A joint resolution creating a special joint congressional investigating committee was adopted on April 4, 1938. By its terms the committee was directed "to make a full and complete investigation of the administration" of the T.V.A. Act. In particular it was requested to investigate 19 more or less specific points, some of which grew out of Mr. Morgan's charges, while others were inserted by friends of the T.V.A. seeking to establish the facts of power company interference with the T.V.A. program. Enumeration of these 19 areas of investigation was not to exclude examination of any other matters pertaining to the administration and policies of the organization.

Three Democrats and two Republicans from each house of Congress were appointed, making a ten-man committee. Senator A. V. Donahey of Ohio, a weak and colorless figure with no particular ties to the Roosevelt administration, was named by the committee as its chairman. The vice-chairman was Representative (later Senator) James M. Mead of New York. The four Republican members of the committee, who were particularly important in furnishing the drive and the political animus necessary to a thorough job of investigation, were Senator Lynn J. Frazier of North Dakota, a "radical" on the power and government ownership issue; Representative Charles A. Wolverton of New Jersey, who proved to be an exceptionally able and tenacious investigator; and two routine and undistinguished politicians, Senator James J. Davis of Pennsylvania and Representative Thomas A. Jenkins of Ohio. The committee named New Dealer Francis Biddle, later Solicitor General and Attorney General of the United States, as its general counsel. To conduct the engineering phases of the investigation the services of T. A. Panter, of the department of water power of the city of Los Angeles, were secured.

The committee heard its first witness on May 25, 1938, and held its last meeting on December 21 of that year. It sat in Washington, in Knoxville, and in Chattanooga, and in addition made a tour of all the T.V.A. projects. It received 6200 pages of testimony, filling 14 volumes. Exhibits filed totalled 588. Witnesses included not only Mr. Arthur Morgan and all important T.V.A. officials, but also representatives of utilities, of fertilizer interests, and even of the National Association for the Advancement of Colored People.

The final report of the committee was submitted to Congress on April 1, 1939. The majority report was signed by the five Democrats on the committee [40] plus Republican Senator Frazier, who presented brief findings generally favorable to the T.V.A. on each of the points which Congress had instructed the committee to investigate. The findings were buttressed by a 200-page discussion and analysis of the purpose, administration, finances, and program of the Authority, prepared on the basis of the testimony which the committee had received.

Three Republican members of the committee submitted a minority report, generally unfavorable in character. They found that T.V.A. administration had been "neither economical nor efficient"; that the accounting methods were "indefensible"; that the power program did not "pay its way"; that the majority of the board "were determined to make a favorable showing for the T.V.A. without always giving all the pertinent facts"; and that there should be a "complete reorganization" of the Authority.[41] Representative Jenkins submitted a separate dissenting statement in which he charged the committee's general counsel with having hampered the investigation.[42]

This division of the committee largely along party lines was perhaps unfortunate, though hardly unnatural or unexpected. A congressional investigating committee is not an ideal fact-finding instrument. But such an investigation does provide one of the most effective methods possible for instrumenting and emphasizing the

40. One Democratic post was vacant at the close of the investigation.
41. *Report of the Joint Committee,* pp. 271–75.
42. For a general summary of the report, see D. L. Marlett, "TVA Investigation," 15 *Journal of Land and Public Utility Economics* 212–24 (1939), and "TVA Investigation; Minority Views," *ibid.,* pp. 360–64.

public responsibility of an administrative agency. The light which this particular inquiry threw revealed an organization which had made numerous mistakes and errors in judgment, which had been on occasions overzealous, which had a few stupid or incompetent or irresponsible employees, but which had done on the whole a competent and honest job, and which in several fields had been responsible for creative accomplishment touching a new high level in American public administration.

CONTROL BY THE GENERAL ACCOUNTING OFFICE

The General Accounting Office, headed by the Comptroller General of the United States, was created by the Budget and Accounting Act of 1921 to serve as the agent of Congress in auditing government expenditures.[43] The Comptroller General's "audit" differs, however, in two important respects from what is commonly understood as the auditing function. First, his audit examination involves both the fidelity and the legality of transactions. In fact, the principal concern of the audit is to determine whether receipt and expenditure transactions meet the statutory requirements and are properly authorized by law. All disbursements made by accountable officers of the various government agencies are required to be justified by submitting to the General Accounting Office, usually on a monthly basis, the vouchers and all related documents necessary to explain and support each transaction.

The second feature of the Comptroller General's position is his power of fiscal control and his ability to enforce his audit. By reason of his authority to "settle and adjust accounts" he can not only review administrative transactions but can also refuse to approve payment in such transactions as he feels to be unjustified or illegal. This uniting in a single office of the diverse functions of controlling ex-

43. The most complete study of the General Accounting Office is that by Harvey C. Mansfield, *The Comptroller General* (New Haven, 1939); there is a monograph by the same author entitled "The General Accounting Office" in the *Report* of the President's Committee on Administrative Management, pp. 171–201. See also John McDiarmid, *Government Corporations and Federal Funds* (Chicago, 1938), Chap. 6; C. H. Pritchett, "The Relationship of the TVA to the Comptroller General," 15 *Tennessee Law Review* 265–279 (1938).

penditures and of conducting an independent audit is unorthodox, and questionable on the ground that it gives control over administration without responsibility for administration. This control extends also to Treasury receipts and issues. By a refusal to countersign accountable warrants drawn on the Treasury by administrative agencies, the Comptroller General can shut off the funds of any accountable officer.[44] The Comptroller General, then, is not simply or even primarily an auditor, but a control officer from whose decisions and legal interpretations there is no effective method of appeal.[45]

For a government corporation which is seeking to establish its own system of accounting and auditing, and which claims immunity from many of the statutes which it is the job of the Comptroller General to enforce, the question of relationship to the General Accounting Office is of paramount importance. It is thus surprising to discover that the drafters of the T.V.A. Act paid little attention either to the problem of audit or of relationship to federal statutes. Earlier Muscle Shoals bills had made provision for a governmental audit by the General Accounting Office and a commercial audit by private accountants. In 1933, however, Senator Norris eliminated the commercial audit from his bill and drafted a section requiring the Comptroller General to audit the transactions of the corporation at least once each fiscal year, and to report the results to Congress and the President, with special report on any transaction or condition in conflict with the legal powers or duties of the corporation.

These provisions seemed to contemplate a different type of audit from that regularly made by the Comptroller General. No authority was given to "settle and adjust" the corporation's accounts, and the making of an annual audit report was contrary to the usual continuous audit procedure. However, there were no specific provisions in the statute such as had previously been used by Congress

44. Harvey Mansfield comments that this control "is in effect the appropriating power of Congress, freed from the salutary influence of democratic controls" (p. 244).
45. The President's Committee on Administrative Management came to the conclusion that the present auditing system needed to be radically modified. Their recommendation that the post of Comptroller General as at present constituted be abolished was one of the issues in the bitter battle over administrative reorganization in 1938.

to keep the Fleet Corporation and the Reconstruction Finance Corporation out of General Accounting Office control. There was no attempt to indicate the extent of the corporation's accountability or its position under federal statutes, except for certain specific exemptions, principally from the civil service laws. The faulty drafting of the Act laid the basis for the controversy that subsequently developed with the Comptroller General.

The first issue to arise concerned the kind of audit to be made. The original assumption of Comptroller General John R. McCarl was that T.V.A. was subject to the regular audit, and his office requested, soon after organization of the T.V.A., that monthly accounts current with supporting schedules be sent to Washington, along with all paid checks and executed copies of contracts. Officials of the T.V.A. had contemplated that there would be a field audit of their accounts at corporation headquarters in Knoxville, but as a measure of cooperation they agreed to submit skeleton accounts to Washington. Without the supporting evidence the Comptroller General could not pass on the legality of the various expenditures.

The Comptroller General apparently accepted the Authority's claim to special field audit, and sent a crew of auditors to Knoxville to conduct a post-audit of transactions for the fiscal year 1934. He subsequently repented of this decision, and attempted to persuade the T.V.A. to send its full accounts to Washington for audit. In February, 1935, having failed to convince the T.V.A. that it should give up rights which it clearly enjoyed under the statute, General Accounting Office auditors were sent to Knoxville presumably for a permanent continuous post-audit.

Although an agreement was thus reached as to the place of audit, more fundamental differences were soon to be disclosed. In April, 1935, the Comptroller General completed and made public his audit report on T.V.A. transactions for the fiscal year 1934. The feature of this lengthy document was a detailed list of payments, totalling $2,013,327, to which the auditors registered exceptions. The report also contained financial statements, general discussion of the organization and activities of the T.V.A., and miscellaneous unorganized and critical comment on the Authority's financial and purchasing practices.

The material contained in the audit report, and the hostile tone that characterized it, made it of great value to opponents of the T.V.A. In Congress and in the press the report was presented as proof that there had been inefficiency in operation, reckless waste of public funds, and even fraud on the part of those administering the corporation's business. Senator Austin charged that the audit had revealed "defalcations," "violations of the law," and the "most astounding state of affairs that has ever occurred in the handling of the public money of the United States." [46] The T.V.A. board was called before the House Military Affairs Committee in connection with the report.

Actually the report made no charges of fraud or misapplication of funds. The exceptions registered were of the same type as the Comptroller General constantly makes to transactions of regular government agencies in cases where his office feels that statutory authority for an expenditure is lacking or that government regulations are not being observed. In many cases an explanation was all that was needed. Many exceptions were obviously erroneous or based on inadequate evidence or faulty judgments.

Fundamentally, however, there was one basic issue on which the two parties disagreed, and that was whether the T.V.A. was subject to regular federal statutes and regulations in its procurement and in the general conduct of its fiscal affairs. The Comptroller General had from the beginning maintained that the T.V.A. was bound by these statutes and was required to follow ordinary government practices, and the audit report furnished the first real occasion for him to challenge the Authority's assumption of corporate administrative freedom. The position of the T.V.A. was that, because it was a corporation, "the acts of Congress relating to contracts, expenditures, and accounting and budget control, which refer only to government departments, agencies and/or bureaus, are not legally applicable to or binding upon it." The Authority held that "upon all

46. 79 *Cong. Rec.* 7134 ff. (1935); quoted by McDiarmid, *op. cit.,* p. 132.

questions of its status, powers, and duties, the Act of Congress by which it was created and which constitutes its charter is controlling, and that wherever the letter or spirit of that Act is in conflict with general statutes or Government regulations, such statutes or regulations must yield to the basic law." [47]

In spite of this contention, the T.V.A. did in practice attempt to conform "with all general statutes and Government regulations governing the use or expenditure of public funds insofar as such compliance does not substantially interfere with the efficiency of our operations." Thus, in the important field of procurement, the system adopted was based upon that used by the Navy Department; government forms were employed, and the necessity for advertising, competition, and award to the lowest responsible bidder was recognized. However, corporation officials assumed that they had a degree of discretion which could be exercised when good business judgment demanded it and, relying on this interpretation of the corporation's powers, they made a number of purchases by methods which were apparently at variance with the procedures prescribed by federal statutes as interpreted by the Comptroller General. For example, low bids were rejected in cases where a slightly greater expenditure would secure a much superior product or one with excess capacity, where the experience of the low bidder was inadequate, where it was desired to secure different makes of equipment for comparative purposes to guide future buying, where previous experience had proved the low bidder's equipment to be unsatisfactory, and so on.

Similarly in other fields the T.V.A. established administrative procedures which appeared to contravene general federal statutes. Because the corporation was subject to suit in the courts, it adopted a procedure for handling claims brought against it, so that as many cases as possible could be settled by compromise out of court. The T.V.A. carried on its extensive land acquisition program entirely with its own personnel, and did not act through federal district at-

47. Quoted from unpublished T.V.A. reply to Comptroller General's audit report for fiscal year 1934.

torneys, nor condemn land through the Department of Justice, nor secure the Attorney General's approval on the title of all lands purchased, as the statutes require regular government agencies to do.[48] Printing services were occasionally secured from private firms, although the general requirement is that printing for government agencies be performed at the Government Printing Office.[49] All such deviations from regular federal practice were challenged by the Comptroller General.

This controversy obviously needed the attention of Congress, which happened to be engaged at the time of the audit report on amendments to the T.V.A. Act. In both houses there were proposed specific amendments giving the Comptroller General complete authority to settle and adjust the accounts of the T.V.A., and requiring the corporation to comply with federal statutes. These were rejected, but no language was added which would clarify the audit provision in the act. So the two parties were left to fight out their own battle. The Comptroller General immediately notified the T.V.A., in September, 1935, that he was discontinuing the field audit, which he contended had proved unsatisfactory. For justification in attempting to revert to regular auditing procedure, he pointed to a provision in a recently-adopted T.V.A. appropriation act requiring all moneys available to the T.V.A. to be "covered into and accounted for as one fund." [50] In other words, the General Accounting Office contended that although both houses of Congress had voted down specific proposals to establish regular auditing control over the T.V.A., they had unwittingly approved such control by the two words "accounted for" in an appropriation act.[51] T.V.A. officials chal-

48. 40 U.S.C.A. 255–57. See H. J. Hitching and P. P. Claxton, Jr., "Practice and Procedure in Eminent Domain Cases under the TVA Act," 16 *Tennessee Law Review* 952–59 (1941).

49. 44 U.S.C.A. 111.

50. 49 Stat. 597; for the history of this provision, which was sponsored by T.V.A. officials to simplify their accounting, see House Doc. 181, 74th Cong., 1st sess. Harvey Mansfield comments that "Mr. McCarl proceeded to effect a personal repeal of the Amendment Act" (p. 241).

51. The Comptroller apparently recognized the weakness of this position, for in a later report to Congress he justified the change solely on the basis of reducing the audit cost. See *Annual Report of the Acting Comptroller General*, 1937, p. 68.

lenged this interpretation of the law, and countered with compromise proposals, but they were met with an ultimatum to the effect that the Comptroller General would not continue to approve advances from the Treasury if there was further resistance. Faced with the threat of having its funds cut off, the T.V.A. had no choice but to capitulate, and the submission of accounts to Washington was begun in February, 1936.

The agreement thus reached did not extend to the question of the Authority's accountability under federal statutes and the Comptroller General's power to enforce his audit, upon which controversy continued. When the new auditing procedure was instituted, the Comptroller General stated that the accounts of the corporation would be "settled and adjusted as other accounts but in the light, of course, of the wide statutory authority vested in the Directors of the Tennessee Valley Authority." [52] In actual practice, however, difficulties continued, even in respect to purchasing, where Congress took special action to insure a reasonable degree of freedom for the corporation. When the T.V.A. Act was being amended in 1935, several proposals to make the Authority subject to regular government purchasing statutes (principally Section 3709 of the Revised Statutes) were turned down in favor of an amendment adopted "to meet the special requirements of the Authority." [53] The new provision required the corporation to make awards on the basis of competitive bidding, except in cases of emergency, in the securing of repair parts or supplemental equipment, and in the procurement of supplies or services not exceeding $500. The T.V.A. was also authorized to take into account, in comparing bids, such factors as quality, time of delivery, and the bidder's experience and responsibility. The procedure thus required was substantially that which the corporation was already employing.

The Comptroller General, however, did not interpret these new provisions as broadening in any important respects the corporation's discretion in procurement. He continued to consider the T.V.A. as

52. Unpublished letter, January 20, 1936.
53. 79 *Cong. Rec.* 10792 (1935).

bound to follow regular government procedures, and to enforce Section 3709 of the Revised Statutes upon the corporation, which was thus handicapped in its goal of achieving a speedy and flexible procurement system. Chairman Morgan in 1936 protested against the "red tape" and "bureaucracy" of the corporation's purchasing procedure.[54] He spoke particularly of the difficulty of drafting specifications, which must accurately describe the Authority's needs but not be so tight as to exclude competition or to favor one particular manufacturer.

Similarly in other fields the General Accounting Office appeared to make no allowance for the corporate status of the T.V.A. or to modify its regular requirements even though insistence upon them led to absurd consequences. The purchase of books of ice tickets at a discount was excepted because it involved the advance of government funds. The purchase of necessary personal equipment for T.V.A. employees, such as boots, slickers, gloves, and goggles, was disapproved on the ground that such material can be furnished by the government only in emergency or to temporary employees. The General Accounting Office objected to the T.V.A. pay roll voucher form, and excepted the entire pay roll for one month on the ground that sufficient supporting detail had not been given.[55] The Authority's practice of contracting with experts for their services in land condemnation cases and paying them in proportion to the value of their services was objected to by the General Accounting Office on the ground that the experts could be subpoenaed and compelled to give their testimony at the cost of only the nominal court witness fees—a point of view which the T.V.A. chief counsel branded as "utter nonsense." [56]

While the Comptroller General reluctantly admitted that, because it was subject to suit, the T.V.A. might be permitted to compromise some claims brought against it, he insisted that his office

54. Speech of July 29, 1936.
55. 16 Ops. Comp. Gen. 239.
56. Hearings before House Military Affairs Committee on H.R. 4961, "Amending the Tennessee Valley Authority Act," 77th Cong., 1st sess., p. 103 (1941).

must give final approval to any such settlement. The approach which the General Accounting Office took to the compromise of claims may be illustrated by the following example. Hardin County, Tennessee, had agreed to pay a stipulated sum to the T.V.A. for the privilege of entering certain county students in a school run by the T.V.A. for children of its employees. Payment was refused and the T.V.A. filed suit. But the T.V.A. lawyers came to the conclusion that even if a judgment was obtained, collection would be difficult since the county was without funds that could be reached by execution. Consequently they negotiated a settlement, accepting $3,500 in cash in settlement of the $4,444.45 claim. This very satisfactory outcome was denounced by the General Accounting Office as illegal and unauthorized.[57]

Following the adoption of the regular auditing procedure in 1936, General Accounting Office exceptions to T.V.A. transactions and expenditures such as those just indicated accumulated at the rate of several thousand a year. The procedure was simply that the Comptroller General would notify the T.V.A. of the transactions to which objection was made, and the T.V.A. would then attempt to supply additional information or to make an explanation which would satisfy the objection. The explanations might or might not be considered satisfactory.[58] In the latter case, the Comptroller General did not attempt to compel recovery on the transaction, as he normally would under his regular audit powers. This failure to seek a show-down seemed to indicate that the General Accounting Office was not sure of its power to "settle and adjust" the corporation's accounts. There was a method of enforcement which the General Accounting Office clearly did have, however, and which it was required by the T.V.A. Act to exercise—namely, an annual audit report to Congress. After the first ill-fated effort in 1934, however, no

57. *Ibid.*, p. 100.
58. For example, of the exceptions totalling over $2,000,000 for the fiscal year 1934, all except $89,585.70 had been withdrawn by the General Accounting Office by 1938 (83 *Cong. Rec.* 3115 [1938]), and by May, 1942, only $92.85 in exceptions remained.

such reports were prepared or sent to Congress. In his regular annual report to Congress for the fiscal year 1937, the Acting Comptroller General did indicate that his office was working on these reports. He noted that during the fiscal years 1936 and 1937 his office had taken exception to the astounding total of 7,964 T.V.A. transactions, involving expenditures of $15,542,459.70. About one-third of the exceptions were released, he reported, "after proper explanation or recovery." [59]

This report was accepted by some members of Congress as an additional reason why the T.V.A. needed a congressional investigation, and Senator Bridges made the ridiculous accusation that the T.V.A. had been "suppressing" the Comptroller General's audit reports.[60] Accordingly, when the investigating committee was established, the joint resolution charged it with determining "whether the Authority had interfered with the Comptroller General's audits of the Authority required to be submitted annually to Congress."

The committee received full information on the relationships of the General Accounting Office and the T.V.A. from representatives of the Comptroller General and from the Authority's comptroller, Mr. Kohler.[61] The Acting Comptroller General outlined the development of the whole controversy, contending that because of the refusal of the T.V.A. to submit its paid checks to the General Accounting Office,[62] because of alleged refusal of access to T.V.A. files and records, and because of "the position taken by officials of the Authority," it had been "extremely difficult to conduct an audit of the financial transactions involved. . . ." [63] A representative of the General Accounting Office who had been responsible for the T.V.A. audit was examined by the committee, and contributed such astounding pieces of nonsense as that Henry Ford had offered $100,-000,000 for Muscle Shoals, and that the regular types of commercial

59. *Annual Report of the Acting Comptroller General, 1937*, p. 68.
60. 83 *Cong. Rec.* 3102 (1938).
61. *Hearings*, pp. 4405–4694, 5893–5949.
62. For the reasons why the T.V.A. preferred to retain its cancelled checks in Knoxville, and for an example of General Accounting Office red tape, see *Hearings*, pp. 5906–7.
63. *Ibid.*, p. 4434.

audit conducted by private auditing firms are worthless, "rubber-stamp" affairs.[64]

Mr. Kohler, following for the Authority, condemned the "hearsay and fantasy" which the General Accounting Office employees had presented to the committee, and frankly expressed his belief in the "incompetence" of the auditors [65] sent to examine the T.V.A. records. He explained to the committee why the Comptroller General's "audit" was of no value to him as a financial executive. The things he expected of a real audit were that it be timely; that it be made at the offices of the Authority; that it examine the Authority's system of internal check; that it give a comparison of operating results with those of business enterprises; that it be made by persons having varied and constant touch with business affairs who would be able to make recommendations on financial, accounting, and management policies; and that examination of individual transactions should not be considered as the sole end of the audit, but should always be made "with the thought in mind that individual transactions may exemplify proper or improper controls, strong or ineffective policies, or intelligent or weak administration. . . . Administrative catharsis is not automatically effected by disclosures of peccadilloes but by the study and refinement of methods which will reduce their occurrence." [66]

The majority of the congressional committee accepted for the most part the T.V.A. point of view. The conclusion reached was

> that the fundamental difficulty lies in the fact that General Accounting Office procedures are unsuitable for the examination of the affairs of a government corporation. The General Accounting Office conceives its functions to be that of controlling each item of expenditure made by the agencies under its juris-

64. *Ibid.*, p. 4468, 4505.

65. "Investigators" is a better term, since very few members of the General Accounting Office staff are certified public accountants, and their work is primarily legal investigation of expenditures. The amateurish balance sheet included in the T.V.A. audit report demonstrated their unfamiliarity with such commercial accounting techniques. The representative of the General Accounting Office admitted to the committee that if they were required to make a "commercial audit," it would be the same kind regularly made (*Hearings*, p. 4505).

66. *Hearings*, p. 5902.

diction. Its examination bears less relation to efficiency, than to conformity to the forms of law, as interpreted by itself. Its facilities do not lend themselves to an audit of the books of a corporation, or to presenting a report conveying useful information as to the efficiency and honesty of the management.[67]

The committee felt that if the existing audit relationship was to continue, it should be a periodic commercial audit in the field, with legal questions being determined by the Attorney General. The committee believed it preferable, however, for the General Accounting Office audit to cease, and it recommended the substitution of "an audit by a commercial firm responsible to the Congress and selected annually by a special joint congressional committee appointed for the purpose." [68]

It appeared that these recommendations were to have some effect when ex-Senator Fred Brown, who had been a member of the investigating committee, was appointed Comptroller General in April, 1939. The new head of the G.A.O. agreed that T.V.A. should discontinue submission of detailed accounts to Washington, and ordered the field audit resumed. Revision and consolidation of the G.A.O. audit reports for the fiscal years 1935 through 1938, which had been hurriedly submitted to the investigating committee at its insistence, were discussed, and it appeared that agreement might be reached on the issues raised by them.[69] However, Mr. Brown's health forced him to resign his office, and his successor, Lindsay Warren, proved to be of a different mind. On November 23, 1940, the T.V.A. presented to him a recommendation that the G.A.O. discontinue its exception procedure and instead "appoint a firm of certified public accountants of national reputation to make an annual audit of the accounts of the Authority. . . ." [70] If the exception procedure was to be continued, the T.V.A. made several suggestions for improving

67. *Report of the Joint Committee*, p. 131.
68. *Ibid.*, p. 133.
69. The T.V.A. replies to the audit reports for these four years, as well as to that for the fiscal year 1939, were prepared and submitted to the G.A.O. in June, 1941.
70. Hearings, House Military Affairs Committee, on H.R. 4961, 77th Cong., 1st sess., p. 21.

and facilitating its operation. In a long reply Comptroller General Warren endorsed the legal position taken in the past by his office holding the T.V.A. subject to the full control of the Budget and Accounting Act, and gave notice that the regular audit procedure must be resumed, although promising that he would review the differences between the T.V.A. and his agency in the light of the special corporate position of the Authority.[71]

The T.V.A. replied on February 12, 1941, to the effect that the position taken by the Comptroller General was "inconsistent both with the express provisions of our governing statute and the intent of the Congress," and stating that since a stalemate had been reached on this question of law, the Authority had proceeded to bring the matter to an issue by requesting the Treasury Department to revise the procedure of releasing T.V.A. funds. Since the Comptroller General's power over the T.V.A. rested on his ability to cut off its funds by refusing to countersign accountable warrants, the T.V.A. asked the Treasury to issue it funds on settlement warrants instead.[72] The Treasury's general counsel agreed that settlement warrants could be used, but said they would have to be accompanied by certificates of settlement from the General Accounting Office.[73] The Treasury Department referred the matter to the Department of Justice, and on June 9, 1941, the Attorney General ruled that the T.V.A. was not accountable to the General Accounting Office, and consequently that settlement warrants could be used.[74] Consequently, on June 16 the T.V.A. requested the Treasury to transfer $5,000,000 to the T.V.A. checking account on settlement warrant. The request was submitted to the General Accounting Office for certification that the balance remaining in T.V.A. funds was sufficient to cover the request.[75] The Comptroller General did not propose to be circumvented in this manner and held up this request, stating that he was seeking to discover whether there was any au-

71. The entire communication is printed in *ibid.*, pp. 17–29.
72. *Ibid.*, pp. 14–15.
73. *Ibid.*, pp. 77–95.
74. *Ibid.*, pp. 72–77.
75. *Ibid.*, p. 114.

thority of law for him to issue such a certificate, and that if the
T.V.A. needed funds in the meantime, they would have to continue
using the established system of accountable warrants.[76]

Meanwhile, on June 2, 1941, the Comptroller General had
thrown the whole matter into the lap of Congress, reporting in a
letter to the Speaker of the House the disagreement, and suggesting
that Congress adopt an amendment to the T.V.A. statute clearly exempting the T.V.A. from his control, or clearly subjecting it to such
control.[77] A bill was immediately introduced to give effect to the
latter suggestion, but eventually a compromise satisfactory to both
sides was reached. The T.V.A. was to be made definitely accountable under the Budget and Accounting Act, but with the following
proviso:

> Provided, That, subject only to the provisions of the Ten-
> nessee Valley Authority Act of 1933, as amended, the Corpora-
> tion is authorized to make such expenditures and to enter into
> such contracts, agreements, and arrangements, upon such
> terms and conditions and in such manner as it may deem
> necessary, including the final settlement of all claims and litiga-
> tion by or against the Corporation; and, notwithstanding the
> provisions of any other law governing the expenditure of public
> funds, the General Accounting Office, in the settlement of the
> accounts of the Treasurer or other accountable officer or em-
> ployee of the Corporation, shall not disallow credit for, nor
> withhold funds because of, any expenditure which the Board
> shall determine to have been necessary to carry out the provi-
> sions of said Act.
>
> The Corporation shall determine its own system of admin-
> istrative accounts and the forms and contents of its contracts
> and other business documents except as otherwise provided in
> the Tennessee Valley Authority Act of 1933, as amended.[78]

This amendment, which became law on November 21, 1941, meant
that the T.V.A. would lose the advantage of its field audit. However,
the Authority was to be limited only by the provisions of the T.V.A.

76. *Ibid.* (telegram of June 24, 1941).
77. *Ibid.*, pp. 13–16.
78. 55 Stat. 775–76.

Act in authorizing expenditures and settling claims, and if any exception was taken to an expenditure, it could be wiped out by a certification on the part of the T.V.A. Board that the expenditure was necessary to carry out the provisions of the Act. Thus the long disagreement was terminated with a reasonable victory for the cause of corporate freedom, and with a result as satisfactory as it is possible to get short of a fundamental revision of the powers and procedures of the General Accounting Office.

In addition to the governmental audit by the Comptroller General, the T.V.A. has also, since 1938, employed a firm of certified public accountants to make an annual commercial audit of the Authority's accounts. This audit includes an examination of the corporation's balance sheet and supporting schedules, review of the system of internal control and accounting procedures, and test examinations of T.V.A. accounting records. The certification of the accountants' examination is included along with the Authority's annual financial report.

T.V.A. IN THE COURTS

A vital element in the government corporation concept has been liability to suit in the courts. Section 4 (b) of the T.V.A. Act provides that the agency "may sue and be sued in its corporate name." The result is that the T.V.A. may more easily be held accountable for its acts in the courts than ordinary government departments which have the protection of governmental immunity. It is true, however, that most of the important court actions brought against the T.V.A. have been of the type to which any government agency is subject. The suability of the corporation perhaps rendered it easier for some litigants to get the agency into court, but usually they would have been able to seek redress in some other fashion had the Authority itself not been subject to suit. Thus Arthur E. Morgan was able to test the President's power to remove him by bringing suit against the corporation for back salary in the chancery court for Knox County. But if this avenue had not been open, he could have proceeded as did the ousted Federal Trade Commissioner,

William E. Humphrey, to bring suit in the United States Court of Claims. The Authority's liability to suit has been important chiefly in laying the corporation open to claims of various sorts, necessitating the adoption of procedures for compromising and adjusting damage claims out of court, and in making the salaries of its employees subject to garnishment proceedings.[79] The procedure for condemnation of land needed by the Authority is specified in section 25 of the T.V.A. Act.[80]

The great bulk of the important T.V.A. litigation has been in connection with the power program, to which reference has already been made. During the early period the favorite method of attacking this program was by alleging its unconstitutionality. In the first five years of the Authority's existence, 41 cases were instituted in the courts involving the constitutional issue.[81] The T.V.A. was named as a party defendant in 19 of these suits; in the other 22, the defendants were either municipalities or cooperatives seeking to purchase T.V.A. power, or the Public Works Administration which planned to loan or grant them the funds with which to secure the necessary power facilities. In all of the cases the courts either eventually held the T.V.A. Act to be constitutional, or disposed of the suit favorably to the Authority without passing directly on the constitutional question.[82]

A total of 38 preliminary injunctions was sought against the T.V.A. during its first five years, of which 12 were denied and 26 granted. Of the latter number, 25 were later dissolved, and one was made permanent. These temporary injunctions greatly hampered the development of T.V.A. power operations. The Authority esti-

79. That liability to suit in the case of a government agency includes the right to bring garnishment proceedings was finally decided by the Supreme Court in *Federal Housing Administration* v. *Burr*, 309 U.S. 242 (1940). For a review of earlier decisions on this point, see John Thurston, *op. cit.*, pp. 56–58.

80. In 1942 Senator McKellar sponsored an amendment which would have transferred such cases from a court-appointed commission to juries of local citizens.

81. *Report of the Joint Committee*, pp. 62–3.

82. The three basic Supreme Court decisions were *Ashwander* v. *T.V.A.*, 297 U.S. 288 (1936); *Alabama Power Co.* v. *Ickes*, 302 U.S. 464 (1938); and *Tennessee Electric Power Co.* v. *T.V.A.*, 306 U.S. 118 (1939).

mated losses to consumers and to itself by reason of the injunctions granted as over $13,000,000.[83]

Apart from the constitutional issue, questions growing out of the position of the T.V.A. as a corporation and its relationship to general statutes affecting federal agencies, constituted perhaps the most interesting type of issue litigated. Earlier in this chapter attention was called to the two contrasting lines of Supreme Court decisions with respect to whether government corporations were to be treated in law as a part of the government or apart from the government. The extent to which this issue was raised in the suit brought by the Authority's ousted chairman has already been mentioned.

A problem in the same field was presented in the case of *Pierce v. United States*,[84] decided by the Supreme Court in 1941. The issue was whether a private individual who falsely represented himself as an employee of the T.V.A. in connection with a money-raising scheme had violated the federal statute covering false representation as "an officer or employee acting under the authority of the United States, or any department, or any officer of the Government. . . ." The court held that this language did not cover the case of an individual pretending to act under the authority of a government owned corporation. Support for this view was gained from the fact that, subsequent to the offense involved in this case, Congress had amended the statute specifically to cover corporations owned or controlled by the United States.[85] Reliance was also placed upon the earlier precedent of *United States v. Strang*,[86] in which the court had held that an employee of the Fleet Corporation was not an agent of the United States within "the true intendment" of another section of the Criminal Code.

In general, the burden of proof must be on any government agency which seeks release from normal governmental procedures.

83. *Report of the Joint Committee*, p. 66.
84. 62 S.C. 237 (1941).
85. 52 Stat. 82 (1938).
86. 254 U.S. 491 (1921).

But a trading enterprise differs so substantially from an ordinary government department as to be perfectly justified in seeking recognition of these differences, particularly in its financial arrangements and controls. Indeed, a failure to make such modifications is almost certain to handicap seriously the work of the agency.

This review has shown the T.V.A. to be in some measure successful in securing consideration for its peculiar needs. Whether the result should be described as "corporate freedom" is dubious, however, for as the writer has pointed out in more detail elsewhere,[87] the concept of the government corporation has been largely drained of its meaning in recent years. To the extent that the T.V.A. has been able to secure a certain measure of administrative elbow-room, the reason was not its corporate status so much as congressional conviction that successful operation of the Authority required it. The T.V.A. certainly has not achieved "the essential freedom and elasticity of a private business corporation," which the congressional committee so hopefully forecast in 1933. That is, in fact, a goal to which a government agency cannot and should not aspire, for it is not consonant with the claims of public responsibility. But the T.V.A. has been granted a reasonable measure of autonomy which it has on the whole used so wisely as to defeat all efforts to force its administration back into the regular departmental mold.

87. "The Paradox of the Government Corporation," 1 *Public Administration Review* 381–89 (1941).

9: Personnel Administration

> "I am beginning to suspect that one reason why these Federal corporations are created is for the purpose of evading the operation of the national civil service laws."—*Senator Bruce (1924)*

IN NO FIELD has the T.V.A. achieved greater success than in the administration of its personnel program and policies. And, apart from the controversy among the board members, no area of T.V.A. administration has received greater attention from the public generally. The Authority's corporate freedom from traditional civil service methods, the determination of its directors to establish a new deal for labor in the T.V.A., and the work of an especially competent and enlightened personnel department, have combined to form a unique and universally-recognized record of accomplishment in the personnel field.

THE PERSONNEL PROBLEM IN THE T.V.A.

The most important factor conditioning the personnel problem in the T.V.A. has been its freedom from the federal civil service system. The question as to whether the personnel of the Muscle Shoals corporation should be appointed under regular civil service procedures was fought out as early as 1924 in the U.S. Senate. The first Norris bills did not specifically exempt the corporation from civil service, but such a status was clearly implied. In 1924 Senator W. Cabell Bruce proposed to amend the current Norris bill so as to place the corporation under civil service, and in the extended debate which the amendment aroused the case for and against civil service in a government enterprise was put very well.[1]

1. 66 *Cong. Rec.* 188–93, 269–72, 296–301 (1924).

Senator Furnifold M. Simmons stated the principle that the civil service laws should cover only purely governmental functions, and that when the government "engages in private business, then it subjects itself to the rules that obtain and apply to private business." He felt that the proposed corporation would be greatly handicapped under civil service, and wanted to know how it could "efficiently function under the handicap of having its employees selected by an outside agency, applying a test which probably no man engaged in that particular business in a private way would apply." [2] It was contended that the Civil Service Commission was not accustomed to supplying the type of business and professional personnel which the corporation would require. Perhaps the most effective case against civil service in a government enterprise was made by Senator James W. Wadsworth, who was opposed to the Norris government operation proposal. He said:

> If we are to impose restrictions and subject the whole thing to civil-service rules, the management of the corporation will have lost that most valuable privilege which should inure to every business man who is to be held responsible for the success of a business undertaking—he will have lost the right to hire and fire. . . . .You may apply civil service rules . . . if you please; but do not hope to pay dividends. [3]

Senator Bruce's position was that without the civil service requirement positions in the corporation would be filled on a political and patronage basis. In defense of the practicability of his plan he pointed out that "many applicants seeking positions of the most highly specialized or technical character are subjected to competitive examination at the hands of the United States Civil Service Commission." [4] It is interesting to note that Senator Norris at first accepted the Bruce amendment,[5] but later decided that civil service would detract from the efficiency of the corporation. He took the position, and was almost alone in doing so, that a merit system was

2. *Ibid.*, p. 190.
3. *Ibid.*, pp. 190–91.
4. *Ibid.*, p. 188.
5. *Ibid.*, p. 186.

possible outside the protection of the civil service. All of his measures contained provisions requiring appointments and promotions to be made on the basis of merit and efficiency, and forbidding the application of political tests or qualifications. He proposed to put sanctions behind these provisions by requiring publicity for all requests relating to appointments or promotions, and by making it a misdemeanor for political considerations to influence the official action of any member of the board. In this way he hoped to escape the dilemma which Senator Wadsworth said was inevitable in government operation, namely, having civil service and inefficiency, or having no civil service and a spoils system.

The final T.V.A. Act embodied the Norris plan for this new form of merit service. The Authority was specifically exempted from operation of the civil service laws, but the selection and promotion of personnel were required to be made on the basis of merit and efficiency.[6] The Authority was thus given freedom to set up its own system of recruitment, with the expectation, at least in some quarters, that independence from the Civil Service Commission would enable the corporation to adopt more effective methods of selection. The injunction against political influence, it must be admitted, assumed an honesty and good faith in administration which was scarcely justified by past experience or the prevailing political mores.

The special character of the T.V.A. personnel problem was established by other factors peculiar to the organization. A range of positions exceptionally wide for a government agency had to be filled—engineers of all kinds, chemists, fertilizer experts, agriculturalists, foresters, regional planners, architects, economists, not to mention the staffs for legal, medical, purchasing, personnel, fiscal

6. Section 6 of the T.V.A. Act provides: "In the appointment of officials and the selection of employees for said corporation, and in the promotion of any such employees or officials, no political test or qualification shall be permitted or given consideration, but all such appointments and promotions shall be given and made on the basis of merit and efficiency. Any member of said board who is found by the President of the United States to be guilty of a violation of this section shall be removed from office by the President of the United States, and any appointee of said board who is found by the board to be guilty of a violation of this section shall be removed from office by said board."

and other administrative services. Moreover, the Authority's decision to carry on its construction operations by its own forces, rather than through private contractors, meant that it had to assume the obligations of hiring and managing a trades and labor force of thousands of skilled and unskilled workers. The distinction between this trades and labor force and the white collar group (called "salary-policy" employees) must be kept in mind.[7] Composition of T.V.A. personnel by classes, at the end of the fiscal year 1941, was as follows:

Salary Policy Employees	
Professional and scientific	1,492
Subprofessional	1,182
Clerical, administrative, and fiscal	2,758
Educational	29
Inspectional	192
Custodial	938
Trades and Labor Employees	
Annual employees	1,917
Hourly employees	13,998
Total	22,506

T.V.A. personnel administration has had to face two emergency periods. The first came immediately after the organization was set up. There was at that time little conception of the size the agency might attain. The original assumption was that Norris Dam would be the only large construction project undertaken, and that the peak employment would not exceed 5,000 persons. Actually, more than three times that number were employed within two years. Following this initial spurt, total T.V.A. personnel fluctuated seasonally between ten and fifteen thousand for five years. Then the national defense program ushered in a second emergency period, which saw T.V.A. personnel grow from 14,000 in the middle of 1940 to 22,500 one year later, and to 40,000 by mid-1942. Both of

7. The salary-policy employees are paid on the basis of annual salary rates. Trades and labor employees are for the most part paid on the basis of hourly wage rates, but permanent trades and labor employees in maintenance, operating, and manufacturing activities are on an annual salary basis.

these periods of rapid expansion set a severe test for the Authority's recruiting system.

Finally, the personnel problem in the T.V.A. has been complicated by reason of the geographical distribution of the Authority's activities over the length and breadth of the Tennessee Valley, and by the necessarily temporary character of the construction projects, requiring a constant process of recruitment and transfer. An appreciation of these difficulties makes all the more significant the outstanding success which the Authority has achieved in the personnel field.[8]

ORGANIZATION FOR PERSONNEL ADMINISTRATION

From the beginning, the T.V.A. policy was one of concentrating control over personnel policies and methods and performance of personnel services in a central personnel department. Such centralization was almost inevitable if the directors were to fulfill the duty imposed upon them by the act to maintain a merit service in the T.V.A. The inauguration of this system was not without its difficulties, however, because so many of the Authority's supervisors and administrative officials were drawn from the engineering field or other branches of private employment, where they had been accustomed to full freedom and direct action in hiring and firing employees and workmen, in regulating wage rates, and in handling problems of employee relations. The transition to a system where such personnel matters were under the control or required the participation of a central personnel agency was not an easy one. In the early days there was undoubtedly a feeling among the engineering and construction supervisors that they were being bound in

8. The most useful general summary of T.V.A. personnel administration is that issued by the T.V.A. in 1942 as Management Services Report No. 1, "Personnel Administration in the Tennessee Valley Authority—Interpreting the Experience of Eight Years" (mimeographed). See also Lee S. Greene, "Personnel Administration in the T.V.A.," 1 *Journal of Politics* 171–94 (1939); Leonard D. White, "Survey of the Personnel Department, T.V.A.," Senate Doc. 56, 76th Cong., 1st sess., part 2, pp. 65–86 (1939). Testimony on T.V.A. personnel matters appears in the joint committee hearings at pp. 1544–69, 3136–3293, 3360–77, and 3397–3429. An unpublished doctoral dissertation on the subject was prepared by R. Ward Stewart at Harvard University in 1938.

red tape and subjected to delays and controls by personnel officials who did not understand their problems or talk their language. But eventually there was general recognition of the necessity for establishing regularized procedures which would give fair consideration to all applicants for employment, ensure equal pay for equal work, and in general guarantee the equality of treatment required when public rather than private funds are being expended. For its part the personnel department bent every effort to emphasize its service rather than its control functions, and continuously studied its organization in order to develop more effective methods of cooperation with the line departments.

Upon the organization of the T.V.A., Chairman A. E. Morgan selected as the first director of personnel, Floyd W. Reeves, professor of educational administration at the University of Chicago.[9] Under Mr. Reeves' direction the major personnel policies were worked out, and divisions were built up for handling the principal personnel tasks—employment (including classification), training, labor relations, records, safety, and health and medical work. In addition, the personnel department was given responsibilities outside its primary field for which there was no other convenient place —the division of camp management and the post of library coordinator were in the department, and the health and medical section handled public health problems as well as employee health. The director of personnel was also head of a separate social and economic research division. Eventually, however, the extraneous functions were sloughed off, and the personnel department shook down into four major divisions—employment, classification, personnel relations, and training.

In the development of personnel department organization, the two problems which received more attention than any others were (a) central office-field office relationships, and (b) personnel department-line department relationships. The field office problem

9. Since Mr. Reeves' resignation in 1936, the post of director of personnel has been held by three men, Gordon Clapp, Arthur Jandrey, and George Gant. In each case the appointee had served as assistant to the preceding director, and had secured his training in public personnel administration within the T.V.A.

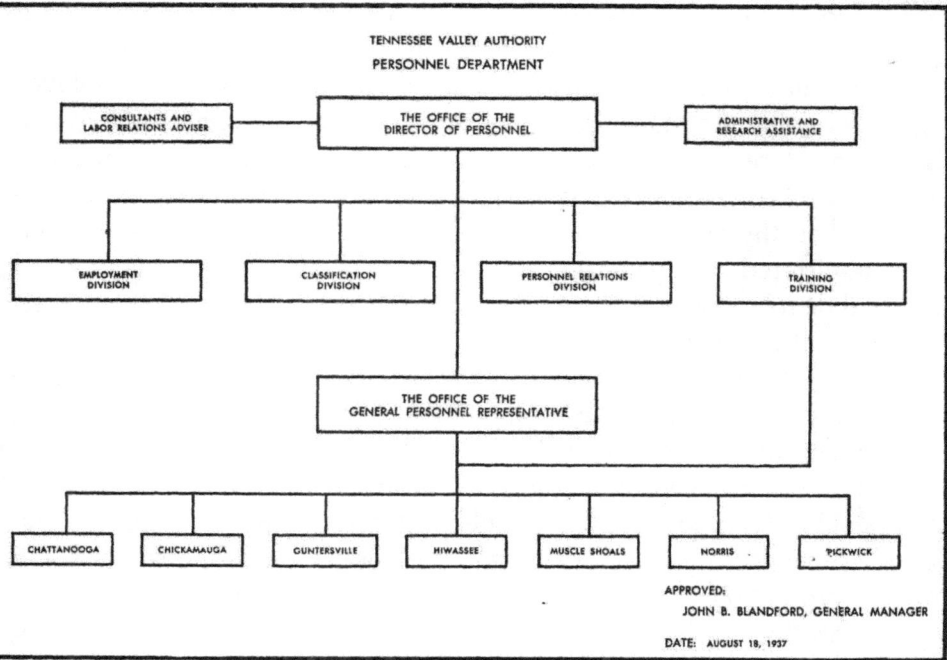

TENNESSEE VALLEY AUTHORITY
PERSONNEL DEPARTMENT

CONSULTANTS AND LABOR RELATIONS ADVISER

THE OFFICE OF THE DIRECTOR OF PERSONNEL

ADMINISTRATIVE AND RESEARCH ASSISTANCE

EMPLOYMENT DIVISION · CLASSIFICATION DIVISION · PERSONNEL RELATIONS DIVISION · TRAINING DIVISION

THE OFFICE OF THE GENERAL PERSONNEL REPRESENTATIVE

CHATTANOOGA · CHICKAMAUGA · GUNTERSVILLE · HIWASSEE · MUSCLE SHOALS · NORRIS · PICKWICK

APPROVED:

JOHN B. BLANDFORD, GENERAL MANAGER

DATE: AUGUST 18, 1937

arose because of the distribution of T.V.A. construction and operating projects throughout the Valley, necessitating a certain decentralization of employment, training, and other personnel responsibilities. Personnel field offices were set up at all important centers of T.V.A. activity, in charge of personnel representatives who were responsible for the direction of all phases of personnel work, except training, in their field areas.[10]

10. The training division, which was operating a broad program of employee training and community educational services, at first maintained its own separate system of branch offices. For representative statements describing the T.V.A. training program, see Management Services Report No. 1, pp. 17–21; A. E. Morgan, "The Man on the Job," 24 *Survey Graphic* 112–16 (1935); F. W. Reeves, "TVA Training," 7 *Journal of Adult Education* 48–52 (1935); Charles E. Ferris and Richard O. Niehoff, "For Practicing Engineers," 11 *ibid.* 431–34 (1939); Maurice F. Seay, "Adult Education," *Bulletin of the Bureau of School Service* (University of Kentucky, 1938), Vol. X, no. 4; Walter H. Kaiser, "Taking the Library to the Worker," 10 *Library Quarterly* 50–59 (1940); Gordon R. Clapp, "Supervisory Training in the T.V.A.," Civil Service Assembly Pamphlet No. 3 (1936).

The responsibilities of the field personnel representatives included the selecting of trade and labor employees from examination lists, advising with supervisors on appointments and transfers, handling minor grievances, participating in developing employee recreation programs, informing supervisors of personnel policies and procedures, and keeping Knoxville informed of developments. The central office of the personnel department, on the other hand, furnished the examination registers of trade and labor candidates, administered compensation and salary determinations, conducted labor relations and handled major grievance cases, established personnel forms, and defined procedures.

Coordination of central office and field activities early became a problem. At first the solution was sought in annual conferences, which all members of the personnel department were called in to attend, and in visits of various central office representatives to the field areas. Subsequently the office of general personnel representative was set up and made responsible for general administration and coordination of the field activities.[11] The general personnel representative visited the field offices regularly, discussing problems, solutions, and improved approaches, and sent out occasional general memoranda. To the central office divisions he made suggestions as to methods for facilitating more effective action in the field. Conferences of the field representatives were held in the central office three or four times a year, with carefully prepared agenda and different personnel representatives serving in rotation as chairmen of the conferences. The work of a typical field officer was described in 1936 as follows:

> 75% of the time is spent in interviewing and selecting candidates for various positions. In the less important positions he exercises final judgment. The filling of more important positions is discussed through frequent contacts with the Employment Section in Knoxville. He makes frequent contacts with supervisory personnel to discuss their personnel requirements. The

11. In addition to this relationship, the field representatives were functionally responsible to the central office employment, classification, and personnel relations divisions in performing duties in those respective fields.

remainder of the time is spent on matters pertaining to employee relations, gathering classification data, assisting the Branch Head of the Training Section in organizing in-service training and job training programs.[12]

By 1938, procedures had become relatively standardized so that central control of the field offices was more automatic and less administrative supervision was required. Improved central registers were concentrating responsibility in the central office, and field reporting procedures were more adequate. Consequently it was found possible to abolish the office of general personnel representative, the field offices being made administratively responsible to the chief of the employment division. Moreover, the administrative separation between training and other personnel functions in the field was ended. Employee training was made the job of the regular field offices, community educational services were transferred out of the personnel department entirely, and the central office staff of the training division became principally responsible for educational relationships. The closer connection between personnel and training officers in the field proved valuable to all parties concerned.

The further development of personnel field organization is merged with the problem of personnel department-line department relationships, to which we may now turn. There has never been any real question in the T.V.A. as to the validity of the original decision to centralize personnel functions in a single department.[13] But adoption of this policy gave the personnel department the responsibility for making its services of the greatest possible use to the line super-

12. Quoted in a memorandum prepared by Milton V. Smith, Richard O. Niehoff, and Lee S. Greene, "Relationships between the Field and the Central Offices in the Personnel Department," August 23, 1941. The discussion above relies in large part on this memorandum.

13. There was, it is true, a measure of decentralization in the engineering organization, in that the general office engineer maintained a control over, or a clearing house for, personnel actions in the engineering departments. But actions which he approved were then handled by the personnel department in the regular way. The personnel files which the engineering organization maintained in its early days were subsequently transferred to the personnel department. The problem of personnel decentralization is discussed in an able memorandum by Ethel L. Reagan and Henry C. Hart, "Departmental Personnel Officers," October 24, 1940, to which the author is indebted.

visors, and reducing personnel red tape. In planning their procedures the personnel officials assumed that line supervisors tended to regard personnel administration as a single problem, and felt that they would be annoyed at having to deal with different divisions in the personnel department and with different technical experts on the various phases of their personnel problems. Solutions were sought which would avoid these difficulties, but it was not until 1940 that a satisfactory one was found in the device of "personnel officers." These officers, while located within the personnel department and responsible to it, were to serve in fact as directors of personnel for the operating departments. Each personnel officer represented the personnel department as a whole in its relationships with a line department, and all contacts between that department and the personnel department were to be through the appropriate personnel officer. He was responsible for seeing that each personnel action affecting his assigned department received coordinated consideration from the specialized divisions in the personnel department. He was expected to become thoroughly familiar with the organizational structure and personnel needs and resources of his assigned departments, and to place this knowledge at the service of the specialized personnel divisions when they had an employment or classification or labor relations or training problem affecting those departments. It was the personnel officer's job to see the personnel problem of a particular line department as a whole, in the same way that the department head saw it, but from the vantage point of the central personnel department.

When the system of personnel officers was first established, they were delegated a considerable measure of responsibility for carrying on training and labor relations activities in their respective jurisdictions. On employment and classification matters, however, they were for the most part simply channels to the specialized personnel divisions where the actual decisions were made. But in 1941 delegations in these two latter fields were also approved, carrying the plan to its logical conclusion. Under the new arrangement, the four specialized divisions really constituted the "central personnel agency," responsible generally for policy formation, the setting of standards, internal personnel management planning, and external managerial aspects of personnel administration, and performing these functions free from the heavy load of individual personnel transactions. The personnel officers, for their part, were the agents of policy execution, handling individual personnel actions, furnishing direct and expeditious service to the line departments, and giving final answers within the lines of the policies established by the central personnel divisions.[14]

In making the plan of delegation effective, it was the task of the employment division to provide the personnel officers with eligible registers, certified lists, and other criteria and procedures designed to maintain adequate standards of merit and efficiency. In the same way the classification division provided class specifications and job descriptions to guide the personnel officers in the proper allocation of positions. In order to ensure that standards of merit and efficiency were maintained under the new system, it was decided to inaugurate periodic personnel surveys or reviews as the best means of gauging the effectiveness with which personnel policies were being executed. The surveys were to be made under the supervision of the classification division, and were to cover the entire program of placement, classification, training opportunities, employee-management relations, and administrative and management analysis.

As put into effect in 1941, personnel officers, under the supervision of a chief personnel officer, were assigned to the departments of chemical engineering, power, management and planning, and engineering and construction, with three additional personnel officers for the Kentucky, Cherokee, and Hiwassee field offices of the engineering and construction departments. For the field offices it will be noted that the new plan involved little change except in

14. Since the above discussion was written, further reorganization (December, 1942) has given even greater operating responsibilities to the chief personnel officer. The employment and classification divisions have been abolished, their operating functons being taken over by the personnel officers and a new examining section under the chief personnel officer, and their work in the field of personnel standards, surveys, and research being assumed by a new "personnel services staff" under the director of personnel.

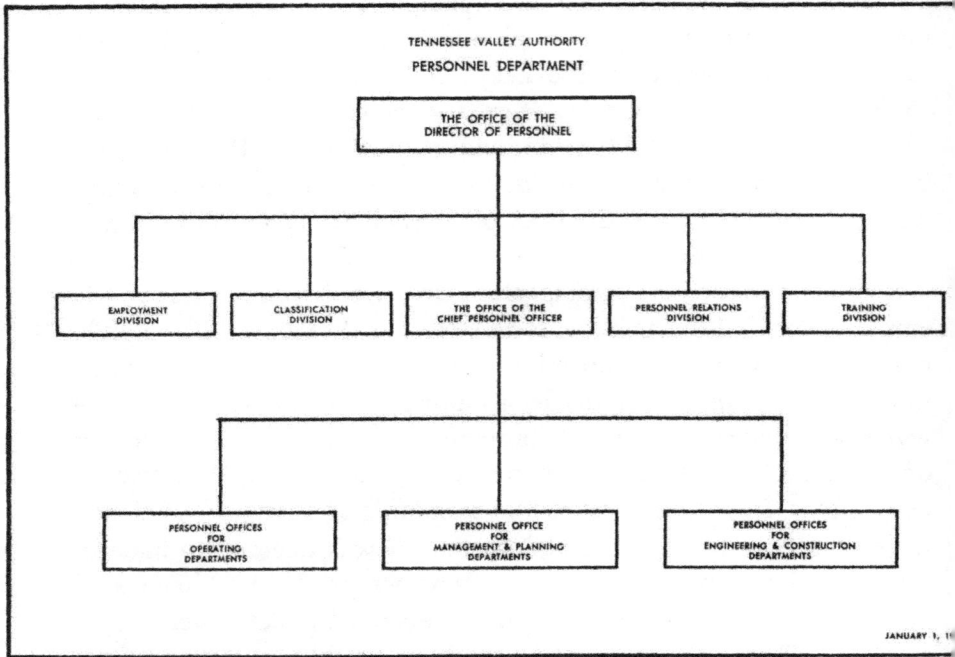

degree of delegation; indeed, the personnel officer device was in essence an application to the rest of the Authority of the type of decentralization first applied in the field offices.

THE T.V.A. MERIT SYSTEM

Selection of personnel in the T.V.A. does not rely heavily upon that time-honored mainstay of civil service, the written examination. Instead, relative ability of applicants is judged by an admittedly subjective process involving analysis of past employment record, training, and other evidence submitted by candidates, supported by reference letters and personal interviews.[15] In discarding

15. Written examinations are used, however, to measure general intelligence and aptitudes where potential ability is a major qualification or where experience is lacking. Such tests have been increasingly used in recent years, with decreasing availability of applicants with established records of experience. Performance tests

written examinations, with their resultant "closed" registers and numerical ranking of candidates according to mathematical scores carried two places beyond the decimal point, the T.V.A. cut itself off from the protection which such mechanical devices give against personal favoritism and political jobbery. But by the same token it opened up the possibility of doing a creative job in the placement field, unhampered by the mechanics and formalism of traditional civil service methods. Fortunately, it was this latter possibility which the T.V.A. chose to exploit. The methods adopted deserve examination in some detail.

Since the T.V.A. is not able to recruit by the usual process of announcing examinations,[16] it must use other methods. The fact that the Authority was set up during a period of widespread unemployment and that its program was well-publicized, made it unnecessary at first to take many positive steps to stimulate applications.[17] But as a long-term policy, and to take care of the situation in specialized fields where sufficient qualified candidates did not apply, the T.V.A. had to adopt a more definite program of publicizing employment opportunities and of searching for individuals with the skills needed. For this purpose contacts were established with universities and graduate professional schools, professional associations and journals, outstanding private enterprises, and government agencies. Advertising was resorted to on occasions, principally in the engineering journals. Registers of the Civil Service Commission were used, though when the T.V.A. first began operations these registers were in many cases too old to be of much assistance. For several years T.V.A. representatives visited colleges and universities in and around the Valley region during the spring to recruit outstanding seniors. By methods such as these, the Authority was assured that its application files were fairly complete and representative of the

are used for typists and stenographers, welders, and draftsmen. Officers in the public safety service are selected through a written test and oral examination.

16. Announced examinations have been employed in the trades and labor field, as will be explained.

17. Engineers had been hard hit by the depression, so that the T.V.A. secured applications from many outstanding men in that field who ordinarily would not have considered employment at government salaries.

available personnel. However, the coverage was not as wide as that which the U.S. Civil Service Commission secures for positions in the regular civil service.[18]

The T.V.A. does establish registers of applicants, but these differ in two important respects from the ordinary registers which civil service commissions customarily maintain. In the first place, individuals may apply and have their names placed on a register at any time; in other words the registers are continuously open.[19] Second, applicants are not ranked on the registers in accordance with a mathematical rating or score; they are unranked registers. Both of these features result from the absence of written examinations, for which is substituted an analysis of experience and training of the applicant as shown on his application blank. The process of analysis involves first a determination of the occupational field or fields in which the applicant is qualified. The T.V.A. has developed a classification of basic occupational groups and sub-groups or series (for example, civil engineering group, one of the subdivisions of which would be the highway engineering series). These classes correspond only very roughly to those used in the federal civil service or to the Authority's own system of titles, for the purpose of the classification is to furnish a bridge between the diverse occupations existing in private employment, as they appear on the application blanks, and standardized T.V.A. positions.

In addition to the occupational classification, the applicant's records are analyzed quantitatively and qualitatively—quantitatively with respect to years of training, experience, age, and past earnings (ordinarily four levels are used), and qualitatively into from three to five groups with respect to the evidence of ability shown. In this way overrefinements of numerical ratings are avoided. The results of the analysis are recorded on a card in the appropriate occupational file, and these files constitute the registers

18. This was one of the reasons given by Leonard D. White for recommending that the T.V.A. be brought under the civil service act. See his survey of the T.V.A. personnel department, *op. cit.* The T.V.A. file of applicants now totals 600,000.

19. Closed application procedures are occasionally used to prepare special registers.

used in making appointments. It will be observed that this process is similar to that of the unassembled examinations which civil service agencies are accustomed to use for higher positions. The T.V.A. practice differs, however, in that positions at all levels are filled in this manner, and that no rank order is established on the registers.

When requisitions for personnel are received in the personnel department, placement officers specializing in particular fields of T.V.A. employment secure from the files the records of those applicants who appear to be best fitted for the job in question.[20] After the selection has been reviewed by several employment officers, the complete files on those chosen for consideration (normally from two to six) are sent to the requisitioning department. The choice made there must be reviewed and approved by the personnel department. In this entire selection process the appropriate personnel officer takes an important part, and gives final approval for the personnel department on appointments below the $3800 entrance level. Appointments at the $4600 level and above cannot be finally approved in the personnel department, but must go to the general manager's office for review.

The appointment process outlined above is the normal one, but there are variations.[21] Review of the files may fail to bring to light any qualified candidate, or the requisitioning officer may reject all the applicants submitted for his consideration. In such cases it is necessary to secure additional applications by some of the methods previously described. The requisitioning official may have a rather definite idea as to the man he wants, and may request the employment division to secure an application from him. Any persons designated in this way, however, must go through the regular

20. Systematic statements of the qualifications required, check lists, and a weighting of qualifying factors are used wherever possible to supplement the judgment of employment officers. Examination scores, where available, are used as an index of ability and are considered along with other factors. A passing score is required for eligibility in cases where mental capacity or other abilities can be gauged by written tests. The number of candidates certified varies with the supply of qualified candidates and the degree to which the best can be identified.

21. During the fiscal year 1938, two-thirds of the 673 new appointments to annual positions were initially recommended by the personnel department, in the manner described.

procedure of having their qualifications compared with those of other applicants, and their appointments will not be approved by the personnel department unless their records justify the selection.

The regular procedure is also likely to be modified materially in filling the more important positions in the Authority. These must of necessity be handled on an individual basis, with personal interviews, field trips, and consultation with well-informed outsiders. For example, when the position of chief engineer was to be filled after Chairman Morgan's removal from that post, the board of directors approved the establishment of a special advisory examining board, composed of outside experts, to appraise the qualifications of candidates.[22]

It may be noted that the T.V.A. is not affected by veterans' preference legislation, nor is it bound by the statute requiring apportionment of positions among the several states according to population. In practice, however, the entire country has been the area of selection, except for trades and labor positions.[23] The T.V.A. has enforced a stricter anti-nepotism policy than has prevailed in the regular classified service.

In operating outside the civil service and without the protection of ranked registers and the "rule of three" in certification, the T.V.A. has exposed itself to influences of all kinds inimical to the "merit and efficiency" standard. Yet these pressures have been resisted in a way that few would have believed possible.[24] According to all the evidence, patronage requests have been consistently ig-

22. Compare with W. A. Robson's plan for the British Broadcasting Corporation, which would require that an *ad hoc* committee be set up to fill all important posts, the committee to include in each case persons from within the corporation and outside assessors with some knowledge of the field of work. "The B.B.C. as an Institution," 6 *Political Quarterly* 479 (1935).

23. The Authority has been criticized in the South on the ground that too few of its employees, particularly in the higher positions, were from that section. See comment by G. F. Milton, "A Consumer's View of the TVA," 160 *Atlantic Monthly* 653–58 (1937).

24. For example, President Hoover said, in vetoing the Muscle Shoals bill in 1931: "These directors are manifestly to have a political complexion and apparently the entire working force is likewise to have such a basis of selection, as the usual provision for the merit service required by law in most other Federal activities is omitted." Senate Doc. 321, 71st Cong., 3d sess., p. 5.

nored.[25] Mr. James A. Farley, who should know, wrote that A. E. Morgan "never consulted Democratic Senators." [26] Senator McKellar from Tennessee, who has few peers in this line of work, stated in the Senate that "I do not know of a man I have recommended who has been appointed by the T.V.A.; not one." [27] Representative Maury Maverick wrote: "Woe be to him who applies for a job with the endorsement of a Congressman or Senator. The directors have little comprehension of the political mind; and the personnel department, wholly inexperienced in dealing with the politicos, writes unnecessarily sharp letters." [28]

If there has been scarcely a chemical trace of political influence in T.V.A. appointments, it is undoubtedly true that there have been limited opportunities for the play of personal favoritism, or amicism. It would be a mistake to make too much of this point, however, for even the civil service system, with ranked registers and the rule of three, is not immune to judicious manipulation. In the T.V.A. there has been on the part of administrators on some occasions a preference for candidates whose abilities they knew from prior acquaintance as opposed to unknown applicants. This is not in all respects an undesirable practice nor completely contrary to the merit and efficiency principle.

Thus far, attention has been directed to the selection process used for the professional, administrative and clerical staff. The recruitment of skilled and unskilled labor for construction projects has been handled in a different fashion, by the use of workmen's examinations. When the Knoxville offices of the T.V.A. were opened in 1933, employment officials were literally overwhelmed by thousands of applicants. At first, an attempt was made to deal with these men by the usual interview method, but this process proved

25. The *Washington Post* said editorially on October 8, 1933: "The scramble of politicians to get jobs for their friends, according to Dr. Morgan, is impeding the work of the Authority. Apparently the merit system is being employed as a measure of self-defense against this army of political job hunters as well as a means of insuring efficient service."

26. Quoted by L. D. White, Senate Doc. 56, *op. cit.*, p. 70.

27. 83 *Cong. Rec.* 962 (1938); quoted by L. D. White, *ibid.*

28. "T.V.A. Faces the Future," 89 *New Republic* 64 (1936).

expensive and at the same time failed to yield sufficient qualified workers in certain occupational fields. Furthermore, most of the applicants were residents of the area immediately surrounding Knoxville, whereas it was desired to spread employment throughout the Valley area so far as possible. An examination seemed the best way to meet the problem, and in addition it offered an effective method for excluding political influence in hiring.

The first workmen's examination was given in the fall of 1933, and included a mechanical aptitude test, and tests of ability to follow printed and oral instructions. All three were devised by and used on the recommendation of the director of research for the U.S. Civil Service Commission. Examinations were conducted on four days in 138 cities and towns throughout the Valley, and 38,807 applicants were examined. The examinations were supervised by local U.S. civil service boards of examiners where such existed, and by local school officials in other centers.

The resulting register of workmen was used in selecting laborers for the Norris, Wheeler, and Pickwick projects, although workmen were not hired entirely on the basis of the examination score. Final selection of personnel was made at each recruiting point by trained interviewers who had at hand the applicant's score on the examination, his experience record, and his occupational rating. In general, only applicants who attained an examination score of 60 or more were considered for employment. Exceptions to this rule were made in trades in which it was difficult to find workmen, and also in later months when the registers had been depleted.

This use of examinations in selecting laborers proved generally successful.[29] Attempts were made to check the effectiveness of the tests by statistical analysis, which showed that workmen who had made high scores were in general considered more efficient by their foremen than workmen with low scores. Likewise, workmen receiving high scores received more promotions and fewer demotions, and were less frequently laid off. Because of this satisfactory ex-

29. See testimony of Floyd W. Reeves, T.V.A. director of personnel, in *Minutes of Evidence,* Commission of Inquiry on Public Service Personnel (1935), p. 585.

perience, a second examination was given to 81,000 men in 1936, when the T.V.A. was ready to proceed with its second group of dams. The process was repeated in 1938 and 1939 as the T.V.A. construction program was carried into new areas.[30]

When the Cherokee Dam and other emergency projects were authorized by Congress in 1940, the vital need for speed was too great to permit use of the examination technique. Moreover, there was no longer a surplus of applicants. From among its own employees the T.V.A. was able to supply 85 per cent of Cherokee's supervisory staff and about three-quarters of its skilled workmen. The need for additional employees was publicized throughout the area by every conceivable method, and 25,000 applications were received. Applications, filed in duplicate, were given a four-point rating in Knoxville on the basis of the applicant's experience. One copy, bearing the coding and rating, was dispatched to the field personnel office to serve as the employment register. Construction began on Cherokee the day after the dam was authorized, and 3,700 men were placed on the job in the first four months. This speed is estimated to have saved two months at the start of the project, and is one of the reasons why the T.V.A. was able to build Cherokee Dam faster than any structure of that size had ever been built before. Yet even in this rush, all selections of personnel were made by comparison of the experience record of the applicants. There was no provisional employment or hiring at the gate. The same methods have been used at the other emergency projects.

A special problem has been faced in connection with Negro employment. From the beginning the T.V.A. policy has been that Negroes should be employed in approximately the same ratio as prevails in the population area where the work is carried on. Thus in 1935 the T.V.A. employees were almost 20 per cent Negroes in the northern Alabama section, but less than 2 per cent in the Norris area, where few Negroes live. In general, Negroes constitute about 10 per cent of the population in the Tennessee Valley, and the

30. In addition to the general tests of mechanical aptitude, mental alertness, and construction knowledge, the last two examinations included 14 optional special tests for the major building and metal trades.

T.V.A. has maintained its ratio of Negro employees slightly above this figure.[31]

The T.V.A. policy, however, has been quite unsatisfactory to Negro organizations, which have bitterly attacked its alleged "lily-white" attitude. Their objections have been based on the T.V.A. practice of segregation for colored workers on construction projects, the use of Negroes in separate crews, and the failure to use Negroes in the higher-paid skilled labor and white-collar positions. The Authority's defense is that it must operate within an existing situation, with limits fixed by public opinion in the area, trade union rules, and so on. The T.V.A. has not believed it practical to pioneer very much in this field. On the credit side, however, is the Authority's non-discriminatory wage scale, and its use of Negroes in a few types of positions where they have not been generally employed. The T.V.A. is fully aware that it is adhering to its 10 per cent standard for Negro employment only by reason of its construction projects, and that it must develop new opportunities for Negroes if the 10 per cent figure is to be maintained after the construction period ends.[32]

PERSONNEL MANAGEMENT

The Authority's exemption from regular civil service procedures extends also to the fields of classification, compensation, service ratings, and to most other aspects of personnel management. The general policy of the T.V.A. in this field has been, however, to adopt practices which were not too dissimilar from those in the regular government service.

The importance of a standardized duties classification as the soundest basis for an equitable compensation plan, and as an important aid in recruitment, in fiscal control, and in administrative management generally, was recognized in the T.V.A. almost from the beginning. But, as in all the government agencies set up on an

31. At the end of the fiscal year 1935, Negro employees were 12.7 per cent of the total, and at the close of fiscal 1938 the figure was 11.5 per cent.

32. In 1941, only 6.2 per cent of the total annual employees were Negro, and only 3.6 per cent of the relatively permanent annual non-trades and labor positions were held by Negroes. On the other hand, 14 per cent of the relatively permanent annual trades and labor positions were occupied by Negroes.

emergency basis in 1933, work had to get under way without waiting for the development of a classification plan, which cannot be improvised on the spur of the moment. The result was, as Herbert Emmerich reported, that "most of the emergency units were subject right from the beginning to all the evils and difficulties which lack of a classification plan entails. Salaries were arbitrarily fixed by supervisors and division heads, and varied with jobs of equal responsibility even within an agency." [33]

To remedy this situation, President Roosevelt issued an executive order fixing a salary-standardization schedule for employees of the emergency agencies.[34] Adoption of the schedule was left to each of the organizations; no reviewing or revising agency was established to supervise their classification work. Although this order was made specifically applicable to the T.V.A., its officials took the position that the T.V.A. Act made the fixing of compensation wholly an administrative matter within the discretion of the board. Consequently the schedule was adopted only in part, for positions below $4,000.[35]

The adoption of a salary schedule did not solve the problem of classification, however. Classification work was performed by personnel officials as incident to their other duties, and by consulting the report on the classification of the federal field service which had been prepared in 1930 by the Personnel Classification Board and by other methods they were able to keep the Authority generally in line with federal standards. The weakness in the system was that procedures were not regularized and that adequate and systematic classification records, job descriptions, and analyses were lacking. Efforts of the personnel department to build up written classification records were made difficult by the fact that most officials and

33. "Personnel Problems in New Federal Agencies," 189 *Annals of the American Academy* 119, 123 (1937).

34. Executive Order 6440, November 18, 1933.

35. This action was later criticized by the Comptroller General, who contended that the order should have been complied with in its entirety. The special position of the T.V.A. was apparently recognized by the President, however, for his second Executive Order on the same subject specifically exempted from its provisions all employees of the T.V.A. and its affiliates (Executive Order 6746, June 21, 1934).

supervisors, having come from private employment, were without previous experience with duties classification, and tended to regard it as part of the governmental red tape which the T.V.A. should avoid. It was not until after an inspection of and report on T.V.A. classification work had been made late in 1934 by Ismar Baruch, classification expert of the U.S. Civil Service Commission, that agreement was reached as to the necessity for systematic classification procedures. A separate classification unit was shortly thereafter established in the personnel department.

The classification plan adopted by the T.V.A. follows in its main outlines the system effective in the regular federal service.[36] Six services are recognized—professional; subprofessional; clerical, administrative, and fiscal; custodial; inspectional; and education.[37] Classification of positions in these services is made on the basis of a comparison of their duties and responsibilities with standards established for the classified civil service, with the specifications proposed for the federal field service by the Personnel Classification Board, and with other positions involving similar work in the T.V.A. Titles of positions have been coordinated so far as possible with the standard titles used in the federal service. Because of the construction program there are many engineering positions which are common to private enterprise but practically unknown in the federal civil service. In such cases the T.V.A. has given due weight to the classifications customary in private employment.

Classification of annual employees has proceeded along two general lines. In the first place, classification procedures must be applied when requests for change of status or requisitions for new positions are received. Every employment requisition is accompanied by a classification sheet carrying the title and salary recommended for the position by the department initiating the request. If it is a position not previously described, the form must give a de-

36. Paragraph 8 of the T.V.A. Employee Relationship Policy provides: "In the classification of annually rated positions due regard will be given to standards of classification and rates of pay prevailing in the classified Federal service."

37. For a chart showing grades and representative titles, see T.V.A. *Annual Report, 1940,* p. 328. Trades and labor positions are handled separately.

scription of the duties and a statement of the minimum experience, training, and education desirable. It is the task of the personnel department to determine whether the proposed title and salary are commensurate with the duties to be performed.[38] The formulation of class specifications was deliberately postponed at first, but with the delegation of classification responsibilities to the personnel officers in 1941, their use became necessary.[39]

The second method of applying classification procedures is a systematic classification survey or audit of an entire organizational unit.[40] Surveys, involving on-the-job interviews with employees and supervisors, had been made throughout the entire organization by 1938. Thereafter they were repeated as warranted, but more emphasis was placed upon classification audits, which require less exhaustive investigations than do surveys.

Traditionally classification analyses were supposed to go no further than assuring correct description of duties and equal pay for equal work. But it has become increasingly apparent that the more comprehensive type of classification analysis, which studies organizational relationships as well as individual positions, affords an instrument which can be used effectively in providing staff assistance in the study and solution of organization problems. Mr. Clapp, former T.V.A. director of personnel, has described some of the contributions which a classification investigation can make to improvement of administrative structure:

> Confusions on the part of incumbent personnel may be discovered; definite conflicts in authority and overlapping of responsibility may be evident; in some instances a supervisor will discover with the aid of the classification investigator that a

38. Each allocation is reviewed by a classification officer to whom has been assigned responsibility for the particular department, as well as by one to whom has been assigned a group of occupations related to his own field of training and experience. Thus the allocation is reviewed both in relation to the organization and to the occupation.

39. In 1941 a preliminary volume of 176 class specifications and representative job descriptions was made available to personnel officers at all T.V.A. locations.

40. Occasionally a classification survey is made on an occupational basis, covering, for example, all secretarial positions or all cost engineering positions throughout the Authority.

subordinate is assuming responsibilities and performing duties quite contrary to the delegation made by the supervisor. Stalemates in the administrative machinery previously known to exist may be revealed where, until discovered in concrete terms, the real causes had been little more than a guess. And on a broader scale, gaps and voids in authority and working relationships caused by faulty organization structure may for the first time be reduced to factual definition.[41]

In recognition of this situation, the classification division in the T.V.A. has since its establishment been definitely charged with the responsibility of advising supervisors and making recommendations to the general manager on matters of organization. In connection with the increased delegation of responsibilities to personnel officers in 1941, the classification division was charged with conducting the periodic personnel surveys and reviews for which that plan provided. At the same time a more definite arrangement was made for the provision of organization analysis and management research services by the classification division. A staff assistant to the chief of that division was made responsible for maintaining a file of organizational material, and serving as a specialist in matters of administrative and management analysis.

With respect to compensation of personnel, the only limitation in the T.V.A. Act was that salaries should not exceed $10,000. The executive order of November 18, 1933, made it clear, however, that the emergency organizations were expected to observe regular federal salary levels. This order established a salary schedule with 19 grades, ranging from $840 to $8,000, and indicated by comparison with the classified service the general level of positions to which the various rates would apply.[42] The outstanding characteristic of this schedule was that it provided only one salary rate for each grade, in contrast with the practice under the Classification Act of 1923, which assigned to each grade a salary range, with a minimum and maximum salary and a number of intervening steps.

41. Gordon R. Clapp, "A New Emphasis in Personnel Administration," 189 *Annals of the American Academy* 111, 113–14 (1937).

42. As noted, the T.V.A. adopted this schedule for positions below $4,000; above that level it was revised by the insertion of seven additional salary grades.

The T.V.A. salary schedule, patterned on this plan for the emergency agencies, was defective in that it made no provision for salary increases except in the case of actual promotions to more responsible positions. For those employees who served well but could not be promoted, the incentive of a salary increase was nonexistent. Equally serious was the effect on the classification system. Many supervisors, wishing to give merited rewards to their employees, would request promotions when the duties assigned remained the same or were not sufficiently increased to justify the new classification. Another objection to the schedule was that T.V.A. employees were underpaid in comparison with the regular civil service, because T.V.A. rates were in most cases the same as the entrance rates for similar positions under the Classification Act, and therefore substantially lower than the average or middle rates for such positions.

Revision of this schedule was obviously needed. The machinery was created in 1935 when the Employee Relationship Policy was adopted, containing a provision for annual revision of salary schedules and for employee participation in the process. The Knoxville organized office employees quickly presented to the management a well-considered proposal for adoption of a system of salary steps within grades such as was provided in the regular federal service, for the most part using the exact Classification Act salary ranges. The union, however, did not want the T.V.A. to adopt the system of efficiency ratings which goes along with the plan of salary increases in the civil service. To do away with the necessity for ratings, the union proposed that salary increases within grade be automatic, and that they be awarded annually to all employees giving satisfactory service until they reached the top of their grade. If the management insisted on the adoption of a service rating plan, the union proposed that it be confined to those employees who distinguished themselves in some way, either to the advantage or disadvantage of the Authority.

These proposals had an important effect in shaping the salary plan finally adopted. Under the new plan, effective in 1937, annual positions were classified on the basis of regular federal grades and entrance salary rates, with a few exceptions.[48] The regular federal plan on salary steps within grade was not adopted, however. Only three salary rates were established for each grade (below $7,500), to be known as the entrance, standard, and maximum rates.[44] New appointments would be made at the entrance rate; after a year of satisfactory service an employee would be eligible for, and would receive, an automatic increase to the standard rate; after not less than an additional year of unusually satisfactory service, the employee would be eligible for an increase to the maximum rate.

This plan did involve a rating scheme, but one quite different from that employed in the regular federal service. The service of all employees was to be reviewed semi-annually by their supervisors and reported as unusually satisfactory, satisfactory, or unsatisfactory. It was assumed that the service of most employees would be satisfactory, in terms of their skills, knowledge, capacity, quantity and quality of work, and conduct; no special reports were required on satisfactory employees. If a supervisor found an employee unsatisfactory on the above criteria, however, he was required to fill out a special report giving specific evidence of the deficiencies, and to recommend transfer, demotion, or dismissal from the T.V.A. Likewise, for employees thought to have given unusually satisfactory service, individual reports were required showing specific evidence of unusual or exceptional achievement, unique contribution, or outstanding resourcefulness. In no case, it will be noted, was any mathematical rating or calculation required.

A board of review was established in the personnel depart-

43. Three intermediate grades (between P–1 and P–2, P–2 and P–3, and P–3 and P–4) were introduced in the lower levels of the professional service because of the numerous levels of responsibility present in the T.V.A. specialized engineering organization. Also, three new grades were inserted in the top levels (with salaries of $7,250, $8,750, and $9,500) to provide for additional administrative levels and to facilitate recruitment of personnel for major technical and administrative positions requiring industrial background. It was also necessary to create new classes to fit occupations new to the public service.

44. Thus for a P–1 position, the entrance rate was $2,000, the standard rate $2,300, and the maximum rate $2,600.

ment which was to review the semi-annual ratings (particularly those of unsatisfactory or unusually satisfactory), to approve or disapprove them, and to notify all employees of the granting or denial of automatic increases. Employees rated unsatisfactory were given an opportunity to appeal their rating, the appeals to be heard by an advisory board consisting of two management representatives appointed by the director of personnel from outside the personnel department, and two representatives of employees selected at each location where the board met. The board's finding was advisory to the director of personnel, who made the final decision.

Experience with this salary and rating plan has been satisfactory on the whole. As might have been anticipated, supervisors have proved reluctant to give employees ratings of unsatisfactory, for the consequence is that the employee must be transferred, demoted, or discharged.[45] Also, the supervisor may have to face the ordeal of a hearing before the advisory board if the employee appeals. The first rating period in 1937 saw three appeals of this sort; one was upheld by the advisory board, one was reversed, and the third was withdrawn by the supervisor concerned after the hearing had begun.

Some dissatisfaction has been expressed over the three-step salary plan within each grade. As noted, the second step is reached after one year of service, and further advance to the third step is almost impossible because of the strict limits imposed on the granting of ratings of unusually satisfactory.[46] As a result, the stopping point is reached too quickly, and thereafter the sense of advancement is lost, and the pressure on the supervisor to reclassify the employee to a higher grade is increased. As the T.V.A. settles down to the stability of an established organization, and opportunities for rapid advancement lessen, this factor becomes more important,

45. For example, only two employees out of more than 4,000 rated were marked unsatisfactory at each of the two rating periods in fiscal 1939. One of the four employees so rated appealed to the advisory board.

46. At the close of 1941 only 13 out of 8,602 salary policy employees were paid the maximum rate. Of course many employees who might have attained this rate were instead promoted to a higher grade.

and suggestions have been made for increasing the number of steps by one or two.[47] The seven-step federal plan has not been favored, on the whole.

The T.V.A. has not considered it desirable to develop formalized promotion procedures, primary reliance having been placed on the judgment of supervisors.[48] The rapid expansion of the organization in the past has provided most employees with ample opportunities for advancement, and has lessened the need for attention to the problem. For example, during the 12-month period beginning November, 1939, when the number of annual employees averaged 6,500, a study showed there were 2,868 promotions, or one for every 2.3 employees.[49] This rate is many times that to be found in stable civil service systems.

While the opportunities for promotion are thus seen to be great, there are other matters to be considered. For the principle of merit and efficiency would be violated by promotions made on the basis of personal favoritism, or without adequate consideration of all qualified employees. The personnel department has announced the general policy of using the entire organization, rather than single organizational units, as the recruitment area for promotions and transfers, and of giving employees an opportunity to bring their qualifications to the attention of personnel officers in connection with vacancies. However, the posting of all vacancies, which would seem to be the surest way of attaining this latter goal, has not been adopted as a general policy, only 21 vacancies having been so publicized during the period from July, 1936, through 1940. The principal assurance of fair treatment in promotion consequently comes through the personnel department's policy of searching the files of employees as well as considering outside applicants when positions

47. The problem has been very completely considered in a memorandum by O. Glenn Stahl, "The Structure of a Compensation Plan," November 7, 1940.

48. The term "promotion" as used here refers only to increase in grade, not to increases of salary within grade.

49. Reported in a memorandum prepared by Charles F. Glass, Donald D. Fowler, and Rudolf Bertram, "Factors in the Formulation and Administration of Promotion Policies, with Special Reference to the TVA," January 16, 1941. See L. D. White's comments on the T.V.A. rate of promotion, op. cit., pp. 78–79.

are to be filled.[50] Promotions do not of course become effective until approved by the personnel department.

There can be no question that the T.V.A. has very consistently followed the policy of recruitment for higher positions by promotion from within. During the one-year period referred to above, when 2,868 promotions were made, there were only half as many new appointments to annual positions (1,494). It is easy to see the promotion system at work in the filling of the higher positions in the T.V.A. When the post of general manager became vacant in 1939, the director of personnel, Mr. Gordon Clapp, was promoted to it. The position of director of personnel has become vacant three times, and on each occasion it was filled by the promotion of the assistant director. The record is much the same throughout the Authority. The wisdom of this policy is self-evident, and it has enabled the T.V.A. to retain most of its key men.

Finally, it should be noted that supervisors have the right to fire their employees, but only for just cause, for reasons stated in writing. No definite period of notice is required by the Employee Relationship Policy. Such action by a supervisor separates an employee from the pay roll, but the approval of the personnel department is necessary before his discharge becomes finally effective, and it may prove possible to transfer him to some other position in the organization. Employees who feel that they are being terminated without cause or for improper reasons may appeal to the personnel department for an investigation.[51] The personnel department conducts "exit interviews" with employees leaving T.V.A. service, which cover the reasons for leaving and other matters useful in guiding the management of personnel relations. In the case of lay-offs, which are frequent because of the seasonal nature of T.V.A. employment, the policy is to release the less promising employees first.[52]

50. The personnel department has experimented with placement surveys, with the object of obtaining a detailed picture of the qualifications available in organizational units in relation to the present and future personnel needs.

51. There were eight such appeals in fiscal 1936, two in 1937, nine in 1938, and one in 1939.

52. Employees laid off and those injured in line of duty are entered in a special placement file.

LABOR RELATIONS AND COLLECTIVE BARGAINING

The directors, of the T.V.A. planned from the beginning to make a new deal for labor a part of the T.V.A. program. The original decision to build the T.V.A. dams by force account, rather than by contract, meant that the T.V.A. was willing, and even anxious, to shoulder the responsibilities that would go with the direct management of such large groups of construction workers. The T.V.A. accepted willingly the necessity of dealing with the craft unions representing the great majority of the skilled workers on these projects. A recent statement of the Authority's credo in this field deserves to be quoted at length:

> The convictions on which the Authority's policies of employee relations are based . . . start from the assumption that employees will react as normal individuals living in a democratic environment. It is taken for granted, therefore, that employees desire to participate in the determination of the conditions of work. These desires become a creative force if accepted in good faith and given an opportunity for effective expression. If the normal impulses of employees are ignored or repressed, a chain of negative responses will unconsciously dull the edge of efficient and imaginative performance, or perhaps even break out dramatically in strikes or widespread grievances.
>
> In an organization as large as the Authority, employees can effectively exercise their collaborative role only through representatives chosen by and responsible to them. So organized, the extent of their participation in matters of joint concern is limited merely by the intensity and continuity of their interest, the effectiveness of their organizations, and the delegated powers of the agency. It is properly an administrative responsibility to maintain these relationships.
>
> It follows that any enhancement of the responsible status of the employees' chosen representatives contributes to good management. The right of a majority of employees in an appropriate unit to select the representatives of all is such a principle. Another is the right of employees to designate whatever leadership they choose, whether from within or without the agency. Employees, moreover, have the right to define the methods and

objectives of their own organizations free of limitations imposed by the employer.[53]

This attitude toward the problems of labor relations was evident in the original T.V.A. grievance procedure. When the construction program first got under way, T.V.A. officials were afraid that the labor policy which it was intended to enforce might not be understood properly, either by the supervisors or by the workers. For this reason employees were allowed to come directly to the personnel department with their grievances, and a labor relations section was established to aid in maintaining proper individual and collective relations between supervisors and supervised employees. It was the duty of this office to investigate complaints, at the instigation of either supervisors or employees, to make reports to the parties concerned, and to secure the best settlement of differences. During the fiscal year 1935 there were 94 formal complaints registered with the labor relations section. Obviously, this policy of encouraging employees to come directly to the personnel department with their grievances was contrary to the regular and more desirable "up the line" process of handling complaints, and it was abandoned as soon as it was felt that employees understood the T.V.A. policy and were in a position to protect their own interests.[54]

After about one year of operation T.V.A. management officials felt the need of formalizing the regulations and procedures applicable in the field of employee relationships. The board of directors issued a statement to the following effect:

It is desirable that the Authority shall formulate a policy governing employee relationships, and provide machinery for its administration throughout the organization, so that every employee whether supervised or supervisory may appraise his own acts and those of other employees by recognized and accepted standards. Otherwise there may be no consistent policy,

53. Management Services Report No. 1, p. 23. When the white-collar office employees began to consider the formation of a union in 1934, Chairman Morgan wrote an open letter to all such employees calling attention to their right to organize.

54. The Authority's experience with grievance procedures has been discussed in an unpublished Master's thesis prepared by Arthur Quadow at the University of Chicago, entitled "Grievance Procedures in the Federal Service" (1941).

and attitudes which happen to be brought from other jobs by various subordinate managers, foremen, straw bosses, and workmen will determine the spirit of employee relationships.[55]

Work was begun on the statement of such a policy in September, 1934, and a proposed draft, representing the combined efforts of the board, management officials, and outside consultants, was presented to the employees in July, 1935. All employees were urged to study the statement and to formulate suggestions and criticisms. Then during the following month conferences were held by the management at six centers of T.V.A. activity throughout the Valley, for the purpose of discussing the policy with the employees. An impartial chairman, Mr. Otto S. Beyer, then director of labor relations for the Federal Coordinator of Transportation, was brought in to serve at these hearings. There followed further revisions and a final conference with representatives of the craft and white-collar unions, following which the board of directors adopted the policy on August 28, 1935.

The Employee Relationship Policy was thus, as the board said, a product of "collective conference and understanding." It was not, however, a signed contract between the management and employee representatives, but rather a unilateral declaration of policy, a statement on the part of management of the principles which it proposed to follow in its labor relations. One of the obligations was that no new rule in this field would be adopted or existing rule revised without an opportunity for employee representatives to confer with the management.

Important provisions in the policy protecting labor's right to organize and bargain, but excluding the closed shop, were as follows:

> 3. For the purposes of collective bargaining and employee-management cooperation, employees of the Authority shall have the right to organize and designate representatives of their own choosing. . . .
> 4. No employee of the Authority and no one seeking employment shall be required as a condition of employment, transfer,

55. Introductory statement in draft of Employee Relationship Policy, June 20, 1935.

promotion, or retention in service to join or to refrain from joining any organization or association of employees.

5. There shall be no discrimination against representatives of
employees of the Authority nor shall employees suffer discrimination because of membership or non-membership in any
organization or association of employees.

6. The majority of the employees as a whole, or of any professional group, or craft, or other appropriate unit, shall have the
right to determine the organization, person or persons who shall
represent the employees as a whole, or any such professional
group, or craft, or unit. . . .

One of the most interesting developments under the Employee
Relationship Policy has resulted from the provision for annual revision of rates of pay through a conference procedure. A system of
annual wage conferences has developed, in which management and
labor representatives meet to discuss rates of pay in trades and on
labor jobs in the T.V.A. for the following year. The skilled workers
on T.V.A. construction projects, as well as its power, chemical plant,
and maintenance employees, are nearly all affiliated with the American Federation of Labor, and their unions have created a Tennessee
Valley Trades and Labor Council to represent them at these conferences and to coordinate their bargaining relationships generally with
the T.V.A.[56] Management representation at these conferences is
through a committee on wage and salary policy appointed by the
general manager, and since 1940 the director of personnel and the
president of the Trades and Labor Council share responsibility for
conduct of the conference machinery.

The task before the annual wage conference is, strictly speaking,
that of determining what is the "prevailing rate of wages for work of
a similar nature prevailing in the vicinity," for the T.V.A. statute
obligates the Authority to pay not less than that prevailing rate, with
due regard also to be given to rates secured through collective
agreements. Consequently, as a preliminary to each wage conference the T.V.A. personnel department must collect wage data in the

56. There is no bargaining with C.I.O. unions, since none is a duly constituted
representative of an appropriate bargaining unit.

Tennessee Valley area, which are compared with standards at other federal projects and in the building and construction trades generally. These systematic wage surveys have practically eliminated disagreement between management and labor as to the factual situation. At the conference the unions present their own wage briefs with requests for wage adjustments and supporting material. After full discussion by all interested parties, management representatives make their determination on pay schedules to be recommended to the general manager and the board for adoption. If the union representatives are dissatisfied with the rates set, the statute permits them to appeal to the Secretary of Labor, whose decision is final.[57]

Until 1941, these annual conferences devoted much time to problems other than wage rates, such as classification, hours of work, leave regulations, and working conditions. Now these matters are largely taken care of by other machinery. Classification matters have been removed entirely from the wage conference to be disposed of as they arise by a standing joint committee. Changes in working conditions are left to direct negotiation. Out of the wage conferences have come other special conferences. It was one of these which led to the famous General Agreement of 1940, which deserves discussion.

Experience under the Employee Relationship Policy as adopted in 1935 had been eminently satisfactory to all parties concerned. But after five years both labor and management felt, in the words of the T.V.A. general manager, that "something was missing." [58] The Tennessee Valley Trades and Labor Council, believing that it knew where the gap was, suggested to the T.V.A. management that a signed agreement be negotiated and formally executed by the T.V.A. and its organized employees. One of the terms which labor wanted in such an agreement was the closed shop. The T.V.A. management was advised by counsel that its authority to sign such an agreement was very doubtful, since the statute prescribed that appointments

57. This machinery has been used twice. In the first appeal, the Secretary upheld the union. The second appeal was pending in mid-1942.
58. Address by Gordon R. Clapp, "Collective Bargaining in a Federal Regional Agency: The TVA as an Example," October 28, 1941.

must be made on the basis of merit and efficiency. The closed shop would consequently be illegal "unless a factual showing could be made to support the proposition that lack of membership in a union was *prima facie* evidence of lack of merit and efficiency in the employee or prospective employee." [59]

While thus excluding the closed shop as a possibility, the T.V.A. management still felt that there was a case for a signed labor agreement. Collective bargaining [60] and machinery for labor-management cooperation were not necessarily dependent on acceptance of a closed shop. Both parties agreed to carry on the discussions, and were able to reach a satisfactory conclusion. On August 6, 1940, the T.V.A. and 15 unions representing T.V.A. employees in the trades and labor services signed an agreement which had the following declared purposes:

> . . . to set up . . . conference machinery and procedures to determine rates of pay . . . as well as hours of service and conditions of work of the employees; to adjust all disputes growing out of grievances or out of the interpretation or application of established labor standards agreed upon between the council and the Authority; and to promote intensive labor-management cooperation between the Authority and its employees.

And the introductory statement continued in these words:

> The public interest in an undertaking such as the TVA always being paramount, the Authority and the Tennessee Valley Trades and Labor Council on behalf of the employees further agree that pending the determination or adjustment of any issue arising between them by means of the conference machinery and procedures hereby set up and during the life of this agreement, the Authority will not change the conditions incorporated in written schedules or recorded understandings be-

59. *Ibid.*

60. There has been considerable controversy as to whether "collective bargaining" in the ordinary industrial sense is possible in a government agency. The term is used here with full recognition of the limits necessarily imposed on the discretion of a government administrator by his public responsibility.

tween the Authority and the council out of which the issue arose, and the council or its member organizations will not encourage or sanction employees' leaving the service.[61]

The Employee Relationship Policy, with some necessary modifications, was accepted by the parties and made a part of the new signed agreement. The bulk of the document dealt with the machinery for handling five major employee relations problems. First was the question of jurisdictional disputes, which the T.V.A. agreed were to be settled by the unions themselves, the T.V.A. however reserving the right to assign work in those cases where the unions were unable to reach a jurisdictional agreement. Second, machinery for handling disputes growing out of grievances was set up. It involved first a joint conference between union representatives and the director of personnel; if that failed, then a board of adjustment composed of two members from each side; and finally, an impartial referee whose decision was to be final. Third, the agreement made specific provision for the annual wage conferences. Fourth, it contemplated the establishment of joint cooperative committees on the various T.V.A. projects to promote better understanding and more effective joint action, with Valley-wide cooperative conferences to be held at least twice a year to review the actions and programs of the local committees. Finally, a central joint council on apprenticeship, established in 1938, was recognized by the agreement.

This contract was, as the *American Federationist* referred to it, a "history-making labor agreement," both in form and in spirit. Organizations of government employees have never enjoyed the full privileges of other labor organizations because of the peculiar position and responsibilities of their sovereign employer. Not only has the right of public employees to strike been generally denied, but other characteristic instruments of the organized labor movement, such as the closed shop, collective bargaining, and signed labor contracts, have been held not to be appropriate to the field of public

61. The agreement is printed as an appendix to the *Annual Report, 1940*, pp. 99–103.

employment.[62] In a letter of August 16, 1937, President Roosevelt wrote: "All Government employees should realize that the process of collective bargaining, as usually understood, cannot be transplanted into the public service." In 1941 the National Institute of Municipal Law Officers, after a survey of existing practices in the municipal field, concluded that "no city has ever signed a collective bargaining agreement with a labor union representing city employees similar to the agreements entered into between private industry and labor unions." [63]

The general T.V.A. policy of handling labor relations ran definitely counter to this limitation of the rights and powers of organized government employees. As already noted, the T.V.A. did feel that its statutory position prevented any closed shop agreement in the Authority, and the question of the "right" of T.V.A. employees to strike has never been brought to an issue. But the Authority has, within its statutory and governmental limits, bargained collectively with its employees. It is often contended that there is nothing for employees to bargain about in the public service, since rates of pay, hours of work, leave privileges, methods and standards of selection of employees, and general employment conditions are fixed by statute, and cannot be modified by the administrative officers in charge. This is of course true in large part for government agencies in a regular civil service system, but as a corporation exempt from civil service the T.V.A. has had somewhat greater discretion in these fields. In particular, the wage conference procedure already described comes very close to being genuine collective bargaining. But even apart from this corporate flexibility, the T.V.A. felt that there were other matters with which a program of union-management cooperation could be concerned, such as departmental rules

62. For a general discussion of this subject, see Leonard D. White, *Introduction to the Study of Public Administration* (New York, 1939), Chap. 28; Sterling D. Spero, "Employer and Employee in the Public Service," in *Problems of the American Public Service* (New York, 1935); *Employee Relations in the Public Service* (Civil Service Assembly, 1942).

63. *Power of Municipalities to Enter into Labor Union Contracts—A Survey of Law and Experience* (Washington, 1941), p. 23.

and regulations, grievances, training opportunities, improvement of efficiency, safety of employees, and the general problems of methods, quality, integrity, and results of administration within the limits set by Congress. Experience in the T.V.A. seems fully to have justified this conception, and it is worth noting that President Roosevelt, who had denied the possibility of collective bargaining in 1937, at the inauguration of the Chickamauga Dam in 1940 praised collective bargaining in the T.V.A. and the "productive partnership between management and labor."

In signing a labor contract with organized employees, the T.V.A. was again taking a very advanced position, although not an unprecedented one. During the first World War the U.S. Shipping Board and the U.S. Railroad Administration operated under contractual relations with unions of their employees, and more recently the Inland Waterways Corporation, the Panama Canal, the National Labor Relations Board, and other government agencies have done likewise. The National Institute of Municipal Law Officers has attempted to prove that, in the municipal field at least, such contracts are invalid. But their analysis seems to be pointed to closed shop provisions, rather than at the contracts themselves.[64] There is no conceivable legal objection to the kind of contract the T.V.A. signed on August 6, 1940, and its significance in establishing "a definite concept of management's responsibility to labor and labor's obligation to management"[65] is very great.

In dealing with its employees the T.V.A. has had its share of the problems created by rival employee representation. The Employee Relationship Policy left the matter of bargaining units wide open by providing that "the majority of the employees as a whole, or of any professional group, or craft, or other appropriate unit" shall have the right to be represented. In case of dispute as to who are the duly

---

64. As pointed out in Mr. Clapp's address of October 28, 1941. The report of the Law Officers Institute has been subjected to a powerful rebuttal by Arthur W. Macmahon, "Collective Labor Action in City Government," 23 *Public Management* 328–34 (1941). The State, County and Municipal Workers of America, C.I.O., published in March, 1942, a legal memorandum in support of the power of municipalities to enter into collective agreements.

65. 39 *Journal of Electrical Workers and Operators* 477 (1940).

authorized representatives, the personnel department is to attempt to adjust the dispute, holding an election if the parties agree. Such elections have taken place on two occasions. While the Policy intended to establish an avenue of appeal to the National Labor Relations Board, the Board has declined to take jurisdiction of such disputes except at the request of all parties concerned.[66]

It is the special task of the personnel relations division in the personnel department to keep supervisor-employee relations running smoothly, without taking over either supervisory or employee representation functions. Thus, supervisors may consult the personnel relations staff concerning the suitability of a certain collective bargaining unit or the course to follow when confronted with conflicting demands by competing unions. The personnel relations officer is likewise the "maintenance mechanic" charged with keeping in good working order the machinery for negotiation and cooperation set up by T.V.A. management and labor.

The success of the Authority's labor policies can be seen most concretely in the record of strikes and work stoppages on T.V.A. projects. On this gigantic construction program there have been only four stoppages in eight years. None was authorized by the Trades and Labor Council, and only one was approved by the international union involved. The longest stoppage, from three days to a week at the various projects, was called in 1939 by a craft union over a jurisdictional question. A second stoppage was caused by racial antagonism at Kentucky Dam, and occurred in November, 1940, shortly after the new labor agreement had been signed. Within three and a half days international representatives of the unions and officers of the Trades and Labor Council succeeded in persuading the strikers to return to work and to adhere to the principles of the

66. The white collar employees of the Authority have not been as interested in organization and collective bargaining as the trades and labor employees. However, there has been a strong union in the Knoxville offices since 1934. All three of the principal federal employee organizations (U.F.W., N.F.F.E., and A.F.G.E.) have units in the T.V.A. The engineers, traditionally indifferent to unionization, have formed their own unaffiliated Engineers' Association. The Public Safety Service Employees Union (A.F.L.) has been acknowledged as collective bargaining agent for T.V.A. guards and guides, as has the American Federation of Office Employees on behalf of the general office employees.

new contract calling for orderly settlement of disputes. The other two stoppages, one only 40 minutes long, were confined to one trade at a single project. This remarkable record is testimony to the soundness of the principles on which the T.V.A. labor policy has been based.

THE CIVIL SERVICE ISSUE

The Authority's status of exemption from the civil service, not at all unusual when it was granted in 1933, is now highly exceptional. In fact, when the Ramspeck Act of 1940 broke down the legal barriers to extension of civil service throughout the entire federal service, the T.V.A. was the only permanent agency allowed by Congress to retain its exempt status. This action was testimony to the high reputation which the Authority's merit system has earned.

From many points of view the congressional decision in this matter was a wise one. The Authority's excellent record of achievement in the personnel field has been in considerable measure attributable to its freedom from time-worn civil service procedures and regulations. In many areas extremely valuable experiments in new types of personnel procedures have been conducted by the T.V.A., unhampered by the necessity of conforming to established rules of the Civil Service Commission or of going to Congress for permission to initiate the changes. The recruitment job which the Authority performed in its early days simply could not have been done under the civil service system as it was then operated. For the character of the U.S. Civil Service Commission during the first half of the 1930's was that of a plodding, routine-ridden, policing organization, starved for funds and fresh points of view. As Reeves and David reported, "Its major interest appears to remain in the negative and restrictive activities attendant upon the enforcement of the civil service laws and rules, rather than in a positive and cooperative approach toward improved recruitment, placement, training, and morale-building activities." [67]

67. President's Committee on Administrative Management, *Report with Special Studies*, p. 63.

It may be argued, moreover, as Senator Norris did in urging exemption of the T.V.A. from the Ramspeck Act, that the T.V.A. has developed "a better civil service than is provided for by our civil-service law." [68] What he meant was that in the T.V.A. the civil service principle was imposed even upon the heads of the organization, by reason of the "merit and efficiency" provisions of the T.V.A. Act. The Authority's success in enforcing these provisions has already been noted.

The T.V.A., in presenting its case for exemption from civil service, stressed the fact that its regional character required "that managerial decisions should be made in the valley, where the work was to be done, not in Washington." [69] Taking away from the Authority discretion in selection of its personnel and control over terms and conditions of their employment "would mean the beginning of piecemeal disintegration of a regional administration. . . ." The 15 unions composing the Tennessee Valley Trades and Labor Council joined with the T.V.A. management in arguing that civil service for the Authority would ruin its established system of collective bargaining, for the Authority's discretion and finality of decision on personnel matters would be largely curtailed. It should also be noted that two different investigating groups, the Commission of Inquiry on Public Service Personnel in 1935, and the joint congressional investigating committee in 1938, considered the question of civil service for the T.V.A. and both concluded that continued exemption was desirable. [70]

This all adds up to an extremely strong case for retention of the T.V.A. merit system outside the regular civil service. But there is also something to be said for the opposite conclusion. [71] First of all, the Civil Service Commission of today is not the commission of five years ago. Astounding changes have taken place during that period

68. Hearings before Senate Committee on Civil Service, on H.R. 960, "Extending Classified Civil Service," 76th Cong., 3d sess. (1940), p. 189.
69. *Ibid.*, p. 249. The entire T.V.A. case is found in pp. 244–53.
70. *Better Government Personnel* (New York, 1935), p. 68; *Report of the Joint Committee*, pp. 59–61.
71. See the statements by Commissioner Flemming and K. C. Vipond of the Civil Service Commission in Hearings on H.R. 960, *op. cit.*, pp. 117–35.

which have made the Commission a constructive and developmental force for improved personnel administration in the federal service.[72] And the present war experience, in which the Commission is not being by-passed as it was during the emergency period of 1933–1934, is blowing to pieces whatever was left of traditionalism and stodginess in the Commission.

There is a danger, moreover, that the T.V.A. case for exemption from civil service will prove too much. It is true that the most efficient administration is secured when authority accompanies responsibility, but this is a principle which must often be compromised in a democratic government to secure goals which, at least in peacetime, are even more important than efficiency. While there are assuredly special factors in the T.V.A. situation, nearly every other federal agency could make out something of a case against sharing control over its personnel with a civil service commission separated from management and unaccountable for management's results. Consistency is not to be over-rated as a virtue, but it does have claims. The T.V.A. is the only federal corporation given this exemption, even such a purely business activity as the Inland Waterways Corporation having been brought under civil service.

When the T.V.A. construction program is finished, and it has shaken down into a relatively small and stable operating and planning organization, the case for civil service will be stronger. Senator Norris has stated that he would favor civil service for the T.V.A. under those conditions.[73] Professor Leonard D. White, after his survey for the investigating committee in 1938, recommended civil service for the Authority. The T.V.A. Knoxville union of the United Federal Workers of America, the principal union of T.V.A. white collar employees, concluded in 1940: ". . . it seems that were the Classified Civil Service extended to the T.V.A., the Authority would probably not surrender enough control or independence to harm its

72. See, for example, Arthur S. Flemming, "Emergency Aspects of Civil Service," 1 *Public Administration Review* 25–31 (1940).

73. Hearings on H.R. 960, *op. cit.*, p. 199.

operations to any important degree." [74] If the T.V.A. were brought under civil service, its collective bargaining powers could be protected by statutory amendment, if that proved necessary. [75]

This question, then, has its pros and cons. The author's own opinion is that the Authority's present status should not be disturbed during the war, but that the T.V.A. should eventually come into the civil service system. This conclusion will be strengthened if the central civil service agency in the federal government shows a continued trend toward the service as opposed to the policing concept. The control and responsibility of management in the field of personnel administration should be limited only to the degree necessary in order to secure adherence to proper standards. The central personnel agency should increasingly seek to maintain such standards, not by controlling individual personnel actions, but by surveys, test audits, development of methods for measuring effectiveness in personnel administration, serving as the research center, clearing house, and dynamo for the departmental personnel offices. Into this sort of a civil service system the T.V.A. could fit without losing the qualities in its merit system of which it is justly proud and which it rightly wishes to preserve.

74. From a mimeographed statement prepared by the union, "T.V.A. in the Classified Civil Service?" The T.V.A. employees at that time, however, voted by a large majority against the extension of civil service to their jobs.

75. It is interesting to note that in the pending bill to set up a permanent Columbia River Power Administration, civil service is provided for with just such a proviso authorizing the Administration to deal collectively with its employees and to enter into contracts with their representatives. See S. 2430, 77th Cong.

Conclusion

10: The Meaning of the T.V.A.

> "There is something in the mere cant of a dam, when seen from below, that makes one think of the Pyramids of Egypt. Both pyramid and dam represent an architecture of power. But the difference is notable, too, and should make one prouder of being an American. The first grew out of slavery and celebrated death. Ours was produced by free labor to create energy and life for the people of the United States."—*Lewis Mumford*

THE TENNESSEE VALLEY AUTHORITY is now ten years old. It has worn well. Since 1933 its fame as dam builder, regional planner, power enterprise, and conservator of soil resources has spread around the world. There is something about the work of the T.V.A. that has fascinated thoughtful observers, who have felt that here was a project with meaning and purpose, something of which a nation could be proud. This reaction is not confined to the starry-eyed visitors who come, in the words of Jonathan Daniels, to "oo and ah at the new heaven in the old earth." It appears in a hard-headed newspaper such as the *New York Times*, which after assisting Arthur Morgan's campaign against his co-directors in 1937 and 1938, decided that it should send a reporter down to the Valley to discover just what was happening there. The resulting series of articles was such a pleasant surprise to the editor that the *Times* published an editorial with the remarkable title, "TVA and the American Dream." It is difficult to think of any other federal agency which could have inspired that phrase.

The component parts of the T.V.A. program are not unusual. Other river systems have been developed, though not so completely, by the building of multiple-purpose dams. There are other public power systems in the country. There are other planning agencies, other programs for agricultural improvement and land conservation. And yet nowhere else have these elements been combined in such a purposeful way. No other public instrumentality of our times has seemed to have more symbolic meaning, more usefulness as a tool, more promise for the future.

THE T.V.A. AS SYMBOL

The comprehensive program of river control which the T.V.A. is now hurrying to its conclusion is probably the most impressive physical engineering project since the Panama Canal. At a time when the world is largely out of hand, the T.V.A. symbolizes man in control of his environment and directing his destiny. While there are larger dams elsewhere, there is nothing to compare with this co-ordinated development of 28 dams located throughout a watershed of 40,000 square miles, operated as part of a single system for a single goal—to make the flow of the river and its tributaries do a maximum of good and a minimum of harm. Controlling purposes in working out the operating plan are to keep navigable depths in the river at all times, to allow proper margins for storage of flood waters, and to permit generation of the maximum amount of power consistent with the first two objectives. The flow of the Tennessee is also coordinated with that of the lower Mississippi, in order to mitigate flood and drought conditions. At New Orleans in 1940 low flow in the Mississippi permitted sea water to back up the river to a point where the city water supply was threatened, a situation which the T.V.A. was called on to alleviate by releases from its storage reservoirs 1500 river-miles away.

The imagination is caught, not only by the boldness and completeness of this control plan, but also by the tremendous potentialities of the stored water. Electric power is a force still as exciting, despite a half century of familiarity, as it was to the sensitive mind of Henry Adams who in the great gallery of machines at the Paris Exposition of 1900 began to feel the forty-foot dynamos as a moral force, much as the early Christians felt the Cross. The planet itself seemed less impressive, in its old-fashioned, deliberate, annual or daily revolution, than this huge wheel, revolving within arm's-length at some vertiginous speed, and barely murmuring—scarcely humming an audible warning to stand a hair's-breadth further for respect of power—while it would not wake the baby lying close against its frame. Before the end, one began to pray to it; inherited instinct taught the natural expression of man before silent and infinite force.[1]

A steam-driven dynamo, impressive as it is, does not begin to compare in symbolic quality with a hydro turbine generator. Electric power derived from steam inevitably carries over into the neotechnic era suggestions of the smoke and grime of the paleotechnic age. In order to stoke a steam plant thousands of men must crouch in the earth to dig for coal. Lewis Mumford has written of the psychological benefits of closing up the mining industries, "with their speculative animus, their gambling, their recklessness of human life, their indifference to beauty and order."[2] In a hydroelectric plant the operating technicians do not wrestle with nature in the dirt and the dark. Instead, they control with ridiculous ease the force of the white coal rushing through penstocks and turning quietly humming turbines.

Again, a steam power plant is that and nothing more. Its social consequences lie simply in the amount of power it will make available. But the damming of a river creates an entire new physical environment. Napoleon is reported to have said that man could have no more absolute authority than control over the waters that cover the earth. He who undertakes to wipe out by flood a valley where men have lived plays God, and incurs obligations proportionately heavy. There must be a weighing of consequences, and a new equilibrium must be fashioned to replace the one destroyed.

The symbolic value of the T.V.A. has been heightened by the stirring architectural treatment accorded its projects. Fritz Gutheim

1. *The Education of Henry Adams* (popular ed., Boston, 1927), p. 380.
2. *The Culture of Cities*, p. 327.

has said that architecture and engineering are more completely integral in the T.V.A. than they have been at any time since the two professions became separated. "The job of the architect has been to make sure that the dams look as efficient as the engineers have made them."[3] Anyone who has seen the Norris and Hiwassee dams, with their spectacular height and scenic surroundings, or the long low dams bracketing the wide valley of the main stream, and has walked through the powerhouses and looked over the reservoirs from the vantage points provided for visitors, can testify how well this goal has been achieved.

One need not be an architect to appreciate the clean lines, the sense of strength and regular rhythm in these structures. The achievement in design which they represent can be better understood by considering Wilson Dam, completed only eight years before Norris Dam was begun, yet closer in spirit to the scroll-work of nineteenth century building than to the simple mass of the T.V.A.-designed dams. These structures have the beauty of their function, heightened not by "decoration" or gew-gaws but by such a natural device as allowing the concrete to retain the mark of the grain from the rectangular wood forms into which it is poured, horizontal being contrasted with vertical patterns.

> What you see when you look at these vast engineering accomplishments is architecture. And it is not the accidental architecture of a rock formation, nor the naked architecture of a grain elevator: it is as calculated and as controlled a piece of construction as a temple. You know it is architecture because it is beautiful—beautiful in a way that other dams where there is merely sincere construction are not.[4]

The remarkable sequence of structures for which the T.V.A. has been responsible derives perhaps its greatest symbolic quality from the fact that it represents the achievement of a truly public architecture—created by public employees for a public purpose and public enjoyment. Gutheim calls it "the architecture of public rela-

3. F. A. Gutheim, "Tennessee Valley Authority: A New Phase in Architecture," 33 *Magazine of Art* 522 (1940).
4. *Ibid.*

tions," meaning that: "From the conception of the scheme to its final execution you feel that each decision has been made in the light of the fact that the public would come, look, and judge by what it saw. . . . In the Tennessee Valley we have shown (at a time when many had come to doubt it) that a public architecture can be a great architecture." Lewis Mumford agrees. Here, he says, is "modern architecture at its mightiest and its best. The Pharaohs did not do any better." [5]

THE T.V.A. AS INSTRUMENT

In one sense the New Deal has been a gigantic re-tooling job. The model T administrative equipment of the federal government during the 1920's was simply inadequate to handle the production requirements of the 1930's. There had been so many tasks which badly wanted doing, and which everyone agreed would have beneficial results, but which had not been undertaken because there were no tools available for the purpose. And the tools had not been developed because of a basic unwillingness to think of the federal government as an instrument, or to use it for other than traditional purposes. There was an assumption that what had not been done previously could not be done, and would not be legal. Consider the frustration implicit in this excerpt from the 1930 report of the Army Engineers on the development of the Tennessee River: "While it is possible that a central agency set up with authority to control the operations of all the waterway plants in the Tennessee Basin might secure a somewhat greater degree of efficiency than could be obtained by voluntary cooperation among independent power producers, there appears to be no legal means for establishing such an agency by the United States." [6] In time it was discovered that this desirable goal was not beyond the constitutional reach of the federal government.

5. "Architecture of Power," *New Yorker*, June 7, 1941, p. 58. Gutheim's article is illustrated with exceptionally fine photographs of the T.V.A. structures. Official T.V.A. publications also contain excellent photographs, largely the work of Charles Krutch.

6. House Doc. 328, 71st Cong., 2d sess., p. 23.

Of all the administrative agencies brought into being by the New Deal, none has seemed more significantly instrumental in character than the T.V.A. The reasons lie in its corporate form, its regional character, its broad range of responsibilities looking toward the general goal of regional development through the control of water resources. These are major characteristics of the Authority, and have already been discussed. But properly to appreciate the instrumentalism of the T.V.A. approach to its problems, it is necessary to note how completely the T.V.A. has developed the interrelationships between its major programs and followed through on all the leads opened up by them.

This characteristic can be seen perhaps most clearly in the Authority's treatment of the agricultural problem in the Tennessee Valley, upon the solution of which practically all of its activities have some bearing. Its water control responsibilities give the T.V.A. a concern for keeping the river off the land, and the land out of the river. There is no controversy concerning this goal. The individual farmer, the T.V.A., the nation as a whole all have the same interests in protecting the soil. It is the task of the T.V.A. to translate these interests into effective action. Education of farmers in soil-conserving practices is required. For a generation this has been the responsibility of the extension services of the state agricultural colleges and the county agents. The T.V.A. did not attempt to compete with these services, but instead sought to make them more effective by embarking on a policy of cooperation, formalized in a three-way memorandum of understanding signed in 1934 with the U.S. Department of Agriculture and the land-grant colleges of the Valley states. Subsequent contracts between the T.V.A. and the individual colleges have covered the particular services they are to perform for the Authority. The T.V.A. reimburses the colleges for expenses incurred, and pays the salaries of additional personnel required, such as assistant county agents.

The special contribution which the T.V.A. has to make to the general educational program of the extension services derives from another of its major programs, fertilizer experimentation and production. Its educational problem is how to acquaint farmers in the most practical way with the effect of phosphate and lime on grass and legume crops which will protect and restore the land. The technique developed for this purpose is the test-demonstration farm. Groups of farmers, called together by their county agents, select one of their number to conduct on his farm a demonstration with T.V.A. fertilizers. They participate in working out a program of land use and farm management for the farm. The demonstration farmer agrees to use the phosphate supplied by the T.V.A. only on soil-saving crops and pastures, and otherwise to follow farming practices that will further soil rebuilding. Except for the phosphate and a limited amount of technical guidance, the farmer and his neighbors do all the work, and out of his own pocket he pays for the additional material, livestock, and machinery required by the adjustment, including freight charges on the phosphate. Further, the farmer agrees to keep detailed operating and financial records, and opens his farm and accounts to the observation of all the farmers in his community. Each demonstration farm—and by 1941 there had been 35,000 of them—thus becomes a kind of schoolroom which the whole neighborhood attends.

But education, even through practical demonstrations of this character, is not enough. It does a man no good to know proper farming methods, if he is foreclosed by circumstances from acting on that knowledge. A farmer does not plow up a hillside and put it in corn because he wants to promote erosion. He does not plant cotton on the same land year after year because he wants to burn out the soil. He does it because, under the circumstances, he has no alternatives. He needs the money which these cash crops bring, if his family is not to starve. He can do nothing else until, as Mr. Lilienthal expressed it to Jonathan Daniels, he is given "a choice— a free choice—by making it possible for him to use his land in such a way that he will not only be able to support his family but at the same time protect his soil against depreciation. No need to fear how he'll choose." [7]

7. Jonathan Daniels, *A Southerner Discovers the South* (New York, 1938), p. 71.

Fortunately the task of making choices of this kind available does not fall upon the T.V.A. alone. It is a responsibility of the whole national agricultural program, with its benefit payments and rehabilitation loans. But the resources of the T.V.A. are dedicated to this purpose also. It conducts research looking toward the development of agricultural industries which will use regional resources and relieve the burden on the soil by supplying new sources of income. Thus work has been done on the quick-freezing of fruits and vegetables, on the preparation of flax fiber so that it can be used on cotton mill machinery for the manufacture of linen fabrics, on the processing of sorghum. Other research efforts have been directed to the development of farm machinery adapted to the conditions existing on the Valley farms. A low-cost threshing machine has been devised, and a furrow seeder which plants grain and distributes fertilizer in the same process on hillsides. Electric power has been adapted to income-producing uses on the farm through such devices as an electric hay drier inexpensive enough to be used by the small farmer and capable of increasing considerably the feeding value of hay crops. Electric methods of curing sweet potatoes have been developed. The Authority has designed and demonstrated a type of community refrigerator for groups of families in the country, which can repay much of its cost and improve farm diets by the preservation of meat and other farm products. Six experimental pilot plants have been established to study methods of community and home dehydration of foods.

It is by an aggressive program of this kind that the T.V.A. has made itself into an instrument for the widening of economic opportunity for the farming population of the Valley. To the extent that its powers permit, this sort of approach has characterized all T.V.A. activities. The Authority has sought to discharge its regional responsibility by an extensive program of interrelated physical and social engineering. Land and water and forests and people have all been included in the equation to be solved. Naturally the solution has not been a perfect one. There have been some mistakes. But the instrument has worked. The re-tooling has produced results.

THE T.V.A. AS PORTENT

Finally, the meaning of the T.V.A. derives from the fact that its windows seem to open so broadly on the future. To friend and to foe, the T.V.A. has seemed a sign in the sky, an indication of the shape of things to come. The frenzied editor of the *Chicago Tribune* had this vision:

> There is no longer room to doubt that at Norris the communism of Lenin and Stalin has taken root in the United States for no man in Norris may engage in private business, no man in Norris may work for wages except for the government, no man in Norris may worship in church or build a church to worship in according to his conscience. Can any one doubt that in the inaccessible mountains of Tennessee is being grown the germ culture that is intended to infect America? [8]

It is obviously true that the T.V.A. has something to say on the question of socialization, but today most sober citizens can see that our national problems are too serious to be settled by name-calling, and that collectivism is not usefully treated as original sin. It is more pertinent to consider the T.V.A. as effect rather than as cause, and its significance for the future depends upon what contributions it has to make, in spirit, in mechanism, in administrative competence, to the solution of the dilemmas of the post-war world. [9]

From this point of view the meaning of the T.V.A. lies in the amount of useable and heartening administrative experience it has produced. Public enterprise has been traditionally considered as handicapped by certain inescapable features of government administration. There is the alleged dilemma of operating with personnel selected either by an unimaginative civil service commission or by politicians. There is the red tape of government contracting, the

8. *Chicago Tribune,* November 4, 1934; quoted by Clarence L. Hodge, *op. cit.,* p. 225.

9. It is significant that the example of the T.V.A. is receiving widespread attention in current discussion of post-war reconstruction, and that battle lines are already forming around the issue. Witness the comment of a prominent industrialist who said that he was not fighting "for a T.V.A. on the Danube," and compare James P. Pope, "From Tennessee to World Reconstruction," 2 *Free World* 205-7 (1942).

restrictiveness of government auditing, the necessity of placating Congress if appropriations are to be secured, the political interference that is to be expected. It is thus of particular importance that the T.V.A. has been able to escape both the civil service and the spoilsmen while building up what is probably the most constructive and enlightened public personnel program ever seen in this country, to announce a long-term plan and carry it through with Congressional approval, and to show that public responsibility does not require meek submission to routine and red tape.

Credit for the Authority's excellent administrative accomplishments is in part due to its organizational form, that of a public corporation, which constitutes a bridge between private and public enterprise likely to be increasingly used in the administration of economic undertakings by governments. Its intent is to blend the administrative autonomy and financial freedom of the private business corporation with public accountability and control. The possibilities of the public corporation have been less understandingly explored in the United States than in Great Britain, where the broadcasting system, the transmission of electric power, the London transportation facilities and port services, and overseas air transport have been carried on by public corporations for varying lengths of time.[10] Consideration is now being given to unifying the British railways on a similar basis. In the case of the T.V.A., the implications of the corporate form have not been given effect in its financing, but its corporate status has been of considerable value in the adoption of personnel, accounting, and fiscal control methods suited to its needs, and has also emphasized its regional autonomy.

The public corporation is, of course, only a means and a mechanism. It can serve the totalitarian, corporate, or communist state, as the Russian trusts, the Hermann Goering Werke, and the South Manchuria Company testify. But a country bent on making democracy work will insist that the process of socialization, and the area within which the government becomes the sole institutional capitalist, be limited. Most Americans agree on the necessity for economic

10. See Lincoln Gordon, *The Public Corporation in Great Britain.*

activity independent of the state, and on the impossibility of maintaining democracy and freedom if economic power becomes the monopoly of an absolute state.

The virtue of the corporation is that it can be used to secure public control in fields where that is desired, without unduly promoting the growth of statism. For the possibilities in separation of the public corporation from the government are not merely theoretical. The autonomy which has characterized the T.V.A. is found to a much greater degree in the British public corporations. Even in wartime the British Broadcasting Corporation has been permitted by the government to retain a considerable measure of freedom in control of its policies.[11] In addition to administrative separation from the government, there are possibilities of "mutualizing" public corporations by providing that their directors shall represent and be appointed by management, labor, and other functional groups rather than by the government.[12] In this way an enterprise can be made truly *public* in character, rather than merely a *government* activity. The policy of decentralization which the T.V.A. has followed so successfully is another indication of how a public function can be undertaken without adding to the dead weight of the central bureaucracy.

The long-run significance of the T.V.A. is of course much broader than any demonstration it may have given of the uses of the public corporation. Fundamentally, its contribution has been the basis it has supplied for faith in democratic institutions. It is well to have it proved so dramatically that planning can grow out of popular consensus, and does not need to be the product of supermen, imposed by Hitlerian dictation. It is good to have such a striking demonstration that public control is compatible with efficiency. For one of the most important tasks of a democracy at war is to strengthen the administrative resources of government, to increase

11. Albert John, "The B.B.C. in Wartime," 12 *Political Quarterly* 190–201 (1941).

12. Lewis Corey develops this idea as part of the plan suggested for democratizing monopoly through public corporations in his *The Unfinished Task* (New York, 1942), Chap. 17.

its sense of responsibility, to raise the level of public administration generally, so that it may be adequate to the heavy tasks of the present and future.

The power plants which the T.V.A. built in the face of protests from the faint-hearted that a market would never be found for such huge quantities of power, turned out to be the nation's salvation when aluminum production became the measure of the difference between victory and defeat. Perhaps in somewhat the same fashion the administrative experience of the T.V.A. has built up reserves of governmental competence and of popular respect for the clean and workmanlike job done in the Tennessee Valley, which will stand us in good stead in difficult times to come. Faith is based on works, and Americans who have looked down on Norris Dam in its setting of the hills of East Tennessee may properly feel that the government which could do this can also somehow succeed in meeting the challenge of the times into which we move.

Index

Index

Accounting, for T.V.A. power operations, 92–99; Federal Power Commission control over, 105–107.

Adams, Henry, quoted, 314.

Administrative bulletins, 170–171.

Administrative codes, 183–184.

Agricultural Adjustment Administration, distribution of T.V.A. fertilizer by, 51; mentioned, 54, 143.

Agricultural program, phosphatic fertilizer experimentation, 48–50; demonstrations, 50–51; attitude of private fertilizer industry on, 51–52; national defense aspects, 54–55; relations with Department of Agriculture and land-grant colleges, 134–135; investment in, 142–143; organization for, 156, 177–178; comprehensive nature of, 318–320.

Agriculture, Department of, 132, 135, 137, 139, 140; Secretary of, 11, 14.

Alabama, interest in Muscle Shoals, 13; regulation of T.V.A., 108–109; payments to in lieu of taxes, 111; court decision, 110; Planning Commission, 125.

Alabama Power Co., and Wilson Dam power, 15, 18; foreign capital, 17; stockholders' suit, 60–61; contract with T.V.A., 66; purchase of T.V.A. power by, 67, 74–75; transfer of properties, 108–109; mentioned, 5, 18.

Alabama Power Co. v. *Ickes*, 71.

Alabama Public Service Commission, 86, 108–109.

Allocation, to national defense, 53; problem of, 82, 85, 88–89; progress toward solution, 87–88; alternative theories of, 89–90; alternative justifiable expenditure theory, 90–91.

Alumina, 55.

Aluminum Company of America, Fontana Dam site agreement, 39; operation of company's dams by T.V.A., 40–41; contract for T.V.A. power, 75–76; board conflict over negotiations with, 189–190; mentioned, 79.

Amortization, accounting policy on, 93; of government investment in T.V.A., 239–241.

Annual report, 241–242.

Appropriations, as source of T.V.A. funds, 230–234.

Arizona v. *California*, 60.

Arkansas Valley Authority, proposed bill for, 136 n, 140, 220.

Army engineers, study of Tennessee River, 19–21; and Wheeler Dam, 22, 35; T.V.A. relationship to, 35–36; mentioned, 6, 8, 13, 20, 34, 42, 317.

Ashwander v. *T.V.A.*, 60–63, 65, 68.

Athens (Alabama), 61, 67, 102.

Audit, exemption of government corporations from, 224, 225, 226–227; T.V.A. controversy with Comptroller General over, 249–263. *See also* Comptroller General.

Austin, Warren R., 252.

Autonomy, extent of in T.V.A. status, 216, 221.

tilizer policy, 48; appointment to board, 150–151; chairman of board, 151; allocation of duties to, 156; and T.V.A. organization, 177–178; relations with A. E. Morgan, 187–188, 189, 202; Roosevelt's comment on, 206; investigating committee's comment on, 211.

Mumford, Lewis, comment on Norris town, 123; views on regions, 134 n; quoted, 315, 317.

Municipal power, 67–68, 71–73.

Muscle Shoals, 5.

Muscle Shoals Commission, 13.

Muscle Shoals Inquiry, 11.

Muscle Shoals project, early development, 5; site for nitrate plant, 5–6; navigation and power project, 6–7; as a fertilizer plant, 7–13; as a power plant, 13–18; and unified river control, 18–22; and President Roosevelt, 27–29.

Myers v. *U. S.*, 213, 214.

Nashville (Tennessee), power system, 72.

National Defense Act of 1916, provisions of, 6, 7; mentioned, 4.

National Defense Advisory Commission, 39.

National defense program, contribution of T.V.A. to, 53–55, 75–76.

National Labor Relations Board, 304, 305.

National Power & Light Co., 66, 67.

National Resources Committee, 133.

Navigation, T.V.A. program of, 41–43; investment in, 142.

Negroes, employment by T.V.A., 285–286; training program, 137.

Newlands, F. G., 19.

New York Times, 200, 313.

Nitrate plants, at Muscle Shoals, 6, 10, 11, 13, 53–54.

Nitrates, 5–6; nitrogenous fertilizers, 48.

Norris, George W., interest in Muscle Shoals, 9–10; bills introduced, 10–11; power provisions, 14–15; compromise measure, 15–16; on river development, 19; corporate features of bills, 25–26; Norris-Sparkman amendment, 113; views on board of directors, 152; on removal by concurrent resolution, 214 n; on Bonneville policy, 218; Comptroller General provision, 250; T.V.A. investigation, 246–247; T.V.A. merit system, 268–269; on civil service for T.V.A., 307, 308.

Norris Dam, executive order concerning construction of, 34; storage at, 43; reservoir operation schedule, 44, 46; flood control effect, 47; powerhouse, 67, 69, 77; training program at, 136; mentioned, 36, 39, 155, 324. *See also* Cove Creek Dam.

Norris-Sparkman amendment, 113.

Norris, town of, 122–123, 155, 188.

O'Brian, John Lord, 192.

Odum, Howard, quoted, 134.

Office of Production Management, 40, 55.

Panama Railroad Co., 22, 25, 223–224.

Panter, T. A., 247.

Parker, Theodore B., 172.

Personnel administration, character of T.V.A. personnel problem, 269–271; organization for, 271–278; recruitment, examination, and selection, 278–282; resistance to political influence, 282–283; workmen's examinations, 283–285; classification, 286–290; compensation, 286–287, 290–292, 293–294; service ratings, 291, 292–293; promotion, 294–295; discharges, 295; labor relations, 296–299; wage conferences, 299–300; signing of labor contract, 300–303; collective bargaining, 303–304; representation problems, 304–305; strikes, 305–306; exemption from civil service, 306–309.